Program Management

"The most efficient way to produce anything is to bring together under one management as many as possible of the activities needed to turn out the product." - Peter Drucker – management expert

Programs bring together a variety of projects and ongoing work that are linked by the overall benefits that they bring to an organization and its customers.

By placing projects and ongoing work under the management of a single program manager, duplication of tasks between projects is reduced, and the direction for the outcomes or benefits of the work is closely managed.

This improves an organization's competitive advantage and helps to ensure that time and resources are not wasted on efforts that have little chance of producing beneficial outcomes.

Currently many organizations have their own definitions and understandings of portfolios, programs, and projects.

The differences in these understandings can lead to confusion, so the Project Management Institute (PMI®) has created standardized definitions of all three types of work allotments.

This standardization should reduce misunderstandings and help to generate sets of best practices specific to each type of work.

When in a program environment, the processes differ from traditional project management.

PMI® has developed The Standard for Program Management, which provides a shared lexicon and set of best practices for program management.

Programs have their own associated organizational structure and stakeholders. The Standard for Program Management provides a structure for program management and provides a set of best practices to help you ensure the success of your programs.

As you work through the course, you will learn about the

- importance of programs and program management and how they relate to portfolio and project management,
- relationship between program management and strategic vision and how the program management themes ensure success of a program.

"The future influences the present just as much as the past." – Friedrich Nietzsche, philosopher (1844-1900)

In program management, it is vital to know what has happened, what is happening, and what will happen. The program life cycle helps you to manage and control a program by clarifying where the program is and what needs to be done.

The program management life cycle is a vital tool in managing and controlling a program and its benefits and outcomes.

By using life-cycle phases, a program manager can ensure that the program achieves all the expected outcomes within the time and budget constraints set for that program.

The aim of this course is to provide an understanding of the basic concepts of program life-cycle management.

It provides an overview of:

program life-cycle phases

Program life-cycle phases are used to monitor and control the program's benefits. A program life cycle is made up of five phases - preprogram setup, program setup, establishing a program management and technical infrastructure, delivering the benefits, and closing the program.

program themes

The three program themes that span all the program life-cycle phases are benefits management, stakeholder management, and phase gate reviews. These themes evolve over time and require management throughout each phase of a program

Sorin Dumitrascu

life cycle.

program governance

Program governance involves the continuous
management and control of a program. It spans the
whole life cycle of the program and is initiated to
monitor the progress of the program and the
delivery of the planned benefits from its constituent
projects.

The course examines each of these program life-
cycle phases:

setting up the preprogram

The preprogram setup phase is the first phase of
a program's life cycle. During this phase, the
rationale and broad plans for a program are
developed and assessed.

setting up the program

Once a program passes its first phase gate
review, it moves on to the program setup phase.

Much of the detailed planning for the program
occurs during this phase.

**establishing program management and
technical infrastructure**

In the establish a program management and
technical infrastructure phase, a management and
technical infrastructure must be established. The
organizational structure plays an important role in
establishing a supporting infrastructure that will

back the program and ensure that all the planned benefits will be achieved.

delivering the benefits

The delivering the benefits phase is the longest phase of a program and continues until the program is closed. During this phase, capacity is developed and the program benefits begin to accrue.

closing the program

The close the program phase is the final phase of a program's life cycle. During this phase, contracts and program components are formally closed and program documentation is archived.

This course provides you with an understanding of program life-cycle phases, knowledge of their use in program management, and their contribution to the successful completion of programs.

The executives at Callinsure Insurance Corporation initiated a program to develop a new billing system. During the development, programmer turnover was high and the company had to employ many expensive systems contractors.

After a number of late deliveries, testing was overlooked in favor of the schedule. When the system was ready, it was a dismal failure. Invoices were sent out months late, and payments of claims were late.

Customers canceled their contracts rather than paying the late bills and eventually the company posted a third quarter loss of $50 million. Company stock dropped 20% in a day and some shareholders brought lawsuits against the company.

"All men can see these tactics whereby I conquer, but what none can see is the strategy out of which victory is evolved." - Sun Tzu, author of "The Art of War"

Project management focuses on the tactics of delivering a program's many benefits, while program management provides the strategy for realizing all the benefits of its components.

Efficient program management requires the implementation of specific processes and components. A post mortem of the program revealed a number of critical problems.

One problem was that the company had recently acquired a substantial business with over 12,000 established clients. Unfortunately, the software was unable to compensate for the expanding business capacity of the company, indicating that the program was poorly scoped.

The Standard for Program Management defines program management as the centralized, coordinated management of a program to achieve the program's strategic objectives and benefits.

Program Management

It provides a system for the effective management of a program from initiation through to program closing.

This course will provide program managers with an overview of the program life cycle, themes, and process groups. It will cover the common inputs and outputs and will describe some of the differences between program and project management.

You will learn how to implement a benefits realization plan and how to use the Initiating process group components.

"You can't overestimate the need to plan and prepare. In most of the mistakes I've made, there has been this common theme of inadequate planning beforehand. You really can't overprepare in business!" – Chris Corrigan, businessman and author

Planning is considered one of the most important phases of any program – without a properly defined plan, a program is much more likely to fail.

When programs don't deliver the expected benefits and go over budget or schedule, the consequences for a business can be devastating.

Program planning is an ongoing process that does not end once program implementation begins. As a program progresses through its milestones, new issues arise that require further planning.

When conducting program planning, you need to generate plans for all of the following areas:

- program scope
- resources
- costs
- interfaces and communications transitions
- schedules
- quality
- risk

This course will help you in planning processes for your programs. It covers all the critical plans required for effective program management and guides you in the best practices for developing these plans.

"The path to success is to take massive, determined action." – Anthony Robbins, motivational speaker

Once a program has been initiated and the necessary planning has been done, it's time to begin executing it. After all, no program can be a success without the actions that management takes to execute it.

This course provides program managers with an overview of the processes that can be used to manage a program's execution.

The Project Management Institute's (PMI's®) Standard for Program Management defines the Executing process group as consisting of the processes that drive program work according to the program management plan, and relevant subsidiary plans.

Processes in the Executing process group include performing quality assurance, distributing information, developing successful program teams, and selecting suitable sellers.

Processes in the Executing process group ensure that benefits management, stakeholder management, and program governance proceed in accordance with the program's policies and plans.

In this course, you'll learn about each of the processes in the Executing process group.

"It ain't over 'til it's over." – Yogi Berra, US baseball player and manager

As a program progresses, it's vital that you monitor and control the incremental delivery of its benefits. Monitoring and controlling a program ensures that it's proceeding as expected and that you can adapt to any changes or problems that occur.

The Monitoring and Controlling process group contains processes that enable you to keep tabs on scope, time, resources, cost, and quality. These processes ensure that a program remains within budget and on schedule.

With an end in sight, you may be tempted to rush toward the finish line and forget to wrap up important tasks. That's why the Closing process group contains processes designed to ensure that once a program is finished, it's truly complete.

To successfully close a program, you need to ensure that all activities and projects within the program are formally terminated and that the completed product is handed over to the customer or program sponsor. This brings the program to an orderly end and signifies a time for celebration.

In this course, you will learn how to enhance the success of a program by using

- the Monitoring and Controlling process group
- the Closing process group

In addition to learning how to monitor, control, and close a program, you'll learn how various processes in program management interact and overlap so that the outputs of one process become the inputs of another process.

CHAPTER 1 - An Introduction to Program Management

The Project Management Body of Knowledge (PMBOK® Guide) provides a shared set of standards and practices for project management, and the Standard for Program Management is an extension of the PMBOK® Guide that provides a shared set of standards and practices for program management.

Programs and program management are important to the success of organizations because they centralize the management of resources and benefits across a variety of projects and ongoing operations. This ensures more strategic decision-making and resource allocation.

This lesson provides definitions of and differences between programs, projects, and portfolios, and their management.

A portfolio is a collection of projects or programs and other work, brought together with the purpose of facilitating effective management of that work to meet strategic business objectives. According to the Standard for Program Management, a program is a group of related projects and other work managed in a coordinated way to obtain benefits and control not available from managing them individually. According to the Project Management Body of Knowledge (PMBOK® Guide), a project is a temporary endeavor undertaken to create a unique product, service, or result.

By defining and differentiating between portfolios, programs, and projects, you are able to understand the purpose, focus, and scope of each of these bodies of work. It also allows you to determine the degree of success that each of these entities reaches.

According to PMI's® Standard for Program Management, portfolio management is a centralized management approach to achieving strategic goals by selecting, prioritizing, assessing, and managing projects, programs, and other related work based on their alignment and contribution to an organization's strategies and objectives.

Program management is the centralized, coordinated management of a program to achieve strategic benefits and objectives. It allows for the application of three management themes – benefits management, stakeholder management, and program governance.

According to the PMBOK® Guide, project

management is the application of knowledge, skills, tools, and techniques to project activities to meet project requirements.

The roles, responsibilities, and tasks associated with each of these management positions differ considerably and it is useful to understand these differences.

Through careful planning and informed program governance, benefits management, and stakeholder management, you can greatly improve your program's chances of success.

This lesson will outline program planning and the functions of the planning team. You will also learn how to manage program benefits using a benefits management approach, recognize key program stakeholders, and recognize the functions of the program board.

The Planning team generates plans for all aspects of a program by carrying out all processes listed in the Planning process group. The team requires knowledge of integration management, scope management, resource management, risk management, and procurement management to plan effectively.

Benefits management involves the identification and tracking of benefits throughout a program life cycle. To manage benefits, you need to conduct plan delivery, identify and define benefits, measure and track benefit delivery, and evaluate the program's delivery of expected and unexpected benefits.

Key program stakeholders include customers, program directors, project teams, program teams, a program board, and administrative offices.

The program manager needs to identify all stakeholders and understand their impact and expectations of the program. The program manager also needs to ensure that relevant information is communicated to all stakeholders in a timely manner.

Program governance involves the development, implementation, and monitoring of company policies, structures, and practices for a program. Companies often set up a program board to oversee these functions and to represent the organization.

The board aids with planning, resource availability, monitoring progress, risk assessment, and problems that have escalated beyond the program manager's ability. The program board may also use a program management office (PMO) to

Program Management

define policies, procedures, and practices that all programs need to follow.

The Standard for Program Management

"Without an integrating structure, information remains a hodgepodge of fragments. Without an organizing structure, knowledge is a mere collection of observations, practices, and conflicting incidents." - Jay W. Forrester, in Principles of Systems (1990)

The Project Management Body of Knowledge (PMBOK® Guide) was created by the Project Management Institute (PMI®) to provide a common lexicon and a set of best practices that project managers can use when selecting and running projects.

PMBOK® also serves as a basic reference for project management accreditation exams such as the Project Management Professional (PMP®) certification and the Certified Associate in Project Management (CAPM®) certification.

PMP®

The PMP® accreditation is the most globally recognized credential for project management. To be eligible for a PMP® credential, you need to meet specific educational and project management experience requirements and agree to adhere to a code of professional conduct. The PMP® exam is a computer-based examination that assesses your ability to apply project management knowledge.

CAPM®

The CAPM® accreditation for project management is designed for project team members, entry-level project managers, and qualified undergraduate and graduate students. CAPM® candidates

must first meet specific educational and project management-related experience requirements, and then pass a comprehensive, computer-based examination.

The Standard for Program Management, also developed by PMI®, is an extension of the PMBOK® Guide. It focuses on programs rather than individual projects and places programs and program management in context.

The Standard defines programs, program management, the relationship between program management and project management, and the relationship between program management and portfolio management.

Like the PMBOK® Guide, it provides a common lexicon, program themes, and a set of best practices, but these aspects apply to programs rather than projects.

Sorin Dumitrascu

The Standard for Program Management is also used as the foundation reference document for program management accreditation exams.

Question

Match each purpose to the standard to which it applies.

Options:

A. It provides a common lexicon, program themes, and a set of best practices that can be applied to programs

B. It provides a common lexicon and a set of best practices that project managers can use when selecting and running projects

Targets:

1. Standard for Program Management
2. PMBOK®

Answer

The Standard for Program Management focuses on the lexicon and best practices for programs and program management.

PMBOK® is the Project Management Body of Knowledge, and as such focuses on the lexicon and best practices for project management.

Benefits of program management

A program is a method in which related projects and ongoing operations can be managed. Programs are increasingly used to boost the success of a wide variety of organizations, businesses, and institutions.

Programs and program management are important to the success of organizations in that they:

allow coordinated management of related projects

Program management allows the coordinated management of related projects. For example, it coordinates fund-raising efforts when an organization is using several projects to raise funds. Through this, project resources, deadlines, and activities can be centrally managed so that the overall goal of the program is met.

help to achieve organizational goals

Program management helps to achieve organizational goals by ensuring the selected projects are within the scope of a particular organizational goal. Program management is strategic rather than being based on creating a specific product or service.

facilitate the delivery of products and services

on time and within budget

Program management enables an organization to deliver products and services on time and within budget. It does this by providing a centralized management platform that oversees resource allocation and project deadlines.

allow staffing to be optimized

Program management allows staffing to be optimized by centrally managing the resources for multiple projects and ongoing operations that share specific benefits or strategic goals.

A nongovernmental organization (NGO) is required to raise funds for general operation and for specific projects. For example, an environmental organization has the strategic goal of reducing wasteful energy practices. A fund-raising program groups fund-raising drives for operating costs and for its main projects – running an educational program on alternative energy use and researching methods of sustainable energy use.

This fund-raising centralizes the management of staff members who will be assigned to each project. It enables more effective resource use and strategic planning for timely delivery of project outcomes, as well as ensuring that the fund-raising activities are all aimed at the organization's strategic goals.

Program Management

Question
Why are programs and program management important in the success of an organization?

Options:
1. They allow the coordinated management of related projects
2. They help to achieve organizational goals
3. They improve an organization's ability to deliver products and services on time and within budget
4. They encourage the optimal use of staffing and other resources
5. They prioritize product or service delivery
6. They decentralize administrative tasks

Answer

Option 1: This is a correct option. Programs and program management provide an overview of related projects and manage these projects within the program structure.

Option 2: This is a correct option. By grouping projects according to the benefits that they can provide and aligning these benefits with organizational goals, programs and program management help to achieve organizational goals.

Option 3: This is a correct option. Through their coordinated management of projects, program managers help to ensure that projects have achievable deadlines and the necessary resources that they need to deliver on time and within budget.

Option 4: This is a correct option. Through coordinated management, programs are able to allocate staff and other resources according to the strategic priorities of the organization. This encourages the optimal use of staff.

Option 5: This is an incorrect option. Programs prioritize the generation of benefits, not products or services.

Option 6: This is an incorrect option. Administrative tasks are centralized through coordinated management.

Definitions

The terms "portfolio," "program," and "project" have been used differently in different companies. This can cause confusion in terms of identifying different work components or activities, their organization, and their management.

To avoid this confusion, it is useful to know the standard definitions of each of these three aspects of work within an enterprise.

A portfolio is a collection of projects or programs and other work, brought together with the purpose of facilitating effective management of that work to meet strategic business objectives.

The projects or programs in the portfolio are not necessarily interdependent or directly related. However, the alignment of programs and projects with the strategic goals of the organization should be used to effectively manage work portfolios.

So a portfolio is a measure of an organization's intent, in that it should identify key objectives and classify and rank various endeavors according to business priorities.

According to the Standard for Program Management, a program is a group of related projects and other work managed in a coordinated way to obtain benefits and control not available from managing them individually.

Programs may also include elements of related work outside of the scope of the discrete projects in the program - for example, ongoing operations at a publishing house or automobile manufacturer.

Programs also involve a series of repetitive or cyclical undertakings, such as an annual construction program or the publishing of a newspaper or magazine.

Consider the example of an automobile manufacturer that has a number of portfolios to cover all company efforts and several programs.

Portfolio

The company's vehicle development portfolio has identified several strategic goals and has classified and rated work efforts according to strategic priority. It has a Lean waste reduction project that aims to reduce costs and cycle time for manufacturing processes, and it has a program for the company's annual new model release.

Program

The annual new car model program is divided into projects for the design and upgrade of each major component – engine, interior, and exterior. The program also oversees the ongoing

Program Management

manufacturing on the assembly line.

According to the Project Management Body of Knowledge (PMBOK® Guide), a project is a temporary endeavor undertaken to create a unique product, service, or result.

Thus projects have a clear beginning and an end – when the product or service is completed. So although some projects may take years to complete, they are still temporary.

Some large projects are divided into subprojects – for example, a project to develop a database software package may be divided into a research project, a functionality development project, an interface project, and a documentation project.

However, despite its management of several projects, the database software project is not a program because it is a temporary endeavor to create a single product.

Question
Match each definition to the term it defines.
Options:
A. A temporary endeavor undertaken to create a unique product, service, or result

B. A group of related projects and other work managed in a coordinated way to obtain benefits

and control not available from managing them
individually

C. A measure of an organization's intent that
comprises a variety of unrelated projects and
ongoing work

Targets:

1. Project
2. Program
3. Portfolio

Answer

The PMBOK® Guide defines a project as a
temporary endeavor undertaken to create a unique
product, service, or result.

The Standard for Program Management defines
a program as a group of related projects managed in
a coordinated way to obtain benefits and control not
available from managing them individually.

The Standard for Portfolio Management defines
a portfolio as a measure of an organization's intent
that comprises a variety of unrelated projects and
ongoing work aligned to various strategic goals.

Distinguishing characteristics

Portfolios, programs, and projects interact hierarchically – with portfolios at the top of the hierarchy and projects at the bottom.

Portfolios are active at the conception of work components and are responsible for allocating resources to them. Projects are the end result of this allocation process.

Programs interact between the two to ensure that benefits aligned with a portfolio's strategic goals are implemented through projects.

There are clear differences in focus for the:

portfolio

A portfolio categorizes and ranks bodies of work according to a business's strategic goals. This enables senior management to prioritize resource allocation according to each body of work's alignment with various goals. Thus the focus is prioritization of work according to its alignment with strategic goals.

program

A program focuses on achieving the benefits that its portfolio outlines, and is aligned with a specific strategic goal. Benefits are the outcomes of activities and behaviors designed to meet strategic goals. So if a strategic goal is to increase efficiency in manufacturing processes, the benefits of this may be reduced costs, improved employee morale, and increased customer satisfaction.

project

A project focuses on creating a unique product, service, or result that aligns with the strategic benefits of the program to which it belongs.

A paint manufacturer may have a portfolio that recognizes profitability, customer relations, and workplace safety as the company's strategic goals. This portfolio identifies ongoing operations, projects, and programs that can meet these objectives. The company decides which of these activities best meets the strategic goals and assigns resources to them.

The workplace safety program identifies benefits such as improved skills and capabilities in meeting safety requirements, and it identifies projects that are able to implement these benefits.

The project of creating a new safety training manual, and the project to align practices to the new legal requirements for handling a toxic material, are projects that the program identifies as most able to generate the benefits that have been identified.

Question

A company uses a management team to focus on increased customer satisfaction. The goals for increased customer satisfaction include improved aftersales support and products more closely tailored to customer demands. What is this focus an example of?

Options:

1. A portfolio
2. A program
3. A project

Answer

Option 1: This is an incorrect option. The focus of a portfolio is to identify strategic goals and prioritize resources for endeavors that are most likely to meet those goals. Increased customer satisfaction is an example of a benefit.

Option 2: This is the correct option. Increased customer satisfaction is a benefit – the outcome of activities and behaviors designed to meet strategic goals. Programs focus on achieving the benefits.

Option 3: This is an incorrect option. Projects focus on implementing benefits. The focus of this team is on increased customer satisfaction. How this will be achieved – through aftersales support and product customization – is the realm of separate projects.

Sorin Dumitrascu

The scope of a body of work helps you to differentiate it and identify it as either a:

portfolio

A portfolio's scope is a business scope that encompasses changes with the strategic goals of an organization.

program

A program's scope is broad and changes to meet the business expectations of an organization.

project

A project's scope is narrow and defined by specific deliverables.

A police force's portfolio scope changes with the priorities outlined by the city mayor and other stakeholders.

A program within the police force may be to reduce the number of incidents of violent crime, and included in the scope of this program may be increased presence on the streets, educational projects, reductions in drug trafficking, and an antigun campaign.

Specific projects within the police force will have a narrow scope, such as distributing flyers that provide safety tips for children walking home from school.

Question

A management team at a pharmaceutical company defines the scope of its work as the creation of an improved treatment for asthma.

According to its scope, what type of endeavor is it involved with?

Options:

1. A portfolio
2. A program
3. A project

Answer

Option 1: This is an incorrect option. A portfolio's scope encompasses all strategic goals and activities within the organization. In this scenario, the scope is limited to delivering a specific product.

Option 2: This is an incorrect option. A program's scope encompasses business expectations for specific benefit sets. Creating an improved asthma treatment is a narrow scope that covers delivering a specific product or set of products.

Option 3: This is the correct option. The creation of an improved asthma treatment is narrow and limited to the delivery of the specific product or set of products that help asthma.

Success is measured differently for:

portfolios

A portfolio measures success using the aggregate performance of its components – various projects and programs.

programs

A program measures success using return on investment (ROI) measures, benefit delivery, and in terms of new capabilities that are created.

projects

A project measures success in terms of adherence to product specifications, budget, and timely delivery.

A multinational chemicals company identifies social responsibility as a key strategic objective. It creates a social responsibility portfolio that encompasses two programs – social development and environmental development – and a project to develop a company code of ethics. It measures its success on the overall success of these programs and projects.

At the chemicals company, the environmental program comprises an educational project and an Environmental Protection Agency (EPA) compliance project.

Ongoing work for this program includes research and maintaining a web presence. The program measures its success in terms of benefit delivery – improved knowledge of the environment and of EPA practices – and in terms of the new capabilities and skills that are created through program activities.

The educational project, which belongs to the environmental program, is to create a five-part television series that explores local ecosystems. Its success is measured in terms of whether it meets the project specifications, remains within budget, and is finished according to schedule.

In the chemicals company scenario, there is a distinction in terms of scope, purpose, and measures for each level or category of work.

Social responsibility portfolio

In this case, the social responsibility portfolio is part of a larger portfolio, corporate image, that incorporates other issues such as profitability, and so on. The social responsibility portfolio aligns various projects and programs and allocates resources and priorities to these bodies of work according to changing priorities in terms of the company's strategic goals around social responsibility.

Environmental program

The environmental program encompasses two

current projects and some ongoing work. It focuses on improved knowledge of the environment and new capabilities that allow better environmental practices. Its scope covers any activities that can result in these benefits and it measures its success in terms of return on equity (ROE) and the new skills and capabilities generated through the program.

Educational project

The educational project is temporary and focused on creating a finished product. Its scope is to provide a quality television series that teaches viewers about local ecosystems. The project itself can be divided into subprojects – one for each episode of the series. And its success depends on a good finished product that is within budget and on deadline.

Question

To evaluate a sales drive's success, an automobile company measures improved sales turnover and reduced employee turnover against its investment in the drive.

What should the sales drive be classified as?

Options:

1. A portfolio
2. A program
3. A project

Answer

Option 1: This is an incorrect option. A portfolio's success is measured in terms of the aggregate performance of its components. The measure in the automobile company scenario is ROI.

Option 2: This is the correct option. The measure in this scenario is ROI, one of the measures for a program's success.

Option 3: This is an incorrect option. A project's success is measured in terms of its adherence to product specifications, budget, and timely delivery. ROI calculations, which are used at the automobile company, measure program success.

Projects, programs, portfolio management

Given that portfolios, programs, and projects are such different entities, how they are managed differs quite substantially.

The definitions of each management type help to differentiate them in terms of their purpose, scope, and tasks. The definitions are as follows:

portfolio management

According to the Standard for Portfolio Management, portfolio management is a centralized management approach to achieving strategic goals by selecting, prioritizing, assessing, and managing projects, programs, and other related work based on their alignment and contribution to an organization's strategies and objectives. The work that portfolio managers manage need not be interrelated.

program management

According to the Standard for Program Management, program management is the centralized coordinated management of a program to achieve strategic benefits and objectives. It allows for the application of three management themes – benefits management, stakeholder management, and program governance. The work that program managers manage is interrelated, and program management focuses on these interrelations.

project management

According to the Project Management Body of Knowledge (PMBOK® Guide), project management is the application of knowledge, skills, tools, and techniques to project activities to meet project requirements. Project managers accomplish their goals through the application and integration of the processes of initiating, planning, executing, monitoring and controlling, and closing. The project manager is the person responsible for accomplishing project objectives.

In light of its definition, portfolio management is the management of a set of components grouped to allow effective alignment with business objectives.

Program management is the centralized management of related entities – projects and operational work – to achieve strategic benefits and objectives.

Project management is the application of knowledge, skills, and tools to meet a specified and concrete objective.

The different management types can also be understood in terms of how they interact in context of one another. Once a portfolio has been set up, a program can be initiated.

Sorin Dumitrascu

During the initiating and planning phases of the program, portfolio managers provide the process groups with information such as strategic goals and benefits, funding allocations, requirements and proposed timelines.

During the program's executing, monitoring, controlling, and closing phases, program managers provide the portfolio management team with status information, program performance reports, and updates on budgets, schedules, risks, and issues.

Project management and program management have a similar cyclical form of interaction. During the initiating and planning phases, the program Initiating and Planning teams provide information such as scope, deliverables, budgets, and schedules to the project planning group.

During the executing, monitoring, and closing phases of the project, project managers provide program managers with status information, performances reports, and updates on various project issues.

Question
Match each definition to the term that it defines.
Options:
A. The centralized management of related entities to attain strategic objectives and benefits

Program Management

B. The management of a set of components grouped to allow effective alignment with business objectives

C. The application of knowledge, skills, and tools to meet a specified and concrete objective

Targets:

1. Program management
2. Portfolio management
3. Project management

Answer

According to the Standard for Program Management, program management is the centralized, coordinated management of a program to achieve strategic benefits and objectives.

According to the Standard for Portfolio Management, portfolio management is a centralized management approach to achieving strategic goals.

According to the PMBOK® Guide, project management is the application of knowledge, skills, tools, and techniques to project activities to meet project requirements.

Management differences

The difference between portfolio, program, and project management does not simply lie in what is managed or who each manager manages – a portfolio team, project managers, or a project team – but also in how each manager manages.

Differences between each of the three management roles include focus and leadership styles. Each of the following has its own requirements for focus and leadership styles:

portfolio management

Portfolio management focuses on prioritizing strategic goals and assigning resources accordingly. This requires the monitoring of change in the environment and adapting accordingly. The appropriate leadership style is one that focuses on decision-making for the portfolio, providing insight, and creating synthesis.

program management

Program management focuses on the interdependencies between related projects and ongoing work components. This means embracing change where necessary, and providing insight and leadership. The appropriate leadership style is one that manages relationships, stakeholder politics, and conflict resolution.

project management

Project management focuses on successful task delivery. This requires keeping change to a minimum and a team-player leadership style that motivates and supports through skill and knowledge.

Thus a portfolio manager deals mainly with high-level strategy that integrates various bodies of work and categorizes it in terms of result, risk, and priority. The manager is responsible for creating communication and process plans that correspond to the components of a portfolio.

A program manager focuses on interdependencies between related bodies of work to achieve a specific benefit set. To do this, managers need to carry out high-level planning to provide guidance to projects, and they need to manage relationships.

A project manager manages the specific tasks in a project and does this through detailed planning, technical support, and team motivation so that the task is delivered on time, within budget, and according to specifications.

Project interdependencies within a program may be based on any of the following:

Sorin Dumitrascu

collective capability

In programs that have collective capability interdependencies – such as meeting International Organization for Standardization (ISO) requirements or Environmental Protection Agency (EPA) requirements – program managers focus on ensuring that these capabilities are met in each project and ongoing work endeavor.

common attribute

In programs that share common attributes – such as a customer, seller, technology, or resource – program managers focus on ensuring that the benefits from these common attributes are realized.

risk mitigation

In programs that have risk mitigation interdependencies, program managers must focus on ways of spreading risk so that it is at reasonable levels for an organization. A common example of program risk is competition from companies in the same industry. To mitigate this risk, some of the program projects could be designed to focus on products or services that have a different set of competitors. This strategy spreads the risk across different industries or competitors.

Monitoring tasks that each manager type must

Program Management

accomplish also differs.

Portfolio managers monitor the aggregate performance of portfolio components. For example, they receive and analyze reports on the projects and programs under their supervision to determine the overall success of the projects in meeting various strategic objectives.

Program managers monitor projects and ongoing work through organizational governance structures. They receive progress reports and other reports from project managers and hold regular meetings with these managers.

Project managers monitor and control tasks involved in creating the deliverable. For example, they use tools such as Gantt Charts, schedules, and budgets to ensure that a project is progressing well.

Alex, Catherine, and Sally are managers who all work for a large environmental agency that runs various portfolios that oversee all programs and work that the agency undertakes. There are several programs and numerous smaller projects within each portfolio.

Alex - portfolio manager
"Our agency has a number of portfolios to try to ensure that everything that we do brings us closer to our strategic goals. My work as portfolio manager

43

on the Air portfolio is to generate strategic plans, processes, and communication strategies that ensure we are pulling together in the right direction on the portfolio that tackles air pollution education and lobbying.

I work with my team and with program managers to select appropriate programs and projects. And I take a big picture view of the work we do to assess how successful we are."

Alex is the portfolio manager.

Catherine - program manager

"The program that I run is the Client Services program, which aims to provide quality environmental impact assessments and improve customer relations. Most of my work involves managing relationships and conflict resolution. I ensure that our resources are used optimally and that work is not duplicated.

I tend to use matrices a lot to keep track of all the interdependencies between projects and use a systems approach to work with project interdependencies. I monitor progress through meetings with project managers and by reading reports on progress."

Catherine is the program manager.

Sally - project manager

"My current project is an environmental impact

assessment for a proposed development on a wetland site. The work is quite hands-on, and I work closely with two researchers.

I coordinate tasks, ensure that we are keeping to deadlines, reassess budgets, and write up reports on our progress that I then hand over to Catherine, my program manager."

Sally is the project manager.

The three management types, and the three work types, should not be confused.

Question Set

Differentiating between portfolio management, program management, and project management helps you to clarify roles and responsibilities.

Question 1 of 3
Question

A job advertisement lists the following as its requirements – "The ability to see the big picture and to develop high-level strategic plans. Must have strong insight into the industry and the ability to predict and act quickly on changes."

What position do you think this advertisement is for?

Options:

1. Portfolio manager
2. Program manager
3. Project manager

Answer

Option 1: This is the correct option. Portfolio management focuses on prioritizing strategic goals and assigning resources accordingly. This requires the ability to monitor change, provide synthesis, and to create high-level strategic plans.

Option 2: This is an incorrect option. Although these skills may be useful to a program manager, the focus on strategic planning and change management is more closely aligned to portfolio management than to program management.

Option 3: This is an incorrect option. Project managers need to create operational plans rather than strategic plans. Also they are expected to keep change to a minimum so that their schedules and budgets are not negatively affected.

Question 2 of 3
Question

A job advertisement lists the following as the requirements for the position – "Good technical skills in online documentation, ability to work well in a team, good leadership skills, and knowledge of budgeting and scheduling tools."

Program Management

What position do you think this advertisement is for?

Options:

1. Portfolio manager
2. Program manager
3. Project manager

Answer

Option 1: This is an incorrect option. Portfolio managers require a more strategic focus, and this advertisement is focused more on technical ability.

Option 2: This is an incorrect option. Program managers require a more relational focus, and their main skills should be more tactical than technical.

Option 3: This is the correct option. Project managers require a team-player leadership style, good technical ability, and the ability to create detailed schedules and budgets.

Question 3 of 3
Question

Zoe describes her work as requiring strong conflict resolution and relationship management skills. She sees herself more as a leader than a manager, and relies heavily on her systems-thinking skills.

What position do you think Zoe holds at her company?

Options:

1. Portfolio manager
2. Program manager
3. Project manager

Answer

Option 1: This is an incorrect option. Although these skills would be useful to a portfolio manager, such a position's requirements should focus more on strategic and change management.

Option 2: This is the correct option. Program managers need to manage relationships and conflict. They should be strong and inspiring leaders who can apply systems thinking to view both the big picture and the interdependencies between projects and ongoing work.

Option 3: This is an incorrect option. Although these skills would be useful to a project manager, project management focuses more on operational skills than on relationship management skills.

Understanding planning and themes

The old adage – if you fail to plan, you plan to fail – is true of program management.

The context of program management within an organization is the planning and execution of organizational plans.

Program planning is primarily concerned with aligning a program to organizational goals, spreading risk through an optimal mix of projects, and ensuring that resources are appropriately assigned.

Program execution uses the three themes of program management – benefits management, stakeholder management, and program governance – to deliver benefits and capabilities that organizations can use to sustain, enhance, and deliver organizational goals.

Effective program planning ensures that programs:

strategically align with organizational goals

A program's goals need to strategically align with the organizational goals to get buy-in and to ensure that the resources that it uses are to the benefit of the entire organization.

Management of Easy Nomad, a travel agency,

decides to embark on a program of marketing projects focused on promoting travel to Eastern Europe. In this case, the program is strategically aligned with the organizational goal to increase sales of travel packages to Eastern Europe. All work that falls under this program promotes travel to this part of the world.

consist of a good mix of project investments

Planning programs with a good mix of project investments helps to spread risk and improve the potential for success.

The Easy Nomad program to promote travel to Eastern Europe includes a range of projects aimed at different market sectors – budget, mid-range, and luxury travel. The projects encompass a variety of media such as brochures, radio, television, and paper media.

comprise the optimal use of resources

Planning programs so that they comprise the optimal use of resources ensures lower operational costs, higher profits, and better quality deliverables.

At Easy Nomad, the program manager for the Eastern Europe program decides to use the most resources on mid-range travel packages because they generate the most revenue. The program allocates the least resources on low-budget travel and an average amount on luxury. This is in keeping

Program Management

with the expected returns on these projects.

   To manage changes, organizations use strategic vision to coordinate portfolios and programs. The programs then mobilize projects that deliver operations and benefits.
   A program's success depends on how the organization defines, communicates, and aligns organizational goals with its plans.

   Program teams handle tasks within five categories of program processes – known as process groups. The program process groups are the
   •   •   Initiating process group
   •   Planning process group
   •   Executing process group
   •   Monitoring and Controlling process group
   •   Closing process group
   Program management handles the execution of organizational plans through these themes:

benefits management
   Benefits management involves defining the expected benefits of a program and monitoring the delivery of these benefits throughout the program life cycle. If an organization uses portfolio management, the portfolio formalizes benefits and

then delegates them to programs.

program stakeholder management

Program stakeholder management involves identifying stakeholders – people and organizations affected by or involved in a program – and how a program will affect stakeholders. It also involves creating a communication strategy that engages stakeholders and manages their expectations of the program.

program governance

Program governance involves creating and integrating a delivery and decision-making framework to guide and monitor benefits delivery for a program.

In terms of benefits management for Easy Nomad's Eastern Europe program, the financial and intangible benefits – such as company reputation – need to be delineated and reviewed in terms of how well the program is achieving those benefits as the program progresses.

Stakeholder management involves management and staff within Easy Nomad, as well as tourism and transport organizations and clients.

Program governance involves internal program architecture, policies, procedures, and practices that should be followed in implementing the program.

Program Management

This includes monitoring progress reports and the details of how the program runs.

Through a clear understanding of program management organizational planning and themes, you can help your programs to succeed by:

being aware of interdependencies of projects within a program in terms of:
- • benefits, role players, and resources,
- recognizing how stakeholders affect the program,
- understanding how program governance affects the program,
- understanding how the program relates to organizational strategic benefits.

Program planning is concerned with aligning the program with organizational goals so that the program can deliver benefits and capabilities that enhance organizational goals. This helps to ensure that you understand the strategic direction of your organization and how your program relates to that.

Program planning is also concerned with ensuring that there is a good mix of projects. Additionally, projects share benefit potential and often share resources and use similar processes and procedures covered by program governance. So organizational planning and program management themes highlight the interdependencies between projects. It is these interdependencies that you, as a program manager, manage.

The program stakeholder management theme prioritizes the identification of how stakeholders affect and are affected by a program. And the program governance theme ensures that you consider the affects of program governance on the program that you manage.

Through careful planning and informed program governance, benefits management, and stakeholder management, you can greatly improve your program's chances of success.

Question

How does a clear understanding of program management, organizational planning, and themes help a program to succeed?

Options:

1. You will understand how your program relates to organizational strategic benefits

2. You will be aware of interdependencies of projects within the program

3. You will recognize how stakeholders affect the program

4. You will understand how program governance affects the program

5. You will understand the technical requirements for product delivery

6. You will be aware of strategic industry changes and develop appropriate new goals and strategies

Answer

Option 1: This is a correct option. Program planning is concerned with aligning the program with organizational goals so that the program can deliver benefits and capabilities that organizations can use to sustain, enhance, and deliver organizational goals.

Option 2: This is a correct option. Program planning is concerned with ensuring that there is a good mix of projects. Additionally, projects share benefit potential and stakeholders and often use similar processes and procedures covered by program governance.

Option 3: This is a correct option. The program stakeholder management theme prioritizes the identification of how stakeholders affect and are affected by a program.

Option 4: This is a correct option. The program governance theme within program management helps you to review program governance in light of an organization, its goals, and its stakeholders.

Option 5: This is an incorrect option. Product

delivery and technical know-how for product delivery is an aspect of project management, not program management.

Option 6: This is an incorrect option. This is the scope of portfolio management, not program management.

The Planning team

The program Planning team is formed in the program setup phase of a program and team members are typically finalized during the "establish program management and technical infrastructure" phase of the program.

Thus the team is created after the program has been approved and a program manager has been selected – and before the program is implemented.

The team is expected to carry out the processes grouped in the Planning process group. So, the team creates a program management plan that includes the scope, schedule, costs, resources, quality, and communication plans. These deliverables provide an infrastructure and a road map for the program to follow.

Program planning is concerned with aligning a program with organizational goals, spreading risk through an optimal mix of projects, and ensuring that resources are appropriately assigned.

It also includes planning how the program team communicates with others.

Question

During which program phases is the program

Planning team formed?

Options:

1. Preprogram setup

2. Program setup

3. Establish program management and technical infrastructure

4. Deliver incremental benefits

Answer

Option 1: This is an incorrect option. Preprogram setup occurs before program approval.

Option 2: This is a correct option. The Planning team is initialized during the program setup phase.

Option 3: This is a correct option. The Planning team membership is typically finalized during the "establish program management and technical infrastructure" phase of a program.

Option 4: This is an incorrect option. The Planning team is not necessarily the same group of people that manage program implementation during the delivery phase.

The Planning team requires knowledge of integration management, scope management, resource management, risk management, and procurement management to plan effectively.

Processes performed by the Planning team

Of all the program management process groups, the Planning process group has the largest scope. The team that implements Planning process group processes needs to plan for all aspects of a program.

The Planning team uses their integration management skills to perform the following Planning process group processes:

Develop Program Management Plan

The Develop Program Management Plan process produces a document that consolidates other planning documents to create a comprehensive guide to program execution and control. This guide is the primary output of the Planning team.

Interface Planning

The Interface Planning process identifies and maps interrelationships within a program and between the program and other organizational activities. It creates strategies to establish and maintain interfaces and to identify the risks associated with these interfaces. Interface Planning supports communications and the setup of formal decision-making relationships. It is typically executed in conjunction with the Human Resource Planning process.

Resource Planning

The Resource Planning process determines the people, equipment, and other resources that are needed to perform program activities and how these should be spread across the program. It prioritizes skill gaps and identifies candidates for open positions.

Transition Planning

The Transition Planning process is conducted to ensure that program benefits are sustained once they are transferred to the organization. It identifies transitions that need to occur and provides clear guidelines on how to make these transitions.

Scope management involves two processes – Scope Definition and Create Program Work Breakdown Structure (PWBS).

During the Scope Definition process, the Planning team develops a scope statement that clarifies the boundaries of a program and forms the basis for future program decisions. The team also draws up a scope management plan, which specifies how the program scope should be managed throughout the program.

The PWBS provides an overview of the program and shows how each project fits into it. The PWBS details the deliverables that the program components will produce and the total scope and major milestones of the program. It also includes the program's plans, procedures, standards, and processes.

The PWBS helps to ensure effective control and communication between the program manager and the various project managers within the program. It is also used as the controlling framework for developing the program schedule.

The Communications Planning process determines the information and communication needs of program stakeholders. It specifies who needs what information, when they need it, and how it should be communicated.

Question

The Planning team performs several Planning process group processes that require integration management skills. Match the descriptions to the processes.

Options:

A. Generating a comprehensive outline for the execution and control of a program

B. Identifying and mapping interrelationships within a program and between the program and other organizational activities

C. Ensuring that program benefits are sustained

Sorin Dumitrascu

once they are distributed across an organization

D. Prioritizing skill gaps and identifying candidates for open positions

Targets:

1. Develop Program Management Plan
2. Interface Planning
3. Transition Planning
4. Resource Planning

Answer

The Develop Program Management Plan process produces a comprehensive outline for the execution and control of the program. This document is the key output for the Planning team.

Interface Planning involves the identification and mapping of interrelationships within the program and between the program and other organizational activities.

Transition Planning ensures that program benefits are sustained once they are distributed across the organization.

Resource Planning ensures that there are sufficient resources and prioritizes skill gaps and identifies candidates for open positions.

The Planning team performs the following Planning process group processes, which require resource management skills:

Program Management

Schedule Development

Time management skills are needed for the Schedule Development process, which defines the program components needed to produce program deliverables. This process determines the order in which the components are executed, and estimates the amount of time required to do so. A program schedule uses the PWBS as its starting point.

Cost Estimating and Budgeting

Cost management skills are required for the Cost Estimating and Budgeting process. Cost Estimating aggregates all costs of a program using an estimate made by the program team or an aggregate based on individual estimates of projects and work packages. Cost Budgeting establishes budgets for the program based on the budgets for the individual projects, the nonproject activities, and any financial constraints on the budget.

Human Resource Planning

The Human Resource Planning process documents and assigns program roles, responsibilities, and reporting relationships of individuals and groups both within a program's organization and outside it.

Quality Planning

The Quality Planning process identifies

standards relevant to a program and specifies how to comply with them. This process must occur early in the program to ensure that the required competencies are available throughout the planning of critical program activities and processes.

The Risk Management Planning and Analysis process involves specifying ways to plan and analyze risk management activities for a program and its individual components.

Risk needs to be spread across a program, and critical risks need to be identified and to have an associated risk response plan.

For example, if a supplier to a manufacturing plant discontinues the production of a necessary component part, the manufacturing plant needs to have alternate suppliers available or a plan to begin producing the component itself.

Question

The Planning team carries out several Planning process group processes that ensure the smooth running of a program. Match the descriptions to the processes.

Options:

A. Clarifies the boundaries of the program and forms the basis for future program decisions

B. Details the deliverables that the program components will produce, the total scope of the program, and its major milestones

C. Determines the information needs of the program stakeholders

D. Plans responses and analyzes potential crises and threats to the program

Targets:

1. Scope Definition
2. Create PWBS
3. Communications Planning
4. Risk Management Planning and Analysis

Answer

Scope Definition clarifies the boundaries of the program and forms the basis for future program decisions. It specifies what activities are within the program domain.

The PWBS details the deliverables that program components will produce, the total scope of the program, and its major milestones. So it provides an overview of the program and shows how each project fits into it.

Communications Planning determines the information and communication needs of the program stakeholders. It specifies who needs what information, when they need it, and how it will be communicated.

Risk Management Planning and Analysis involves specifying ways to plan and analyze risk management activities for a program and its individual components. Critical risks should have a risk response plan that the organization can follow if things go wrong.

The Planning team requires procurement management skills for planning program purchases and acquisitions and for planning program contracting.

When planning program purchases and acquisitions, the team determines what to procure and when it should be acquired.

The Plan Program Contracting process identifies potential contracting sources and creates formal contracting documents to implement contracts for suppliers either external to or within the organization.

Contracting at the program level often needs to address legal issues and considerations. This process produces the guidelines for the Program Contract Administration process.

Question

Match descriptions to resource management processes that the Planning team performs.

Options:

A. Determines the order in which program components should be executed

B. Aggregates all costs into a program using estimates made by project managers

C. Assigns program roles, responsibilities, and reporting relationships

D. Identifies program standards and specifies how to comply with them

E. Identifies potential contracting sources and creates formal contracting documents

Targets:

1. Schedule Development
2. Cost Estimating and Budgeting
3. Human Resource Planning
4. Quality Planning
5. Plan Program Contracting process

Answer

Schedule Development determines the order in which program components, needed to produce deliverables, should be executed.

Cost Estimating and Budgeting involves aggregating all costs using estimates and establishing budgets for the program based on the budgets for the individual projects, the nonproject activity, and any financial constraints on the budget.

Human Resource Planning documents and

assigns program roles, responsibilities, and reporting relationships of individuals and groups that are both within the program's organization and external to it.

Quality Planning identifies standards relevant to the program and specifies how to comply with them. This process must occur early in the program to ensure that the required competencies are available throughout the planning of critical program activities and processes.

Procurement management involves planning program purchases and acquisitions and carrying out the Plan Program Contracting process, which identifies potential contracting sources and creates formal contracting documents.

Benefits management basics

Benefits management involves defining the expected benefits of a program and monitoring the delivery of these benefits throughout the program life cycle.

According to the Project Management Institute's (PMI®) Standard for Program Management, benefits management

assesses the value and organizational impact of a program

identifies the interdependencies of benefits being delivered among various projects within the program ensures that targeted benefits are specific, measurable, actual, realistic, and time based

analyzes the potential impact of planned program changes on benefits outcomes

assigns responsibilities and accountability for the actual benefits required for the program

Woodworth Financial Advisors has launched a program called Flexible Finance Loans in partnership with a Media Equipment Retail outlet. Darren Alford is appointed as program manager. This program intends to provide a new capital-lending service that is accessible to individuals and organizations.

The service offers a variety of flexible options

that can be customized to suit each customer, consolidating customers' debt from various purchases into a single, easily managed package.

To analyze how this program is likely to affect Woodworth, Darren and the program management team identify potential benefits or value that the program can bring to the organization. In this case, likely benefits are higher customer satisfaction, increased sales of financial products, and a greater market share.

The value of these benefits must then be assessed to determine whether the program is viable for the organization.

To identify interdependencies, Darren needs to review the projects associated with the new financial service and identify the benefits associated with each project within the program. For example, training employees on the new financial packages will provide higher sales and increased customer satisfaction.

Each benefit must be measurable and have a schedule for its delivery. For example, quarterly sales are expected to increase by 20%, and customer complaints should show a decrease of 50% three months after staff training is completed.

To ensure that benefits are delivered in the quantity expected and within schedule, Darren needs to assign responsibilities and accountability for benefits delivery. The Sales team manager is responsible for increased customer satisfaction and sales, and Darren is accountable for both these benefits.

Additionally, any changes that Darren plans within the program must be assessed in terms of its impact on benefit delivery. For example, a new software system for processing customer calls must be assessed in terms of its ability to reduce the time taken to answer and process calls.

Question

What are the attributes of benefits management according to the Standard for Program Management?

Options:

1. It assesses the value and organizational impact of the program

2. It identifies benefit interdependencies among various projects within the program

3. It ensures that targeted benefits are specific, measurable, actual, realistic, and time based

4. It analyzes the potential impact of planned program changes on benefits outcomes

5. It assigns responsibilities and accountability for the actual benefits required for the program 6. It

ensures that information is communicated when it is needed to whoever needs it

Answer

Option 1: This is a correct option. Benefits management involves analyzing how a program is likely to affect an organization and ensuring that the program will bring value to the organization. This value must then be assessed to determine whether the program is viable for the organization.

Option 2: This is a correct option. Program management works with the interdependencies between programs to reduce work duplication and enhance results. Benefits management identifies shared benefits that various projects and ongoing work bring to the organization and its customers.

Option 3: This is a correct option. To manage benefits effectively, the benefits must be realized or actual, realistic, and measurable to some extent so that they can be assessed in terms of expected and actual delivery of benefits.

Option 4: This is a correct option. When projects or program work needs to change, the changes need to be assessed in terms of their impact on expected benefits before any changes can be signed off.

Option 5: This is a correct option. To ensure that benefits are managed effectively and to ensure that benefits are realized, accountability for the results must be set.

Option 6: This is an incorrect option. This attribute is an aspect of stakeholder management rather than benefits management.

Tangible and intangible benefits

Benefits may be financial or nonfinancial. Examples of nonfinancial benefits are a positive impact on the working environment, company reputation, or customer satisfaction. Some benefits can be easily identified and quantified, and they are known as tangible benefits.

You can directly compare tangible financial benefits in terms of costs or generated revenue and prioritize the benefits accordingly. Nonfinancial benefits – such as decreased staff turnover – generally require more aggressive justification and lobbying.

Intangible benefits are nonfinancial benefits that are not easily quantifiable – for example, improved employee morale. You identify and prioritize these benefits according to their contribution to strategic business goals. The benefits and the objectives need to be stated as clearly as possible.

Links to measurements should be made explicit, however much of the value of this type of benefit is qualitative rather than quantitative.

Financial benefits are always tangible, but nonfinancial benefits can be tangible or intangible. It is important to classify these benefits so that you can better measure them.

Tangible benefits

Financial tangible benefits include decreased costs and increased revenue. Nonfinancial tangible benefits include increased quality of service, decreased staff turnover, decreases in the number of customer complaints, and increases in productivity.

Intangible benefits

Intangible benefits are typically nonfinancial and include increased customer satisfaction, improved staff morale, heightened corporate image, and other qualitative improvements in an organization.

In the Woodworth Flexible Finance program, one of the tangible benefits is increased sales. The company sets targets for the number of sales that it expects - for example an increase of 15% in sales of capital-lending packages by the end of the financial year.

An intangible benefit of Woodworth's Flexible Finance program is increased customer satisfaction. This intangible benefit can be quantified by linking it to decreases in the number of customer complaints and increased sales. Qualitative data can also be generated through questionnaires that customers can fill in.

Sorin Dumitrascu

Question

Identify examples of tangible and intangible benefits.

Several examples may match to a single category.

Options:

A. Decreased staff turnover

B. Reduction in expenses

C. Improved access to information

D. Increased staff morale

Targets:

1. Tangible benefits

2. Intangible benefits

Answer

Decreased staff turnover and reduction in expenses are tangible benefits because they are easily quantified and are measured in integers or percentages.

Improved access to information and increased staff morale are intangible benefits because their value is not easily transferred into quantifiable data.

Phases of benefits management

The high-level objectives of a benefits management strategy include identifying and defining expected benefits of a program, establishing a benefits management structure – including a benefits realization plan – and establishing accountability for benefits realization.

A benefits realization plan includes review points, a benefits delivery schedule, benefit interdependencies between projects, and processes for implementing business changes brought about through these benefits.

At each phase of the benefits management strategy, the program team adds to the benefits realization plan.

A benefits management strategy goes through four phases:

initial planning

Initial planning for benefits management specifies how the benefits will be managed and delivered. These details are provided in the business plans for the program and its projects.

The plan should include key benefits statements, stakeholder analysis, benefit models, and the schedule for delivery. When setting the schedule delivery, you need to structure project phases so that benefits can be delivered as soon as possible.

identifying and defining benefits

Identifying and defining benefits involves categorizing benefits, noting their interdependencies across projects, and aligning them with business strategic goals.

The needs and expectations of stakeholders should be clearly defined, and program outputs should be assessed in terms of their impact on a business.

realizing and tracking benefits

Realizing and tracking benefits requires detailed action plans for the benefit delivery. You should then measure the progress against these plans at each phase of program delivery.

The benefits should continue to be tracked after projects are completed.

reviewing and evaluating benefits

The review and evaluation of benefits involves measuring the benefits achieved against theirtargets as set out in the benefits plan.

Any unplanned benefits that a program generates should be noted and measured throughout the life of the program.

In the initial planning phase, you define expected benefits and plan for how each benefit is to be realized in the benefits realization plan. This involves planning for each benefit using business plans and stakeholder expectations.

Planning for each benefit involves creating key benefits statements, which list the key benefits and explain why the program is being undertaken. The statements clarify anticipated business improvements and classify benefits as quantifiable, nonquantifiable, and financial. Stakeholder expectations are captured and analyzed, and this analysis is added to the benefits realization plan.

During initial planning, you also structure projects in terms of their schedule to ensure that benefits are realized as quickly as possible.

In the initial planning phase of the Woodworth Flexible Finance program, the program team:

plans for each benefit

The plans for each benefit list and classify benefits, such as higher customer satisfaction, increased sales of financial products, and a greater market share. In terms of the increased sales benefit, the plan states that the program should increase quarterly sales by 20%.

In terms of stakeholder expectations, it is noted that the company director is really interested in this program as it is likely to generate new income.

Sorin Dumitrascu

structures the program

To structure the program, it is decided that the schedule for the program will begin with a market research project, and then employee training and a marketing campaign will run concurrently.

Key benefits statements should also include an overview of who should be responsible for delivery of each benefit, what changes are needed to obtain the benefits, and a list of who will be affected by the changes.

More detailed stakeholder analysis is added as the program continues.

In the identifying and defining phase of benefits management, you need to map benefits to program outcomes - for example, Darren maps the program outcome of providing a new capital-lending service for Woodworth's clients to increased market share, increased sales, and improved customer satisfaction.

You also need to note interdependencies across benefits and projects. In the Woodworth scenario, customer satisfaction relies on employee training and is associated with the benefit of increased sales. Program managers can create benefits matrices that show these relationships and add the matrices to the benefits realization plan.

In this phase, program managers should clearly

define the needs and expectations of stakeholders, and assess predicted and actual program outputs in terms of their impact on the business.

In the identifying and defining phase of benefits management, the Woodworth program team links program benefits to the following strategic goals:

to create innovative financial solutions for clients

The innovative financial solutions goal links directly to the program output of providing clients with a flexible finance package that reduces their reliance on capital. This goal is also linked to the program's intangible benefit of increased customer satisfaction. And it links to the tangible benefits of increased revenue and sales.

to provide excellent and friendly service

The goal of providing excellent and friendly service links directly to the program's intangible benefit of increased customer satisfaction and links indirectly to goals of increased revenue and sales.

to develop strategic partnerships with respected companies

The strategic partnership goal links directly to the program outcome of creating a financing solution for the Media Equipment Retail outlet's clients. This is also directly linked to the tangible benefits of increased sales and revenue.

In the realizing and tracking benefits phase of benefits management, you draw up detailed action plans for the benefit delivery and then monitor delivery against these plans. You measure the progress of benefits delivery against these plans at each phase of the program, even after projects are completed.

To ensure measurements are useful, baseline measures of each benefit are taken before the program begins and targets are set for each phase gate review.

For example, the Woodworth program team measures current customer satisfaction levels at 72% and the target at the second phase gate review is 80% – an 8% increase.

To track benefits effectively, the benefits realization plan needs to include specific measures for each benefit.

For intangible benefits - such as improved customer satisfaction - you need to create a quantifiable measure and use this in conjunction with a qualitative assessment of the benefit. For example, customer questionnaires can be used in conjunction with numbers of customer complaints and compliments.

You then prioritize benefits according to their contribution to strategic business goals. In this case, customer satisfaction is directly linked to the "provide excellent and friendly service" business objective, so it is rated as a top priority.

During the review and evaluation of benefits phase, the program's benefits are measured using the measurements developed for them.

For example, customer satisfaction increase is measured at 11%, which is 3% higher than the expected target of 8%. This unexpected benefit is noted and communicated to the appropriate stakeholders.

Case Study: Question 1 of 4
Scenario

Easy Nomad travel agency management has decided to embark on a program of marketing projects focused on promoting travel to Eastern Europe. You have been assigned as program manager for this program and now need to prepare for the benefits management of the program.

Answer each question in the order that it is presented.

Question

What should be included in the benefits realization plan during the initial planning phase of the program?

Options:

1. Definitions of key benefits such as increased revenue and improved strategic relations with Eastern European Tourism departments

2. Interdependencies between projects that lead to benefits such as improved strategic relations with Eastern European Tourism departments

3. Schedules showing the research project completion coinciding with the start of the training and development of strategic relationships projects

4. Information around the overly high expectations of Easy Nomad's rail partner company

5. Benefits target measures such as a 20% increase in sales of Eastern Europe travel packages

Answer

Option 1: This is a correct option. Each benefit needs to be clearly defined before it can be managed or delivered. So the program team uses business plans and other inputs to define key benefits of the program and adds these to the benefits realization plan.

Option 2: This is an incorrect option. Interdependencies are generally identified during the identifying and defining benefits phase of the program benefits management strategy.

Option 3: This is a correct option. The

sequencing of projects needs to be defined so that they are structured in a way that ensures benefits can be achieved quickly and successfully. This sequencing should occur before projects are initiated. Therefore this is an aspect of program structuring that occurs during the initial planning phase of the program benefits management strategy.

Option 4: This is a correct option. Providing a broad analysis of stakeholder expectations is an aspect of planning in the initial planning phase; it is then taken further in the identifying and defining benefits phase. Understanding what stakeholder expectations are can help set benefits management goals.

Option 5: This is an incorrect option. Benefits targets should be added to the benefits realization plan during the realizing and tracking benefits phase.

Case Study: Question 2 of 4
Match the program benefits to Easy Nomad's strategic business objectives. Several benefits may match to a single objective and the same benefit may match to more than one objective.
Options:
A. Increased revenue
B. Increased market share

C. Improved strategic relationships with tourism departments

D. Customer satisfaction

Targets:

1. To provide a wide range of quality travel packages at affordable prices

2. To develop strategic relationships with tourism and travel stakeholders

3. To provide skills training to frontline employees

Answer

The increased revenue and market share are linked to providing a wide range of quality travel packages at affordable prices. Improved strategic relations should also help to ensure this.

Increased market share and improved strategic relations with Tourism departments have a direct link with the development of strategic relationships with relevant stakeholders.

Customer satisfaction is directly linked to the efficiency and friendliness of the service they receive. As such, skills training should improve customer service and customer satisfaction.

Case Study: Question 3 of 4

What should be included in the benefits realization plan during the realizing and tracking benefits phase of the benefits management strategy for Easy Nomad?

Options:

1. The current sales figures and measures for customer satisfaction

2. Benefits target measures such as a 20% increase in sales of Eastern Europe travel packages

3. An explanation of why customer satisfaction levels had not reached their target at the first phase gate review

4. A statement about the high level of support received from the company's partners in Poland 5. The surprising shift in employee morale that has occurred during this phase of the program

Answer

Option 1: This is a correct option. To track and realize benefits, you need to ensure that detailed action plans for each benefit are in place and included in the benefits realization plan. These plans should include baseline measures of each expected benefit.

Option 2: This is a correct option. To track benefits effectively, you need target measures for benefits realization. These must be included in the benefits realization plan during the realizing and tracking benefits phase of benefits management.

Option 3: This is a correct option. At each phase

gate review, you need to note benefit delivery targets that have been met. Any unmet targets should also be noted with reasons for the target not being met.

Option 4: This is an incorrect option. A broad overview of stakeholder expectations should be added at the planning phase of benefits management. This helps set benefits management goals and aids in stakeholder management around program benefits.

Option 5: This is an incorrect option. Unexpected benefits should be noted at the reviewing and evaluating phase of benefits management.

Case Study: Question 4 of 4

What should be included in the benefits realization plan during the review and evaluation of benefits phase of the benefits management strategy for Easy Nomad?

Options:

1. The difference between target levels and the incremental increase in customer satisfaction levels at each phase gate review

2. A description of the surprising increase in employee morale since the program's initiation

3. A note about how rapidly sales increased once

the problems with customer service were addressed

4. The schedule for when the 10% increase in sales revenue should be expected

Answer

Option 1: This is a correct option. When evaluating benefits realization, you need to compare actual benefits measures against the targets set for these benefits.

Option 2: This is a correct option. When evaluating and reviewing benefits, any unplanned benefits should be noted and described.

Option 3: This is an incorrect option. The interrelationships between benefits should be noted during the identifying and defining benefits phase of benefits management.

Option 4: This is an incorrect option. Schedules for delivery are added to the benefits realization plan during the initial planning phase of benefits management.

The program manager's role

Stakeholders play a critical role in the success of a program. But how do you identify and manage these stakeholders?

According to the Project Management Institute's (PMI®) Combined Standards Glossary, stakeholders are persons and organizations – such as customers, sponsors, and the public – that are actively involved in the program, whose interests may be positively or negatively affected by the program, and who may exert influence over the program.

Stakeholder management for program managers encompasses a far broader scope than that of project managers.

There are typically far more people and organizations – both internal and external to the program – who affect and are affected by a program.

The key tasks of stakeholder management are to:

identify how a program affects stakeholders

To identify how a program affects stakeholders, program managers need to understand the positions that stakeholders may take in relation to the program and plan accordingly to ensure the program's success.

create a management plan

Program managers need to create a management plan that incorporates basic change management strategies and a communication strategy to ensure buy-in and to provide accurate and timely information to all stakeholders.

Key stakeholders

Program managers need to be able to identify key stakeholders and to understand the role of these stakeholders in terms of program work and benefits delivery.

The following internal key stakeholders play a management role:

program director

The program director is ultimately responsible for the successful delivery and achievement of program benefits. The director often also plays the role of program sponsor.

program sponsor

The program sponsor – or executive sponsor – is the decision-maker on the program board and is responsible for ensuring that resources are available for a program. This position is often held by the program director.

program manager

The program manager is responsible for the overall management of the program – its planning, implementation, and delivery of benefits. The program manager is also responsible for the setup, management, and delivery of the program.

project managers

Program Management

Project managers are responsible for managing individual projects and ensuring that project deliverables are reached on time and within budget.

Natural Ways is a company that grows medicinal plants to sell in bulk to other companies. It has recently approved a new program focusing on finding African medicinal plants that it can grow and market successfully.

The head of research for the company, Julio Hernandez, is given overall responsibility for the program and is responsible for ensuring that there are sufficient resources for the program. So his role is program director and program sponsor.

Rosa Eisen, the program manager, is responsible for the setup, management, and delivery of the program. Tom Herwig is responsible for identifying optimal growing conditions for identified plants –so he is the project manager for the project that focuses on growing the plants.

In program management, the key stakeholder groups or organizations are the:

program board
The program board oversees and implements program governance, and it provides the infrastructure for quality assurance and governance

for the program. The board defines the functions and responsibilities that will dictate how the program is set up.

program management office (PMO)

The PMO centrally manages administrative functions for the programs in an organization. It ensures that programs use similar processes and follow the same policies and guidelines.

program office

The program office is set up when an organization does not have a mandate to set up a PMO. The program office functions similarly to a PMO by centrally handling administration. However, a program office administers a single program rather than all programs.

performing organization

The performing organization is the organization whose personnel are most directly involved in doing the work of a program.

program team members

Program team members perform program activities such as interface planning, benefits management, and stakeholder management.

project team members

Project team members carry out project activities such as training staff members and developing new products.

customers

Customers are any individuals or organizations that use the results of the program and that will gain from its anticipated benefits.

Although the program manager for Natural Ways will hire consultants and others to assist in ensuring the program's success, Natural Ways employees will carry out the bulk of the work, so Natural Ways is the performing organization.

The program board, headed by Julio – as the program sponsor – defines the functions and responsibilities that specify how the program will be set up. So Julio is ultimately responsible for the spread of projects selected for the program and for ensuring that the program has sufficient resources to create viable products.

Natural Ways' board uses the company's PMO to provide the program team with policies and procedures that it should follow to ensure that it complies with legal and company requirements. Because the company has a PMO, no program office is required for the program.

The PMO provides process documents that ensure that the research team members operate within the legal bounds of the countries from which plants are taken and that they follow approved processes in testing the plant properties.

The Natural Ways program team is responsible for ensuring that marketable plants are identified and grown to extend the company's product line and customer base.

The research project team is responsible for identifying plants that have broad-based or specific healing properties, particularly in boosting immune systems. The horticultural project team is responsible for ensuring that the optimal number of plants are grown within schedule.

The key customers for the program are the retail companies that sell Natural Ways products. Internal customers include the Natural Ways CEO and the vice president of the division.

Additional stakeholders that may be associated with a program include:

- • government regulatory bodies,
- suppliers,
- interest groups,
- competitors.

As program manager for the Natural Ways program, Rosa Eisen needs to ensure that all stakeholders are identified and that the list is documented. She should take time to understand each stakeholder's position and analyze how that may impact the program.

She and her program team also need to draw up a communication strategy to ensure that there is sufficient support for the program and to ensure that pertinent information is available where and when it is needed.

Case Study: Question 1 of 2
Scenario

A nongovernmental organization that assists victims of violence has an ongoing fund-raising program for its core projects – awareness training, counseling services, and advocacy.

Answer the questions in any order.

Question

Match the names of the program personnel to their roles.

Options:

A. June

B. Henry

C. Ruth

D. Tania

E. Martin

Targets:

1. Program director and sponsor
2. Program manager
3. Project manager
4. Program team member

5. Project team member

Answer

June is responsible for the running and funding of the organization, and as such she fulfills the role of program director and sponsor.

Henry is responsible for managing the funding program, and as such he is the program manager. Ruth is responsible for the advocacy project, so she is a project manager.

Tania helps Henry in his work and is a member of the program team.

Martin assists Ruth, so she is a member of the advocacy project team.

Case Study: Question 2 of 2

Match these names to their associated group or category.

Options:

A. Maria

B. William

C. Tony

Targets:

1. Program board member

2. PMO/Program Office member

3. Customer

Answer

Maria oversees program governance and advises

June, and as such is a member of the program board.

William handles program administration and policies for the organization, so is part of the PMO. Tony is a customer in that he and other victims of violence are intended to benefit from the program.

Purpose and context

Program governance provides a framework for decision-making and delivery management for a program.

Its purpose is to control a company's investment and to monitor benefits delivery. It does this through the development, implementation, and monitoring of company policies, structures, and practices for a program.

Program governance tries to ensure that governance at program level integrates with other levels of governance such as operations management and portfolio or project management.

Program governance also ensures that its policies and practices are aligned with the strategic plans of the organization.

Creating a program board is a formal method of overseeing and implementing program governance. The board comprises three key figures supported by the program management office (PMO).

Program sponsor

The program sponsor – also known as the executive sponsor – takes advice from the program management team and key internal and external stakeholders within the board.

He or she is responsible for the decision-making of the board because program boards are seldom consensus based. In some organizations, the program director may also serve in the role of executive sponsor.

Key internal stakeholders

Key internal stakeholders that may be included in a program board are portfolio managers, business change managers, and program directors.

These individuals do not work full time on the board, so they rely heavily on information from the program management team.

Other stakeholders

Other stakeholders that may be a part of the program board include suppliers, customers, or others external to the organization that are affected by the program's outcomes.

Like the rest of the board, these members do not work full time on the board, and they provide advice and other perspectives for the executive sponsor to use in her or his decision-making.

PMO

A PMO may be set up to manage administrative functions and to define policies and procedures for a program to follow.

Typically, a single PMO is set up to centrally manage administrative functions for all programs so that all programs use similar processes and follow the same policies and guidelines. Its role is to support the program board.

Management of Easy Nomad, a travel agency, has decided to embark on a program of marketing projects focused on promoting travel to Eastern Europe. The company has set up a formal program board to oversee and implement program governance.

The board comprises Andrea Horner – an external stakeholder, Ed Miller – the portfolio manager, Gina Rosetti – the program director, and Debora Wade – the program sponsor.

Debora makes the final board decisions once she and the board have discussed issues that the program manager and program team bring to the board.

The program board also has access to a PMO that defines and manages the shared processes, procedures, and policies that all the programs at Easy Nomad must follow.

Question
Who has the decision-making role on a program board?
Options:

Program Management

1. The program sponsor
2. The program director
3. The portfolio manager
4. The business change manager

Answer

Option 1: This is the correct option. The program sponsor of a program board is responsible for decision-making after receiving input from other board members and the program team.

Option 2: This is an incorrect option. A program director may serve on the board as an internal stakeholder, but the program sponsor is responsible for decision-making. In some organizations, the program director may also serve in the role of executive sponsor.

Option 3: This is an incorrect option. The portfolio manager may be a member of the board and provide input on decisions.

Option 4: This is an incorrect option. The business change manager may represent internal stakeholders as a member of the board, but he or she doesn't have the power to make board decisions.

Functions of the board

A program board is set up at the inception of a program, and it continues to function until the program terminates. The board represents an organization's interests and provides the infrastructure for quality assurance and governance for the program.

The eight main functions of a program board are:

program initiation

Once a program has been provisionally approved, the program board initiates the program by issuing a program brief that details the strategic objectives and benefits that the program is expected to deliver.

planning approval

The program board reviews the broad plans for a program and approves these plans – for

example the draft schedule, budget, and benefits management plans.

reviews

The board carries out a number of reviews at significant gateposts during the program life cycle.

These reviews include reviews of program progress, benefit delivery, and costs.

guidance on roadblocks

Program boards provide guidance to program

managers on issues that they are unable to resolve –
for example stakeholder management issues or
changes to resource needs that impact the budget.

resource availability

The program board is responsible for ensuring
that the necessary resources for a program are
available. This includes financing, human resources,
and any technical equipment that the program needs
for it to run efficiently.

**establishment of frameworks and limits for
investments**

The program board establishes the frameworks
for program investments and sets limits on these
investments. This includes time and financial
investments and is associated with risk assessment.

**collection of input for strategic progress
reporting**

The program board needs to provide strategic
progress reports about the program to executive
management and to the portfolio managers or
directors. To do this, the board must gather relevant
information from the program team.

**compliance with corporate and legal policies,
procedures, and practices**

The program board is responsible for ensuring
that the program is compliant with corporate and
legal policies, procedures, and practices. Some of

the work that is required to ensure this may be handled by the PMO.

The Easy Nomad travel agency sets up a program board to create a program brief for the new Eastern Europe program. The brief details the strategic objectives and benefits that the program is expected to deliver – in this case, increased sales, improved customer service, and increased market share.

The program team creates broad plans for implementation and delivery. The board reviews the program plans, ensuring that they meet overall limits in terms of resources and schedules. They adjust budget and scope limits of the plans and then approve the plans ahead of implementation.

The board also commissions the PMO to define the sales and marketing policies and procedures required for the program to meet with corporate and legal requirements.

Question

Wildlife Films has set up a program board for its series of wildlife films focusing on life in the oceans. Which of the following functions does the board need to fulfill over the life span of the program?

Options:

1. Issue a program brief that lists the three expected benefits of the ocean program

2. Approve the draft schedule for the program

3. Set the budget limits on filming expeditions

4. Ensure that the program implementation plans follow the accepted processes within the company

5. Write phase gate schedules and budget plans for the program

6. Draw up a benefits management plan for the program

Answer

Option 1: This is a correct option. To initiate a program, the program board needs to issue a program brief that outlines the objectives and benefits that the program is expected to deliver.

Option 2: This is a correct option. The program board needs to approve plans made by the program team – this includes schedules, costs, and benefit delivery plans.

Option 3: This is a correct option. The program board sets limits on investments. This includes time and financial investments and is associated with risk assessment.

Option 4: This is a correct option. The program board is responsible for ensuring that the program meets corporate and legal requirements in terms of policies, procedures, and practices.

Option 5: This is an incorrect option. The program board need only approve these plans and ensure that sufficient resources are available. The program team needs to create the plans.

Option 6: This is an incorrect option. The program board need only approve these plans, ensuring that they align with the organization's strategic goals. The program team is responsible for creating all program management subsidiary plans.

The Easy Nomad board is also responsible for the following functions:

performing reviews

The board schedules a series of phase gate reviews in the program life cycle. At each of these phase gates, the board receives cost, benefit delivery, and progress reports from the program manager. The board reviews these reports and approves necessary changes or reigns in aspects of the program that are moving outside of the program scope or budget.

During the first phase gate review, the board approves an increase in the marketing budget to accommodate an unexpected increase in paper costs.

collecting input for strategic progress reporting

Using the phase gate reports and through a series of meetings, the board gathers information that members can compile into strategic progress reports on the program for the company directors.

One of the Eastern Europe program's strategic progress reports details the need to change the focus for middle market packages from family trips to ones that cater more to singles and couples.

ensuring resource availability

Using the detailed plans that the board has approved, and the information that it gathers for its progress reports, the board checks what resources are required and lobbies for these resources or otherwise ensures that the resources are available when needed.

For example, the board lobbies for the recruitment of ten additional travel agents who specialize in Eastern Europe to accommodate the increase in sales.

assisting the program manager through roadblocks

When problems escalate or unexpected issues occur, the board discusses the issues with the program manager and provides possible solutions to the problems, or it uses its political weight to help the program manager overcome the difficulties.

So when the Easy Nomad program manager lost

the printing contract with a brochure printing
company, the board used its networks to secure
another contract at a similar cost.

Program boards may be called upon to fulfill
other functions depending on the organization's
needs and structure.

Alternatively, some organizations do not set up
an official program board, but use senior managers
and executives to handle the functions that are
generally handled by a program board.

Question

Wildlife Films has set up a program board for its
series of wildlife films focusing on life in the
oceans. Which of the following functions is the
board responsible for?

Options:

1. Carrying out reviews of the program's
progress during the production of each episode

2. Gathering information on the quality of the
first film from the program manager's reports

3. Coordinating with human resources to ensure
that editing personnel are available when a film is
behind schedule

4. Providing mentoring to the program manager
when she has difficulties with a manager

5. Defining the Television Broadcasting requirements that all programs need to follow

6. Identify how the program outcomes will affect stakeholders and write a report detailing this

Answer

Option 1: This is a correct option. The program board is responsible for reviewing cost, benefit delivery, and progress reports from the program manager at strategic phase gates of the program.

Option 2: This is a correct option. The program board is responsible for collecting input for strategic progress reporting.

Option 3: This is a correct option. The program board is responsible for ensuring resource availability.

Option 4: This is a correct option. The program board is responsible for assisting the program manager through various roadblocks that have escalated beyond the manager's control or capacity.

Option 5: This is an incorrect option. The program board is responsible for ensuring that the program meets legal and corporate requirements. However, if all programs need to follow a set of requirements, the PMO is typically used for centrally administering this. The program board has jurisdiction over a single program only.

Option 6: This is an incorrect option. The

program manager is responsible for this, though the board may assist the program manager in this task.

CHAPTER 2 - Program Life Cycle and Organization

Program management life-cycle phases are important for a successful program because they enable you to manage benefits and control outcomes, manage stakeholders effectively, ensure effective program governance, and control program resources across constituent projects.

In this lesson, you will learn about program life-cycle phases, program themes across the program life cycle, and program governance across the life cycle.

Program management life-cycle phases are used as a tool to monitor and control a program's benefits. The program life cycle is made up of five phases – the preprogram setup phase, the program setup phase, the establishing a program management and technical infrastructure phase, the delivering the benefits phase, and the closing the program phase.

Program management life-cycle phases are used as a tool to monitor and control a program's benefits. The program life cycle is made up of five phases – the preprogram setup phase, the program setup phase, the establishing a program management and technical infrastructure phase, the delivering the benefits phase, and the closing the program phase.

The three themes that span all the program life-cycle phases are benefits management, stakeholder management, and phase gate reviews.

Benefits management is a vital process in the program life cycle. It involves ensuring that all the expected benefits are identified and achieved.

Stakeholder management is focused on managing all the individuals and groups that are affected by the program, as well as ensuring that their expectations are met.

Phase gate reviews evaluate the outcomes of the various program and project life-cycle phases at key decision points and enable program managers to address any deviations from program plans. They also enable managers to determine whether the program must continue, and whether it's ready to enter a new phase.

Program governance involves overseeing a program and its functions throughout the program's life cycle. It involves developing and maintaining a program infrastructure with suitable communication and monitoring systems, as well as overseeing progress and benefits delivery.

The groups or individuals that play active roles

in the program governance process include the program board, the executive sponsor, the program director, the program manager, and project managers. Each of these roles is associated with specific program governance responsibilities.

Programs can be managed in terms of their five life-cycle phases – preprogram setup, program setup, establish program management and technical infrastructure, deliver the benefits, and closing the program.

A clear understanding of the management of these phases improves your program's chances of success. This lesson takes you through the management tasks and the objectives associated with each of the five phases.

During the preprogram setup phase, the program sponsor or program manager needs to develop a rationale for the program, identify and analyze stakeholders, and create documentation such as high- level plans and program charters. The selection committee then reviews the program and accepts or rejects it at its first phase gate review. If the program is accepted, a program manager is formally appointed.

During the program setup phase, the

foundational planning for the program occurs. If necessary, feasibility studies are run and the program is divided into components – if this has not already occurred. The program management plan is developed along with several subsidiary plans and decision-making responsibilities are defined.

In the establishing program management and technical infrastructure program life-cycle phase, a management and technical infrastructure that will support the program and enable the delivery of its benefits must be established.

Key results of this phase include staffing of the organizational structure for the program, and the provision of a program office, a program governance mechanism and control framework, facilities and required infrastructure, and the needed IT and communication technologies.

The deliver the benefits phase is the longest phase of a program and continues until the program is closed. During this phase, you initiate projects, manage the transition to the program's end state, and identify and manage changes that affect the program.

The close the program phase is the final phase of a program's life cycle. During this phase, you need

Program Management

to compile a benefits status review, detail lessons learned, ensure ongoing customer support, and disband the program teams and infrastructure.

Importance of life-cycle phases

"Time and money are running out on agencies that handle projects and programs the old-fashioned way." - Anne Laurent, journalist

How should organizations handle their projects and programs?

Using life-cycle phases in program management is becoming essential in the modern environment because it helps organizations to control, monitor, and realize program outcomes and benefits.

The life cycle of a program can be divided into several phases. According to the Standard for Program Management of the Project Management Institute (PMI®), the function of these phases is to facilitate program governance, enhance control, coordinate program and project resources, and coordinate overall risk management.

Program management life-cycle phases are important for a successful program, because they enable you to:

manage benefits and control outcomes

The phases enable you to manage benefits and control outcomes in a predictable and coordinated manner. They enable you to record, track, and evaluate benefits. They also enable you to predict the ongoing value of benefits and reasons for deviations, and to make suggestions on how gaps can be bridged.

manage stakeholders effectively

The phases enable you to manage stakeholders effectively. They provide a structure for identifying stakeholders, managing stakeholder expectations, and ensuring continued stakeholder support for the program.

ensure effective program governance

The phases enable you to ensure effective program governance by means of phase gate reviews, predefined milestones, and continuous program evaluation. They also enable you to ensure strategic alignment and to monitor and manage opportunities and threats, manage program outcomes, and assist with investment appraisal and benefit assessment.

coordinate resources

The phases enable you to coordinate resources by allocating them across projects, managing program resources according to a program management plan, monitoring resource use, and releasing resources from a program once they're no longer needed.

Candy is the program manager of an events

planning company. To ensure that all events are successful, Candy divides the planning of each event she is organizing into specific phases.

By using program management life-cycle phases, Candy:

manages benefits and controls outcomes

Using life-cycle phases, Candy manages the benefits and controls the outcomes of each event her program team is organizing. She tracks, records, and evaluates the progress on specific events. When the planning for an event deviates from the original plan, Candy is able to identify why and make suggestions on how these gaps can be bridged.

effectively manages stakeholders

Using life-cycle phases, Candy effectively manages the stakeholders involved in each of the events her company is planning. For each event, she secures funds from the main stakeholder – the client. She also delivers regular progress reports to the client and ensures the client's continuous involvement in planning the event.

ensures effective program governance

Candy ensures effective program governance by monitoring the progress of each event her company is planning. She sets specific milestones for each phase of organizing an event and ensures that these milestones are reached. By dividing the program into phases, she is able to evaluate progress regularly, and she makes corrections if necessary.

coordinates resources

Candy coordinates resources in order to save money. She optimizes her company's use of resources – such as a graphic designer, the printer, and tablecloths for different functions – by allocating them across various events as they're needed.

These are the phases of the program life cycle:
- • preprogram setup,
- program setup,
- establishing a program management and technical infrastructure,
- delivering the benefits,
- closing the program.

In this lesson, the following areas will be covered:

program life-cycle phases

The program moves through specific, often overlapping program life-cycle phases. These phases serve as a means to manage and control the program, to manage outcomes, and to achieve the planned benefits.

program themes across the program life cycle

There are three main program themes across the program life cycle – the management of benefits, management of stakeholders, and program governance through phase gate reviews.

program governance across the program life cycle

Program governance across the program life cycle is achieved by using tools such as predefined milestones or phase gate reviews throughout all the phases of a program.

Question

What is the importance of program management life-cycle phases in a successful program?

Options:

1. They enable you to make informed decisions regarding the management of a company

2. They enable you to manage benefits and control outcomes

3. They enable you to effectively manage stakeholders

4. They enable effective program governance

5. They enable you to coordinate resources

6. They enable you to determine all program outcomes

Answer

Program Management

Option 1: This is an incorrect option. You will not be able to manage a company by dividing a program into life-cycle phases. The phases enable you to manage a specific program, rather than the strategic direction of a company.

Option 2: This is a correct option. Using program life-cycle phases, you will be able to record, track, and evaluate benefits, recognize reasons for deviations, and make suggestions to correct them.

Option 3: This is a correct option. Using program life-cycle phases enables you to identify stakeholders, manage stakeholder expectations, and ensure continued stakeholder support.

Option 4: This is a correct option. Using program life-cycle phases enables you to ensure that your program is successful by putting phase gate reviews and predefined milestones in place.

Option 5: This is a correct option. Using program life-cycle phases enables you to allocate resources across projects and to manage these resources according to a program management plan.

Option 6: This is an incorrect option. You use program life-cycle phases to manage the progress and outcomes of a specific program, rather than to manage the outcome of multiple programs.

Program and project differences

You use program management life-cycle phases to manage program benefits and outcomes. Projects are initiated to deliver program benefits.

Some projects deliver products or services that allow benefits to be realized immediately. Other projects may deliver capabilities that must be integrated with the capabilities delivered by other projects before the associated benefits can be realized.

To ensure that a program delivers its expected benefits and complies with established program governance procedures, senior management oversees the program by means of phase gate reviews.

According to the Standard for Program Management, using program life-cycle phases enables you to manage outcomes and benefits. Project life-cycle phases, in contrast, serve to produce deliverables.

Projects deliver capabilities to an organization, whereas program management controls and accrues the corresponding benefits.

Programs and projects differ in terms of their:
life cycles
Programs often have extended life cycles

because some of the program projects end and are integrated into operations while other program projects are just beginning. Projects, on the other hand, have brief life cycles that don't follow an iterative pattern. A project reaches the end of its life cycle as soon as it has created the required product or service.

deliverables

Projects generate discrete deliverables at the completion of their life cycles, and the resulting benefits subsequently flow into the program. Program deliverables are benefits that are built incrementally from a range of discrete project deliverables.

capabilities

Projects generate capabilities. Programs integrate capabilities to create benefits.

A project life cycle is used to assist in the control and management of a project's deliverables. A Guide to the Project Management Body of Knowledge (PMBOK® Guide) states that a program may contain several projects, and that each of these projects may follow its own project life cycle.

You can use a different life-cycle model for each project – depending on its type – in order to achieve its planned benefits.

Question

What are the three key differences between program and project life cycles?

Options:

1. Programs have longer life cycles than projects

2. Programs generate discrete capabilities, whereas projects generate products or services

3. Projects generate discrete deliverables at the completion of their life cycles, whereas programs don't

4. Programs integrate capabilities to create benefits, whereas projects deliver capabilities

5. Project life cycles are iterative, whereas program life cycles aren't

Answer

Option 1: This is a correct option. Programs have an extended life cycle, encompassing several project life cycles. Project life cycles end as soon as the projects have generated the intended products or services.

Option 2: This is an incorrect option. In fact, projects create capabilities that are then integrated through the program into broad benefits.

Option 3: This is a correct option. A project creates a discrete product or service, whereas a program integrates these discrete deliverables into broad benefits.

Option 4: This is a correct option. Projects create capabilities that are then integrated through the program into broad benefits.

Option 5: This is an incorrect option. Projects move predictably through a single life cycle pattern from initiation to completion. Programs initiate and end projects during different phases of their life cycles.

Program and project life cycles

The type of program being managed can influence a program's life cycle, but major life-cycle phases remain the same.

Before a program or project moves on to its next life-cycle phase, a phase gate review takes place. In a phase gate review, the deliverables of the preceding phase are reviewed and approved.

A program management life cycle comprises five phases.

Preprogram setup

In the preprogram setup phase, the primary objective is to establish a firm foundation of support and approval for a program. A business-based selection process is followed to determine whether the organization will approve the program.

The program is initiated with a mandate or brief detailing of the strategic objectives and benefits that the program is expected to deliver. In the first phase gate review, the program is either approved or discarded.

Program setup

In the program setup phase, a program manager is identified, and the scope, objectives, visions, and constraints for the program are generated.

The purpose of this phase is to develop the foundation of the program by constructing a plan that provides direction on how the program will be managed and that defines its key deliverables.

Establishing a program management and technical infrastructure

The purpose of the establish a program management and technical infrastructure phase is to establish an infrastructure that will support a program and its constituent projects.

A program manager and program team need to establish the structure in which work will occur, as well as the technical infrastructure to facilitate that work.

Deliver the benefits

In the deliver the benefits phase, the component projects of a program are initiated, and the deliverables from these projects are coordinated to create incremental benefits.

The duration of this phase is unlimited because the activities it includes are repeated until all the planned benefits of the program have been delivered.

Closing the program

In the close the program phase, a controlled closing of the program, its projects, and its contracts is executed.

Typically, all the program work has been done and the benefits have been delivered prior to this phase. The goal of this phase is to ensure that the closure of the program is smooth and safe.

Consider a pharmaceutical company that wants to develop and manufacture a drug that lowers cholesterol. Management divides the program for the new drug into the five program life-cycle phases:

preprogram setup

During the preprogram setup phase, management needs to decide whether there is a need for the drug, and whether it would be profitable for the company to develop and manufacture the drug.

Then the company needs to create a program charter that outlines the program rationale, mission, and vision.

program setup

When the program charter has been approved, the program moves into the program setup phase.

During this phase, the company needs to develop a program management plan outlining the budget, deadlines, and scope for the program.

establishing a program management and technical infrastructure

During the establishing program management and technical infrastructure phase, managers need to ensure that sufficient resources are available for developing and manufacturing the drug.

By allocating enough resources and funds to the various projects, the company creates a program management and technical infrastructure.

delivering the benefits

The delivering the benefits phase incorporates the initiation and running of the program's projects, such as drug testing, clinical tests, drug manufacturing, and marketing.

Each project is run to build the benefits for the program incrementally.

closing the program

The closing the program phase occurs after all the benefits have been achieved or if the program is ended prematurely for some other reason.

In this phase, the company closes the distribution project and finalizes all program contracts. The manufacture and distribution of the drug is handed over to become part of the company's ongoing operations.

In order to achieve all the planned benefits and outcomes of a program, managers divide it into various projects.

Sorin Dumitrascu

And by dividing projects into phases, project management teams can provide better management control of the ongoing operations.

A project life cycle is characterized by sequential phases, the ability of stakeholders to make final decisions regarding product and cost, and the completion and approval of one or more deliverables.

Because it can take some time for deliverables to be reviewed and approved, several projects can run at the same time. It is common for projects from various program life-cycle phases to overlap.

The main phases of a project life cycle can be described as the:

initial phase

The initial phase of a project life cycle comprises a basic idea, a brief of the products or services the project is expected to deliver, and the appointment of a project management team.

intermediate phase

The intermediate phase continues until all the project deliverables are achieved. A final plan is put in place, and the work needed to create the project deliverables is done. The intermediate phase progresses toward the final phase as the components for the deliverables are completed.

final phase

In the final phase, the deliverables are reviewed for approval. When all the objectives and milestones have been achieved, the deliverables are handed over to the program, and the project is closed.

Management at the pharmaceutical company initiates several projects to achieve the benefits of the drug development and manufacturing program. One of the projects is the clinical trials project, in which a few potential cholesterol-lowering drugs are tested.

The clinical trials project is divided into the following project life-cycle phases:

initial phase

In the initial phase, the project team plans the sizes of the test and control groups and set

schedules and budgets for the generation of acceptable test results.

intermediate phase

During the intermediate phase, the drugs are tested on groups of healthy people using a double-blind technique, where neither the dispensers nor the tested subjects know whether they are receiving the drug or a placebo. The results are recorded and consolidated.

Sorin Dumitrascu

final phase

In the final phase of the project, the results of the trials are reviewed to determine whether or not the drug testing can move on to the next phase – handled by a different project team.

Once all projects are completed, their deliverables are integrated, and program benefits are achieved. Then the program can be closed and considered successful.

Question Set

Programs and projects follow different life-cycle phases. It is important to differentiate between the two.

Question 1 of 3
Question

A software company analyzes the profitability of designing a series of games aimed specifically at women. It analyzes its client base to find new game ideas. Next it designs the games, and software developers develop the code. The games are tested, and then marketed and distributed. This creates a larger market share for the company.

Is this a program life cycle or a project life cycle?

Program Management

Options:
1. A program life cycle
2. A project life cycle

Answer

Option 1: This is the correct option. This is a program life cycle because the life cycle is extended through various projects – research, development, and marketing. The life cycle builds on capabilities generated through different projects to achieve the broad benefit of increased market share.

Option 2: This is the incorrect option. A project life cycle centers around the delivery of a deliverable or product, such as a game aimed specifically at women. However, in this example, the company is involved in a gaming program that consists of multiple projects such as the production of research and marketing results, design of games, and coding.

Question 2 of 3
Question

An IT company is designing software that uploads photographs from cell phones to a web site. The company must decide which software engineers it wants to use for the software and provide the engineers with the product specifications. The engineers need to submit their ideas before doing the actual coding, and then they need to submit the code for approval.

Is this a program or a project life cycle?

Options:

1. Program life cycle
2. Project life cycle

Answer

Option 1: This is an incorrect option. The scenario shows that a single specific deliverable – the software code – is being produced rather than a series of capabilities that lead to a benefit. The phases described aren't iterative or extended, as is typical in a program life cycle.

Option 2: This is the correct option. The work moves through the initial phase in which the specifications and the team are selected, the intermediate phase in which the code is developed, and the final phase in which the code is approved. This is a project life cycle rather than a program life cycle because it focuses on the delivery of a specific product instead of on realizing a broad benefit.

Question 3 of 3
Question

A travel agency is extending its offers to include adventure sport holidays. The agency will first conduct market research, then draw up an action plan, develop relationships with adventure sport providers, and market and sell the packages to a new target market.

Is this a program life cycle or a project life cycle?

Options:

1. Program life cycle
2. Project life cycle

Answer

Option 1: This is the correct option. The travel agency uses various capabilities – such as improved relationships and market research – developed through separate projects to build the benefit of increased sales and a new market presence. This describes a program life cycle.

Option 2: This is an incorrect option. A project life cycle is characterized by sequential phases. The travel agency conducts multiple phases or projects at once to produce an integrated benefit, so this describes a program life cycle.

Benefits management

Three major themes run across all the activities of a program. These themes evolve over time and require management throughout each phase of a program life cycle.

The themes are:

1. benefits management
2. stakeholder management
3. phase gate reviews

Whereas the success of individual projects is assessed using criteria such as completion on time, budget, and adherence to specifications, programs are judged in terms of return on investment and delivery of new capabilities and benefits.

Benefits management involves defining the expected benefits of a program and monitoring the delivery of these benefits throughout a program life cycle.

Programs are planned and initiated to deliver specific benefits. To achieve the desired outcome, benefits must be managed in a coordinated manner.

A helpful strategy for benefits management uses the following five benefits management phases:

1. benefits identification
2. benefits analysis
3. benefits planning

4. benefits realization

5. benefits transition

In the benefits identification phase, expected program benefits and objectives are identified and qualified in the preprogram setup phase, before a program is initiated. So the actual program outputs need to be identified and defined before work can start.

All stakeholders for the program are identified, and appropriate stakeholder support and processes are put in place in order to manage and realize benefits.

The program's objectives should align with those for its constituent projects. And the program's benefits should align with the needs and expectations of its stakeholders, as well as the objectives of the organization.

During program setup, the benefits analysis phase involves drafting a plan for the realization of the benefits. The expected benefits are prioritized, and a way of tracking, measuring, and assessing the expected benefits is determined.

Benefits are analyzed according to their alignment with company objectives, short-term and long-term expected results, required resources and capability, as well as the probability of success in achieving the identified benefits.

Sorin Dumitrascu

The benefits planning phase occurs during the establishing a program management and technical infrastructure phase in program management. During this phase, strategies for realizing benefits are identified. Benefits are tracked, recorded, and evaluated in accordance with the benefits definition and assessment processes established in earlier phases.

The strategies for realizing benefits are then incorporated in the program plan. The purpose of this is to develop a program infrastructure that maps how the projects within the program will deliver the capabilities that will result in the desired benefits.

In the benefits realization phase, a benefits register is maintained to measure the progress of a program and its constituent projects, and a progress report is compiled.

The progress report establishes accountability, indicates expected benefits flow over the duration of the program, forecasts the value of the expected benefits, tracks how many of the planned benefits have been achieved, and allows time to address deviations.

In the benefits transition phase, program work is completed, and its benefits accrue.

Benefits from program components are reviewed and evaluated to determine whether all objectives have been reached. Additional or unplanned benefits are also assessed and coordinated. Then benefits from the program and its constituent projects are consolidated and coordinated to achieve the planned objectives.

The benefits and the responsibility of maintaining the benefits are transferred to the relevant program stakeholders and sponsors. The objectives have been achieved and the program is closed.

Question

Match each benefit management phase to the tasks it includes.

Options:

A. Benefits transition

B. Benefits realization

C. Benefits planning

D. Benefits analysis

E. Benefits identification

Targets:

1. The program reaches its objectives and the program sponsor receives the benefits report

2. A benefits register is used to monitor and measure all benefits

3. A plan to realize and monitor all the expected benefits is mapped in the program plan

Sorin Dumitrascu

4. All the program's benefits are prioritized and measured according to various criteria

5. The expected program outcomes are established and the stakeholders are identified

Answer

The benefits transition phase is used to hand over benefits and the responsibility of maintaining them to the program sponsor and to the stakeholders. The program is closed when all objectives are reached.

The benefits register helps to measure, track, and monitor benefits as they are being realized. This register is used during the benefits realization phase.

Before benefits can be realized, you need to plan how to monitor them and map their expected progress to the program plan. These tasks are part of benefits planning.

To realize all the benefits, you must rank the benefits in terms of importance and establish a method of measuring the benefits achieved. This involves benefits analysis.

Before a program can begin, it needs a direction and the manager needs to know who the program will affect and where to get support. In the benefits identification phase, expected program outcomes are established and stakeholders are identified.

Program Management

Darren is a program manager for MyBudget Software, a company that develops software packages. A new client asks MyBudget Software to develop an accounting package that will enable the client company to downsize its Accounting Department, save on administration costs, and reduce the need for paperwork. MyBudget Software needs to develop the software, provide online and offline training on its use, and develop a support service for users.

One of Darren's main tasks is to ensure that all the expected benefits for this program are achieved. To do this, Darren needs to implement a benefits management strategy.

To control and manage the realization of the program benefits, Darren identifies five phases that will structure his approach to managing benefits:

benefits identification

During benefits identification, Darren identifies the benefits – increased customer satisfaction, increased revenue, and increased employee skills – that the program must deliver. He also identifies the stakeholders contributing to the software development program – technical specialists and the executive managers of his and the client company.

Finally, Darren ensures that the program's

expected benefits align with his company's objectives – providing high-quality products and excellent customer service – and with the needs of the client.

benefits analysis

During benefits analysis, Darren draws up a plan to track, measure, and assess the expected benefits. Then he determines increased revenue and increased customer satisfaction to be the highest-priority benefits. The software application project will generate long-term benefits in terms of broadening the employee skills base.

Finally, Darren ensures that he has all the required resources to run the program.

benefits planning

Darren draws up a plan of how all the program's benefits are going to be achieved, and when the benefits will be achieved and delivered.

He establishes a benefits monitoring plan to track, record, and evaluate all the achieved benefits. Finally, Darren develops a program infrastructure that maps how and when the various projects will deliver the planned benefits.

benefits realization

During benefits realization, Darren collects and measures the performance data from the various projects throughout the program's life cycle. He checks their progress against the benefits delivery targets and maintains a benefits register that helps him measure and monitor the benefits.

As a result, Darren can address deviations from the objectives immediately, without wasting time or money.

benefits transition

In the benefits transition phase, Darren reviews and evaluates the benefits from the various projects to determine whether all the planned objectives have been achieved.

He notes that employee skill levels are higher than expected and that the unplanned benefit of improved employee morale has boosted the company's production levels. Darren formally closes the program and delivers the accounting package to the client.

Case Study: Question 1 of 2
Scenario

Jackie is a program manager for a company that manufactures clothes for a chain of department stores. A client asks the company to manufacture a new range of clothes. To be successful in this program, Jackie applies a structure that includes five program benefits management phases.

Answer the questions in order.

Question

Match each of the first three benefits management phases to an example of how Jackie implements it. Not all examples will be used.

Options:

A. Benefits identification

B. Benefits analysis

C. Benefits planning

Targets:

1. Jackie establishes that the program will increase revenue and market share

2. Jackie decides how best to manufacture and market the clothes and the sequence in which projects should run

3. Jackie creates measures and targets for revenue and market share during the program life cycle

4. Jackie draws up regular stakeholder reports detailing the benefits delivery rates and the progress of the program

Answer

In the benefits identification phase, Jackie identifies the benefits – increased revenue and market share – and the key stakeholders of the program.

In the benefits analysis phase, a plan is drawn up of how the benefits will be achieved, and how they are prioritized.

In the benefits planning phase, a method to measure and monitor the benefits throughout the program is established.

Drawing up a stakeholder report is part of the benefits realization phase.

Case Study: Question 2 of 2

Now match the remaining benefits management phases to examples of how Jackie implements them. Not all examples will be used.

Options:

A. Benefits realization

B. Benefits transition

Targets:

1. Jackie draws up a benefits register to find out whether the benefits are being achieved, and to fix any problems that might occur in the clothes manufacturing process

2. Jackie checks the finished clothes to determine their quality before sending them off to department stores

3. Jackie tracks the continuous benefits of the program after the program has closed

Answer

In the benefits realization phase, a benefits register is maintained to measure the program and project outcomes.

In the benefits transition phase, the delivered benefits are handed over to the sponsor, and the program is formally closed.

Maintaining a schedule to track benefits after delivery is not one of the benefits management phases.

Stakeholder management

To manage program stakeholders successfully, the program manager needs to:

- • identify all stakeholders
- analyze stakeholders to determine how the program will affect them,
- manage stakeholders' expectations.

Program stakeholders are the individuals or organizations whose interests may be affected – either positively or negatively – by program outcomes.

The first step in managing a program's stakeholders is to identify all stakeholders and determine their needs early in the program. A program manager must also identify the impact of stakeholders on the program, and what their input will be with regards to the scope, cost, timing, quality, and success of the program.

Analyzing all the stakeholders entails assessing the influence and importance of each individual stakeholder or group involved with the program. Program managers must ensure that they understand the current position of each stakeholder with respect to the program objectives and expected outcomes.

The impact and power of the various stakeholders are also analyzed and defined in terms of the amount of influence they have on the program outcomes and objectives.

To manage stakeholder expectations, program managers need to develop a strategy to involve the stakeholders in the program. Stakeholders play a significant role in the program outcome.

Stakeholders must be managed individually, by identifying their expectations, ensuring that these expectations are realistic, and then delivering on these expectations.

The program manager must be familiar with the influence, power, and level of activity of each stakeholder, and must manage each stakeholder accordingly.

A change in the program environment can also have an impact on program stakeholders because new stakeholders may be added or existing stakeholders may be removed.

Recall Darren, a program manager for MyBudget Software. He and his team need to develop an accounting software package for a new client. To do this, Darren must know who the program stakeholders are and what their expectations are.

To meet all the stakeholders' expectations, Darren:

identifies and analyzes the stakeholders

To identify and analyze stakeholders, Darren writes a list of individuals and companies involved with developing the software, training users, and building the support framework. He interviews the stakeholders to determine their expectations of the software and its add-on projects, and of its impact on their companies. When Darren has a firm understanding of the influence and expectations of the stakeholders, he is equipped to manage their expectations.

manages stakeholder expectations

To manage stakeholder expectations, Darren ensures that he manages each stakeholder individually. He knows which stakeholders are actively involved in the program, and ensures that their expectations about revenues and functionality are realistic. As the program progresses, he ensures that stakeholders receive monthly benefits reports.

Question

Jackie works for a clothing company that supplies chain department stores. Recently the company secured a contract to manufacture a new range of clothes.

What does Jackie need to do to manage the program stakeholders successfully?

Options:

Sorin Dumitrascu

1. Know who the stakeholders are, ensuring that all those who affect or are affected by the program are identified

2. Assign each stakeholder to a specific task and measure and track their performance

3. Work with each stakeholder individually, ensuring that their expectations are realistic

4. Track the performance of stakeholders and monitor whether they are still needed within the program

5. Review what each stakeholder's current position is and what they expect from the new clothing range

Answer

Option 1: This is a correct option. In order to manage stakeholders successfully, Jackie must identify all the stakeholders that are involved in the program.

Option 2: This is an incorrect option. Jackie must first determine who the stakeholders are and what their positions are in the manufacturing of the new clothing range, and then track the delivery of the benefits the stakeholders expect.

Option 3: This is a correct option. One of Jackie's tasks is to manage stakeholder expectations. Jackie must know each stakeholder and manage their expectations individually.

Option 4: This is an incorrect option. Jackie must track, measure, and evaluate stakeholders' expectations rather than their performance.

Option 5: This is a correct option. Program managers need to analyze stakeholders in terms of their roles and their expectations.

Phase gate reviews

Phase gate reviews are carried out at key decision points throughout the program life cycle, usually by the program board.

During a phase gate review, the deliverables from each phase are evaluated, deviations from the planned objectives are identified and may be corrected, and a decision is made on whether the program can be continued or should be stopped.

The purpose of phase gate reviews is threefold. They enable managers to evaluate the program's progress, to identify and respond to any changes to the program plan, and to decide whether or not the program should continue to the next phase.

To evaluate a program's progress, the program's performance and key deliverables are reviewed to ensure that the program and its constituent projects are still aligned with the organization's strategy, and that the deliverables are aligned with the original business plan.

Program managers are able to identify and respond to changes identified during the evaluation of a program's progress. Underperforming areas or changes in the business climate are identified and then program plans are altered to accommodate the changes.

Program Management

If progress is good and if changes can be accommodated, the decision to continue the program is made. However, if the program is performing badly or can't respond well to change, the program is terminated.

MyBudget Software is developing accounting software and associated support for a new client. Once programmers finish developing the software, Darren, the program manager, must execute a phase gate review before designers begin creating graphics for the software.

In this phase gate review, Darren and the program review board execute the following tasks:

evaluate the deliverables

To evaluate the deliverables, Darren reviews the software package test results against the program targets that have been set for this stage. He determines that the accounting software does not meet all of the client's specifications.

identify and respond to changes

When identifying and responding to change, Darren notes that there is a problem with some of the accounting formulas that has not been addressed in the software. Also, currency types need to be added to the program.

decide whether the program should continue

Because the issues identified can be fixed with only a small change to the program schedule and budget, Darren and the program board decide that the program should continue. However, they determine that the program is not yet ready to continue to the next life-cycle phase, but should be returned so that programmers can add the necessary formulas and currency types.

Question

Jackie's clothing manufacture company secures a contract to manufacture a range of clothes for a new client. The program includes a planned series of phase gate reviews.

What purpose do these reviews serve?

Options:

1. They provide a system for measuring and tracking the program benefits generated through its projects

2. They enable Jackie and the review board to evaluate the quality and styles of the clothes in production

3. They help to identify problems such as increases in fabric costs and enable Jackie to develop responses to these problems, such as using different fabric

4. They provide a forum for the client to test the

quality of the clothes after the order has been delivered 5. They provide a forum for deciding whether the program should continue

Answer

Option 1: This is an incorrect option. Creating a system to measure and track benefits is not one of the purposes of using phase gate reviews. It is an aspect of benefits planning.

Option 2: This is a correct option. One of the benefits of performing phase gate reviews is that it enables Jackie to evaluate the program deliverables at each key decision point.

Option 3: This is a correct option. One of the benefits of performing phase gate reviews is that it enables Jackie to quickly and effectively identify and respond to any changes that impact on the program. For example, he may decide to change the base fabric for garments to reduce costs.

Option 4: This is an incorrect option. Evaluating the quality of the clothes after the program has been closed is not one of the benefits of using phase gate reviews – it forms part of outcome control.

Option 5: This is a correct option. Phase gate reviews enable Jackie and the board to decide whether the program should continue and whether it's ready to move on to the next phase in its life cycle.

Program governance roles

Program governance can be defined as all the activities and processes that individuals – filling executive and management roles – engage in to oversee a program and its functions.

These activities include developing a communication and monitoring strategy, monitoring program progress, and prioritizing and organizing the structures and practices associated with a specific program.

LangFarma, a company that grows herbs and medicinal plants, is merging with a leading health food provider. As a result, a program of change management initiatives has been put in place.

The program is overseen by a program board comprised of three key executives. The executives ensure that all current change activities are aligned with the company's new strategy.

LangFarma's change management program includes employee integration and training projects, a legacy systems project, and a system of internal communications among change initiative teams.

Program governance allows managers to:

monitor the progress of the program

The team monitors the progress of the program by routinely reviewing progress reports, particularly at each phase of the life cycle. Regular team meetings are held where updates on the progress of specific projects – such as the internal communications project – are provided. By monitoring the progress of the program, the team can stay within its time and budget limits.

monitor the delivery of the coordinated benefits

The team monitors the delivery of the benefits using the program governance structure. Benefits, such as containing costs and realigning resources, are tracked by the governance team. This enables them to make changes to the program as it progresses, ensuring alignment with LangFarma's goals and achievement of benefits.

Question

What is the purpose of program governance?

Options:

1. It provides a structure for those overseeing the program to monitor its progress and assess performance

2. It enables program team members to achieve the expected benefits of a program earlier than originally planned, to save time and money

3. It allows those overseeing the program to track the delivery of benefits and adjust the program

as required

4. It enables program team members to make adjustments to time and budget constraints as a program progresses

Answer

Option 1: This is a correct option. The progress of a program is monitored through the use of a phase gate review system at key decision points.

Option 2: This is an incorrect option. Program governance doesn't enable program benefits to be achieved in advance. It allows those overseeing the program to track benefits and adjust program components as necessary.

Option 3: This is a correct option. Program governance provides a framework whereby those overseeing the program can monitor it to ensure expected benefits are being achieved. Such monitoring allows adjustment of the program components so that expected benefits are in alignment with the original business plan.

Option 4: This is an incorrect option. Program governance is about monitoring the progress of programs to ensure that the goals and benefits of the program are achieved.

Successful program governance relies on individuals in each of the following roles meeting

specific responsibilities:
- • program board,
- executive sponsor,
- program director,
- program manager,
- project manager.

The responsibilities associated with each role involved in program governance should be defined and structured according to a program's required outcomes and expected benefits, and the organization's strategy and business objectives.

The program board is made up of the executive sponsor, the key internal stakeholders, and external stakeholders. The program management office (PMO) is a separate entity that supports the program board.

The program board is set up at the beginning of the program and operates until the program is closed.

The program board is responsible for representing the organization's interests, providing an infrastructure for guidance and quality assurance, and making decisions regarding the program's scope, objectives, schedule, and budget.

The program board also assists with resolving issues and risks a program manager may have difficulty dealing with.

Other functions of the board are to initiate the program, to provide planning approval, to perform reviews, to ensure that resources are available, and to decide on frameworks and limits for investments and delivery. The board also needs to ensure compliance with corporate and legal procedures and policies.

An executive sponsor is an individual who supports a program, and is usually the key decision-maker.

The executive sponsor is responsible for directing and overseeing the program, and must create a program environment that leads to successful benefits delivery. The executive sponsor is also responsible for allocating the funds and resources a program requires.

The executive sponsor typically takes advice from the key internal and external stakeholders and the program management team.

A program director is the designated leader of a specific program and has management and administrative authority for the program. The program director may also serve in the role of executive sponsor.

The program director has oversight responsibilities and is responsible for the successful delivery and achievement of the benefits of the program. The program director also accounts for budget, time, and resource management, and ensures that consistent quality is implemented across the program.

Before work on the program can begin, it needs to be authorized by the program director. The program director submits regular reports to the program board, to inform it of the program's progress.

A program manager is responsible for providing leadership and managing a program, its resources, and its funding. The program manager identifies and defines the program's outcomes, controls time and budget constraints, and exercises oversight of the program.

The program manager ensures that the program's outcomes align with the set objectives, and that all the planned benefits are delivered. He or she prepares regular progress reports for the program board to report on the status of the program and its deliverables.

The program manager is supported by the PMO and receives reports directly from a group of project managers.

A project manager is responsible for managing an individual project and needs to ensure that this project's deliverables are provided within time and budget constraints.

The project manager also provides regular status reports to the program manager, and consults the program manager when facing difficulties within the project.

Question

To ensure effective program governance, individuals in each of several program management roles must meet specific responsibilities.

Match each program management role to its responsibilities in program governance.

Options:

A. Program board

B. Executive sponsor

C. Program director

D. Program manager

E. Project manager

Targets:

1. Provides oversight, guidance, and quality assurance

2. Supports a program, providing funding and resources

3. Accountable for program quality, budget, time, and resource management

4. Manages program funding and resources, and

provides leadership

5. Manages a specific program component and its deliverables

Answer

The program board operates for the life span of the program, and its responsibilities include setting up a program governance infrastructure. This infrastructure provides guidance and quality assurance.

The executive sponsor is responsible for gaining support for a program and is also the person who provides funding for the program. This individual is usually the key decision-maker on the program board.

The program director is the leader for the specific program, and as such is accountable for the program's costs, time constraints, and quality.

The program manager manages the program's project managers and all other resources for a program.

The project manager manages an individual project, and must ensure that all the project's benefits are delivered.

Consider MyBudget Software, a company that develops software packages. Poseidon Bank, an international banking group, has asked MyBudget

Software to develop a set of end-user enterprise computer applications that will enable better control of the money the bank handles every day.

Darren has been appointed as program manager at MyBudget Software. Ed, a senior manager of Poseidon Bank, is the executive sponsor, and Margaret, who fills a senior management position at MyBudget Software, is the program director.

William, a senior computer software developer at MyBudget Software, is one of the project managers.

To govern the application development program successfully, the program management team members work together to oversee and monitor the program's progress and benefits delivery.

program board

Ed and Margaret, as executive sponsor and program director respectively, serve on the program board.

They ensure that there is adequate funding and that resources are available for developing the software. They are responsible for quality assurance and ensuring that the software aligns with the objectives they have set. In addition, the board must ensure that the software complies with government regulations.

executive sponsor

Ed, as the executive sponsor, supports the development of the software by funding it. He receives regular progress reports from the program team, and is responsible for making decisions, with help from the key stakeholders and the program management team.

He must also provide the necessary funding and resources to deliver the planned benefits successfully.

program director

Margaret is the appointed leader – program director – for this program. She must authorize the initiation of the program and submit regular progress reports to the executive sponsor and the program board.

She must also account for the money and resources needed for the development of the software, ensure that the software is of a high quality, and ensure that it can perform the expected tasks.

program manager

Darren is the program manager for the development of the software. He manages resources, money, and various project managers.

He controls time and budget constraints and reports to Margaret, the program director. He also ensures that the program's outcomes align with the objectives that the program board has set.

project manager

William, a senior computer software developer, is a project manager for the New Accounts application module.

He ensures that the software is developed in the time limit that the program manager set, and that the software can perform all the planned functions. He also submits regular status reports to Darren, who is the program manager.

MyBudget Software delivered a successful suite of applications, within the required time and money constraints, to Poseidon Bank. The software company was able to do this because it used a specific program governance structure in which roles and responsibilities were clearly defined.

The individuals who directed the development of the suite of banking applications were organized into a team that allowed regular monitoring of the progress of the program and its benefits.

Question Set

Jason, an executive at Gleeson Associates – a management solutions company – has been assigned to oversee the setup of a program governance structure for the company's Six Sigma program.

Jason decides that in order to create a program governance structure, the responsibilities of each individual or group that fulfills a program governance role should be clearly defined.

Question 1 of 2
Question

Match each of three roles in program governance to examples of its responsibilities. Not all examples will be used.

Options:

A. Program board

B. Executive sponsor

C. Program director

Targets:

1. Determines the expected benefits of the Six Sigma program, and how much money Gleeson Associates will need to allocate to the program

2. Provides the program with the funding to develop consultancy skills and to roll out Six Sigma to client companies

3. Authorizes the Training, Internal Communications, and IT Integration projects before they are initiated

4. Defines the outcomes of the Six Sigma program in Gleeson Associates, and ensures that

these outcomes are achieved

Answer

This is an example of the responsibilities the program board must fulfill. The program board must create an infrastructure that provides guidance and quality assurance, as well as making decisions regarding the program's scope, objectives, schedule, and budget.

This is an example of the responsibilities that the executive sponsor fulfills. This individual is responsible for raising the funds for a program and for making key decisions.

This is an example of the responsibilities of the program director, who is accountable for the successful delivery of the program components and the achievement of all the planned benefits. The program director must authorize program work before it proceeds.

This is an example of the responsibilities of the program manager, who is responsible for overseeing and controlling the project managers, budget, and resources.

Question 2 of 2
Question

Match two of the program governance roles with the appropriate examples of responsibilities. Not all examples will be used.

Options:

A. Program manager

B. Project manager

Targets:

1. Reviews the Six Sigma program's work components to ensure that they align with the company's goal of providing excellent service

2. Ensures that the consultant training is completed in time and within the budget that has been set aside for this purpose

3. Authorizes the initiation of a training project at Gleeson Associates

Answer

This is an example of the responsibilities of the program manager, who must ensure that the program's outcomes align with the planned objectives.

This is an example of the responsibilities of a project manager, who must ensure that the deliverables for a particular project within the program are provided within time and budget constraints.

This is an example of the responsibilities of the program director, who must authorize program work before it begins and submit regular reports to the program board.

Managing program life cycles

For ease of management, programs – like projects – benefit from division into specific phases.

Despite some overlap, program phases are discrete entities that should enhance program managers' abilities to ensure optimal governance, control, and benefit delivery.

The Project Management Institute (PMI®) details five phases of a program's life cycle in the Standards for Program Management – preprogram setup, program setup, establishing a management and technical infrastructure, delivering benefits, and closing the program.

By understanding the tasks, goals, and processes associated with the preprogram and program setup phases, you are better able to achieve the program's strategic objectives.

This is because each of these phases requires that you spend time defining and mapping benefits to strategic goals, and that you coordinate the program components in a way that encourages the achievement of the program's strategic goals.

You should also be better able to establish support and direction for the program because you need to lobby for the program in the preprogram and program setup phases. And you need to clarify the strategic direction of the program within its charter and planning documents.

By understanding the tasks, goals, and processes associated with the establish program management and technical infrastructure phase, you will better understand how to establish an infrastructure to support the program.

By following the recommendations for managing this phase, you can ensure that all areas of control and technical infrastructure are in place before initiating the program components.

Through the tasks, goals, and processes associated with the deliver the benefits phase, you will better understand how to achieve incremental benefits of the program. You will be able to combine and sequence component deliverables so that benefits are realized more quickly.

By understanding the close the program phase, program managers can ensure that the program is closed without contractual breaches, that all documentation is up to date, and that there is sufficient support to maintain the program's benefits.

The Easy Nomad Travel agency has approved a program that will promote travel to Eastern Europe. The program director is Gina Rosetti and the program manager is Amrit Khan.

Both Gina and Amrit found that their understanding of the program life-cycle phases helped them to:

achieve the program's strategic objectives

Gina's work in the preprogram phase helped to ensure the program's strategic objectives were clear and aligned with the company's goals. Amrit was able to ensure that all the program work was closely aligned with achieving these goals. Together, they were better able to achieve the program's strategic objectives.

establish support and direction for the program

Gina's lobbying and strategic planning helped to establish support and direction for the program and Amrit was able to build on this foundation during program planning and execution. establish an infrastructure to support the program

Amrit's understanding of the establish program management and technical infrastructure phase helped her to establish an infrastructure to support the program. She ensured that she had adequate software to communicate with and monitor the progress of the different branches of the travel agency. She also ensured that there were clear procedures and guidelines for her team to follow.

Additionally, Gina was able to set up a representative program board to govern the program.

achieve incremental benefits of the program

Amrit's understanding of the deliver the benefits phase of the program helped her to structure and sequence program components optimally, allowing the program team and the various project teams to achieve the incremental benefits of the program.

Question

What are the benefits of understanding how to manage life-cycle phases in a program?

Options:

1. You are more likely to achieve the program's strategic objectives

2. You are better able to establish support and direction for the program

3. You understand how to establish an infrastructure to support the program

4. You know how to achieve the incremental benefits of the program

5. You are better able to measure program benefits accurately

6. You are better able to develop suitable program procedures

Answer

Sorin Dumitrascu

Option 1: This is a correct option. By understanding how to manage the preprogram and program setup phases of a program, you will be able to set clear strategic objectives for the program and to construct a program management plan that is focused on achieving these objectives.

Option 2: This is a correct option. By understanding how to manage the preprogram and program setup phases of a program, you will be able to lobby for support from key stakeholders and construct plans that provide a clear direction for the program.

Option 3: This is a correct option. By understanding how to manage the establishing a program management and technical infrastructure phase, you will be able to ensure that all the necessary governance and control structures for the program are in place. You will also be able to ensure that you have sufficient IT infrastructure to meet communication, tracking, and reporting needs.

Option 4: This is a correct option. By understanding how to manage the delivering the benefits phase of the program, you will have a better understanding of how these benefits can be achieved by careful structuring of the various program components.

Option 5: This is an incorrect option. Measuring

benefits requires technical know-how in terms of benefits management, rather than an understanding of the phases of the program's life cycle.

Option 6: This is an incorrect option. Developing program procedures requires an understanding of processes and regulations rather than an understanding of the phases of the program's life cycle.

Preprogram setup phase

The preprogram setup phase is the first phase of a program's life cycle. During this phase, the rationale and broad plans for a program are developed and assessed. It is at this stage that a program is selected for implementation across an organization.

The selection process is business based. This means that only programs that are helpful in adapting to the current business environment and that are aligned with an organization's long-term strategies and goals are selected.

The process may be formal or informal but typically the program board, portfolio management team, or executive sponsor initiates the program using a program brief that details the program's strategic objectives and benefits.

The tasks associated with the preprogram setup phase can be categorized as follows:

develop the rationale for the program

In developing the rationale for the program, you need to understand the context for the

program – how the program addresses a need for change in your organization.

You need to understand the strategic value of a

proposed program and you need to define and map the program objective to the organization's strategic objectives. Finally, you need to explain why it should be a program rather than a project.

identify and analyze stakeholders

Before finalizing documentation outlining the program's rationale, it is important to identify and analyze stakeholders. By identifying the decision-makers in the selection process and their expectations and interests, you are better prepared to develop the documentation needed to ensure the program is approved.

You should also identify those who influence the selection and those who can influence its success or are impacted by the program benefits, and generate documentation accordingly.

create high-level plans

Once you have analyzed the stakeholders, you need to develop a high-level plan, a business case, and a program charter. The business case should show the program manager's understanding of the needs, feasibility, and justification for the program. The high-level plan should include the program rationale and its mission, vision, and values.

You then develop the program charter using these two documents as inputs. The program charter should include the program vision, key objectives, expected benefits, constraints, and assumptions.

gain approval for the program

The program manager or program sponsor needs to gather stakeholder signatures approving the program charter. Then the executive board needs to approve the program and officially appoint a program manager.

The program sponsor and the program manager then need to identify and commit the resources needed for the planning phase and the program manager needs to draw up a plan for the program setup phase.

LangFarma is a company that grows medicinal plants to sell in bulk to other companies. Despite growing interest in natural and herbal remedies, the growing competition in this industry has led the company's executive management to explore opportunities to extend its product line and customer base.

Julio Hernandez, a portfolio manager for LangFarma, discusses the possibility of a new program focusing on finding African medicinal plants that it can grow and market successfully with an executive manager, Rosa Eisen. Rosa is excited by the idea and expresses interest in managing the program.

Program Management

To develop a rationale for the LangFarma African program, Julio and Rosa discuss the context for the program, agreeing that the company's need to diversify and the growing international interest in homeopathic African remedies provide an excellent base for program approval.

Rosa then develops a set of objectives and benefits for the program, including the extended product line and customer base.

As part of developing a rationale for the program, Rosa needs to demonstrate that the work should be a program rather than a project.

To do this, Rosa needs to answer the following questions:

What shared resources are there across projects?

Rosa identifies the shared resources across the projects as botanists, scientists, nutritionists, plant data, marketing data, and IT infrastructure and software.

What should the program duration be?

Rosa concludes that the program duration should be at least 12 years to allow ample time for research and development.

What participation between corporate entities is required?

Some of the areas where Rosa determines that

participation between corporate entities is required are between the Research, Marketing, Horticulture, and Manufacturing Departments.

What dependencies on deliverables exist between projects?

Identifying the dependencies on deliverables involves working out which project deliverables or products are needed before a subsequent project can begin. Rosa identifies research results and marketing briefs as project deliverables that are required for subsequent projects and to begin the benefit delivery process.

In light of her answers to the previous questions, Rosa concludes that the LangFarma Africa program should indeed be a program rather than a project. The program needs to incorporate both projects and ongoing work, and although it will generate actual products, the benefits that it will generate go beyond the scope of delivering a product.

Question

You believe that the charity organization that you work for needs to initiate a program that supports victims of violent crime. One of the tasks you need to perform at the preprogram setup phase is to develop a rationale for the program.

Program Management

Which steps should you take to do this?

Options:

1. Review crime statistics, what similar organizations are doing, and the current funding climate

2. Align the program's expected benefits for the local community with the organization's objectives

3. Review the expected duration, resource use, and deliverables to determine whether the work should be a project or a program

4. Predict the costs of the program's projects, including the costs of training and recruiting personnel

5. Identify and analyze all the program components

Answer

Option 1: This is a correct option. Reviewing these issues helps you to gain a clear understanding of the context for the program so that you can explain how the program addresses a particular need.

Option 2: This is a correct option. Identifying benefits and mapping them to organizational objectives is crucial to this phase and provides a compelling rationale for the program.

Option 3: This is a correct option. When developing a rationale for a program, you need to specify why it should be implemented as a program rather than as a project.

Option 4: This is an incorrect option. Although a broad sense of what the program may cost could be useful for a program rationale, you don't need to create detailed budgets for projects within the program at this stage.

Option 5: This is an incorrect option. Identifying program components is an aspect of planning that occurs at the program setup phase and is not essential to developing a program rationale.

Before drawing up the required plans for this phase of the program, Rosa and Julio need to identify and analyze the various stakeholders.

The first set of stakeholders to look into are those that are on the approval committee for the program – those people who have a vote as to whether or not the program is initiated.

Finding out where each member of the committee stands and whether the program will have benefits for them is important for lobbying for the program.

The second set of stakeholders are those likely to be implementing the program or receiving the benefits of the program. These stakeholders should be identified and listed for documentation and lobbying purposes.

Once you have identified the stakeholders and performed a broad analysis of them, you begin creating high-level plans for the program.

The main high-level plan should outline the:

context for the program

You use the program rationalization to provide a context for the program, stating why the

program is important in the current environment.

You also need to include the program's objectives and benefits and map these to the organization's strategic goals. This aspect of the plan is vital for the program.

program mission

The program mission states what the program needs to achieve and why it is important.

For example, the LangFarma Africa program aims to research and document indigenous African plants that the company can use and market, grow plants identified as marketable, and create marketable health supplements using the identified plants.

program vision

The program vision details how the program will benefit the organization and provides a view of the desired program end state.

Sorin Dumitrascu

For example, the LangFarma program will serve
to broaden the company's customer base by 30%
and increase its market share by 20%. The program
also aims to increase revenue by 35% within 10
years.

program values

The program values outline how the program
will balance decisions and evaluate trade-offs.

For example, the LangFarma Africa program
intends to prioritize the research section of the
program to avoid risks of unsafe products being
marketed.

In addition to a high-level plan, you need to
develop a business case for the program. You then
use information from the business case and the
high-level plan to create a program charter.

The program charter should include the program
vision, key objectives, expected benefits,
constraints, and assumptions.

The selection committee stakeholders need to
sign off the program charter to initiate and accept
the program.

The committee typically bases its decisions
regarding the program on the following criteria:

- • available resources,
- preliminary budget estimates,

- a benefits analysis that identifies benefits and plans for their realization,
- strategic fit with the organization's long-term goals,
- the risks associated with the program.

Question

You have developed a program rationale and identified and analyzed the stakeholders for a program to support victims of violent crime. You now need to create a high-level plan to help convince the board that the program should be initiated.

What details about the program should you include in the plan?

Options:

1. The current funding climate and local crime statistics

2. The program's aim to respond to increased violent crime by providing counseling and support to victims

3. The program's goal to empower crime victims from the local area through counseling, and to break cycles of violence

4. The point that the program will prioritize women over other crime victims if there is insufficient capacity

Sorin Dumitrascu

5. The expected counseling constraints and the assumptions of the program

6. The results of the economic and ethical feasibility studies assessing the potential program

Answer

Option 1: This is a correct option. This provides the context for the program, so should be included in a high-level plan.

Option 2: This is a correct option. This is an example of the program's mission because it states what the program needs to achieve. The program mission must be included in all high-level plans.

Option 3: This is a correct option. This is an example of the program's vision because it details how the program will benefit the organization and provides a view of the desired program end state. The program vision must be included in all high-level plans.

Option 4: This is a correct option. This is an example of the program's values because it outlines how the program will balance decisions and evaluate trade-offs. Program values should be included in high-level plans.

Option 5: This is an incorrect option. The program's constraints and assumptions should be included in the program charter rather than in the high-level plan.

Program Management

Option 6: This is an incorrect option. Feasibility studies typically occur in the program setup phase. If any studies were conducted before the program setup phase, information regarding feasibility should be included in the business case for the program rather than in the high-level plan.

The results of the preprogram setup phase include:

program approval

The program sponsor needs to secure approval for the program to continue to the next phase of its life cycle. This is accomplished by getting stakeholder signatures on the program charter.

identification and commitment of resources

The program board needs to identify and commit resources required for planning the program in the program setup phase. This includes the official appointment of a program manager for the program.

the plan for the program setup phase

The program manager must develop a plan to initiate the program – the program setup phase plan – using the output of the preprogram setup phase.

The program setup phase

Once a program passes its first phase gate review, it moves on to the program setup phase. During this phase, you use the program charter as a base to continue developing the foundation for the program.

The aim of this phase is to provide a clear direction for the program and to define the program's key deliverables.

Common activities during the program setup phase are:

running feasibility studies

If necessary, you should run any economic, technical, or ethical feasibility studies before you go further with program planning. These studies help to ensure that the program will be viable and any positive results of these studies can be used to secure more support from program stakeholders.

establishing decision-making rules

The team needs to establish decision-making rules, especially for make or buy decisions. Without these rules in place, the program may be stalled unnecessarily or resources may be duplicated.

defining program components

The team needs to define program components

and develop a business case for each project. These business cases need to include technological, investment, regulatory, and legislative factors appropriate for each project.

developing program plans

The team needs to develop program plans. The primary plan at this point is the program management plan. This plan is likely to include several subsidiary plans that cover the entire scope of the program.

gaining support from stakeholders

Throughout the program setup phase, the program manager and program sponsor should continue to lobby stakeholders for their support of the program.

The executive committee for LangFarma wants an economic and an ethical feasibility study to be carried out before the Africa program is implemented. Rosa ensures that these studies are performed before further resources are used on the program.

The study results show that the program could be profitable. However, the ethics study stipulates that profit sharing with indigenous people who traditionally identified the plants for their various health properties must occur.

Sorin Dumitrascu

The program board decides that the program should go ahead after going through the study reports.

The program team establishes decision-making rules for make or buy decisions. Rosa, the program manager, is authorized to make any purchasing decisions for $250,000 or less.

Any decisions for purchases above $250,000 must be made by the program director, Julio, after discussion with the program board.

Next, the program team defines program components – for example, research, testing, growing, manufacturing, and marketing – and develops a business case for each project that outlines technological investments and regulatory and legislative factors.

Key questions that are answered by the program management plan and its subsidiary plans include the following:

- • What are the program components?
- What dependencies are there between deliverables?
- When will the targets for key deliverables be reached?
- What will the program cost?
- What are the risks, constraints, and assumptions?

Program Management

- How will the program be executed and managed?

The planning required during the program setup phase includes the processes in the Planning process group. So plans such as program schedules and budgets are drawn up. The planning team also creates a map of how projects will deliver the capabilities needed to generate program benefits.

Question

Your program to help victims of violent crime has passed its first phase gate review and you have received positive results from the ethical feasibility study.

What do you need to do next for the program?

Options:

1. Provide technological, financial, and regulatory overviews for each of the program's projects

2. Specify the person who is responsible for major purchasing and operations decisions

3. Develop a program management plan, a program budget, a schedule, and a risk management plan

4. Lobby funders and inhouse staff to ensure their ongoing support

5. Conduct feasibility studies on each of the

program components

6. Write a program charter outlining the expected counseling constraints of the program

Answer

Option 1: This is a correct option. During the program setup phase, you need to define program components and develop a business case for each project. These business cases need to include technological, investment, and regulatory factors appropriate for the projects.

Option 2: This is a correct option. During the program setup phase, you need to specify those accountable for and responsible for major decision-making – especially for make or buy decisions within the program.

Option 3: This is a correct option. The program management plan is the primary output for this phase in a program's life cycle. A large proportion of all planning should be completed at this stage.

Option 4: This is a correct option. The program needs to get through the second phase gate review before it can be implemented. So it's vital that you manage stakeholders and lobby for their support.

Option 5: This is an incorrect option. In this scenario, a feasibility study has already occurred so further studies are unnecessary.

Option 6: This is an incorrect option. The

program charter should have been completed in the preprogram setup phase.

Elements of a supporting infrastructure

The third program life-cycle phase is the establishing program management and technical infrastructure phase.

The purpose of this phase, according to the Standard for Program Management, is to establish an infrastructure that will support the program and its constituent projects as they deliver the expected benefits for the program.

When the program has passed through the second phase gate review, a framework needs to be established in which the program work can be done.

The program manager must ensure that the program's objectives align with the organization's objectives and business strategy. He or she must also keep the program's budget and time constraints in mind when creating its framework.

The program manager and the program team must then implement the structure or framework in which the program's work will be executed, as well as a technical infrastructure to facilitate that work.

To provide the supporting infrastructure for a program, the program management office (PMO) ensures the provision of:

program-specific governance

The PMO must ensure that all the program's

relevant policies, processes, and procedures are written up and made available to the program team.

program-specific tools

The PMO must ensure that all the necessary program tools are available to the program team. The tools can include software tools for planning, measuring, and tracking the program's performance and benefits delivery, the relevant finance and planning spreadsheets, and reporting tools.

program facilities

The PMO must ensure that the necessary offices and meeting rooms, as well as all the equipment the program team might need, are allocated to the program.

MyBudget Software is a company that develops software packages. Michael Cassidy, a senior program management consultant, has asked MyBudget Software to develop a software package that will enable him to keep track of his clients, his advice to them, their correspondence, and the clients' progress.

At MyBudget Software, Darren Alford has been appointed as the program manager for this assignment, and he forms part of the PMO. The PMO must ensure that a management and technical infrastructure is established to support the program.

MyBudget Software's PMO has to establish a structure in which all the program's planned objectives can be achieved.

The PMO's tasks during this phase include providing:

program-specific governance

The PMO draws up a grievance procedure and a privacy policy, and distributes these to all the program team members. The PMO also ensures that the program team is familiar with company policy, and Darren prepares a document outlining the deadlines the team should meet.

program-specific tools

Darren draws up a list of everything he thinks the program team might need in order to execute its tasks. The PMO ensures that the necessary computer software, textbooks, information, and specifications are available to the program team. It also provides a tracking sheet for monitoring and measuring the program's progress.

program facilities

The PMO assigns specific offices to Darren and his program team to use for the duration of the program's development. The PMO also ensures that computers, telephones, Internet access, and testing facilities are available to the program team members.

Program Management

    Once the PMO at MyBudget Software has ensured that all the elements of the managing and technical infrastructure are created and in place, the software development program must pass a phase gate review. The program team can then start developing the required computer software.

The program organizational structure

Each program needs a governance structure to support, oversee, track, and monitor the program and its constituent projects. This structure is called the organizational structure. The people assigned to this structure are responsible for making all decisions regarding the program.

In addition to the role of program manager, the key roles in the organizational structure include the:

program board

The program board represents the interests of the organization and is responsible for overseeing the program. The board is made up by the stakeholders, the executive sponsor, the program director, and the portfolio manager. It is supported by the PMO.

executive sponsor

The executive sponsor is supported by the program team and the key internal stakeholders within the program board. She is responsible for direction and oversight of the program, and must provide the infrastructure – such as the necessary funding and resources – to execute the program's tasks successfully.

program director

The program director sometimes fulfills the role of the executive sponsor, and so must ensure that the necessary resources are available to execute the program's tasks. The program director also contributes to the management structure by setting deadlines and budget constraints.

program manager

The program manager represents the program team and all project managers who contribute to the program, and is supported by the PMO. He must manage the program's progress, resources, and all involved in the program's constituent projects. The program manager may request changes to the program's technical infrastructure if necessary.

program team

The program team consists of the program manager and all the project managers involved in the program. It is responsible for executing various tasks that will achieve the program-level benefits.

program office

The program office supports the program manager and governs the program team. It is responsible for overseeing the various project activities, for quality control, and for reviewing the deliverables from the various projects.

Recall MyBudget Software, which is working on the development of software for its client, Michael Cassidy.

Sorin Dumitrascu

Before the company can start actual work on the software package, a managing and technical infrastructure needs to be established.

An organizational structure is created by appointing Darren Alford as program manager, Margaret Greger as the program director, and William Benson as one of the project managers and a member of the program team. The client, Michael Cassidy, is the executive sponsor.

Each member of the MyBudget Software organizational structure has a specific role with its own responsibilities:

executive sponsor

Michael, as the client, provides the funding that is needed to secure the necessary resources to do the program work. He is also responsible for overseeing the new software package to ensure it has the specifications that he requested.

program director

Margaret is responsible for the successful completion of the program. She must ensure that the resources – such as computers, software, people, and money – are available to the program team. She also provides a management structure by deciding on the budget and the deadlines for the development of the software.

program manager

Darren must manage the program's resources, and monitor the progress of the program and all its constituent projects. He is supported by the program office and the program team. He is also responsible for changes to the technical infrastructure, such as additional computers, software, people, and money.

program team

Darren, William, and the other project managers are responsible for overseeing execution of the various tasks that will complete development of the software package.

program office

The program office must review, monitor, and control everyone performing project tasks, such as the software developers and graphic designers. It must also support the program manager, Darren, in his tasks.

Outlining the organizational structure and the key roles in it is important for achieving all the program's benefits within the time and budget constraints.

MyBudget Software was able to deliver the software package in time because everyone involved in the program knew exactly which roles they filled, and what their responsibilities were.

Sorin Dumitrascu

Question Set

A-Plus Pharmaceuticals is a drug development and manufacturing company. A client has asked the company to develop a drug that will lower blood pressure.

Before work on development of the drug can start, a program management and technical infrastructure must be established. By outlining the organizational structure and the key roles of everyone involved, A-Plus Pharmaceuticals can create a supporting infrastructure, and work on the drug can start.

Question 1 of 3

The program board and the program manager play an important role in establishing the management and technical infrastructure. Match the examples of their tasks to the correct roles.

Targets can have more than one option matched to them.

Options:

A. Contributes to the management infrastructure by overseeing the development and manufacture of the drug

B. Requests additional equipment the scientists need, and monitors the drug development process closely

C. Determines the deadlines and the amount of money allocated for the development of the drug

D. Ensures that the program team does not use more money than has been allocated

Targets:

1. Program board

2. Program manager

Answer

The program board oversees the program and is responsible for deciding deadlines and allocating the available funds.

The program manager is responsible for managing program resources. This includes ensuring that the program remains within budget and requesting additional human and physical resources when needed.

Question 2 of 3

Match each role in A-Plus Pharmaceuticals' organizational structure to an example of its responsibilities. One example of a responsibility is not used.

Options:

A. Program team

B. Program director

C. Program manager

Targets:

1. Create a framework for performing all the work that must be done during development of the new drug

2. Set the deadlines and budget constraints for the research and development of the new drug

3. Manage all the equipment and the funds the scientists need, and monitor the progress of the drug development process closely

4. Ensure that the drug is tested intensively and that it can perform all the functions that were planned

Answer

This is an example of a responsibility of the program team in the organizational structure. The program team needs to oversee the execution of all tasks that will result in delivery of the new drug.

This is an example of the responsibility of the program director in the organizational structure. The program director ensures the availability of needed resources, and sets deadlines and budget constraints.

This is an example of the responsibilities of the program manager in the organizational structure. The program manager needs to oversee program execution, including the execution of all projects and their use of resources.

This is an example of the responsibilities of the

program board in the organizational structure. The program board oversees the program.

Question 3 of 3

Match each key role in the organizational structure to the appropriate example of its responsibility. One role is used twice.

Options:

A. Program office

B. Executive sponsor

Targets:

1. Ongoing monitoring and reviewing of the progress of everyone working on the new drug

2. Provides the funding that those involved in the drug development need for research and development

3. Provides the funds and the computer software needed for the initial research and development of the new drug

Answer

The program office supports the program board and program manager by establishing a management infrastructure, which provides processes for monitoring and reviewing the program's progress.

The executive sponsor is responsible for ensuring that there is sufficient funding available for a program.

The executive sponsor is responsible for ensuring that a program has sufficient resources – such as funds and computer software – to meet its delivery targets.

Expected results of the third phase

The establishing program management and technical infrastructure phase is expected to deliver specific results before the program can continue to the third phase gate review, and then to the deliver the benefits phase.

The supporting infrastructure and the relationships within the structure are defined in the program framework and are customized in the program charter and plan.

Expected key results from the establishing program management and technical infrastructure life-cycle phase include:

the staffing of an organizational structure

A program director, program manager, program team, and project managers must be appointed, and the program board must be assembled. Once staffing of an organizational structure for the program is complete, work on providing the required infrastructure for the program can proceed. If additional skill is needed, the relevant persons should be contracted to participate in the organizational structure.

the establishment of a program office

A program office to support the program must

be established. The program office will be responsible for overseeing most of the tasks that must be executed in the third phase, as well as putting the supporting infrastructure in place.

a program governance mechanism

To provide support for an appropriate program governance mechanism, the program board and the program manager must decide on oversight methods for the program. A reporting, reviewing, and approval structure and procedures must be in place before work on the program can start.

a program control framework

A framework and procedures for monitoring, controlling, measuring, and tracking the benefits from the program and its constituent projects must be established.

facilities and required infrastructure

The PMO must allocate the necessary facilities and provide the required infrastructure to support the program and its constituent projects.

IT systems and communication technologies

The necessary IT systems, communication technologies, and other equipment needed to support and sustain the program throughout its life cycle must be available to the program team.

Consider MyBudget Software, the company that

develops software packages. Michael Cassidy, a senior program management consultant, has asked MyBudget Software to develop a software package that enables him to keep track of his clients.

The development of the software package has moved through the first two program life-cycle phases, and is now in the establishing program management and technical infrastructure phase.

During the establishing program management and technical infrastructure phase, MyBudget Software must ensure the delivery of six main results.

Program staffing

To put the organizational structure in place, Margaret Greger is appointed as the program director, and Darren Alford as the program manager. Michael Cassidy, as the client, fills the role of executive sponsor, and William Benson is appointed as the project manager.

With all the roles in the organizational structure for the program filled, program staff can begin work on other tasks included in the establishing program management and technical infrastructure phase.

Establishment of a program office

Margaret, the program director, and Michael, the executive sponsor, form part of the program board.

They must assemble a program office that will be responsible for procuring the necessary resources, allocating funds, and drawing up the relevant procedures.

A program governance mechanism

The program board and Darren, the program manager, draw up documents and processes that detail how the review and approval system for the development of the software are going to be executed. They also decide who must deliver reports on the progress of the software development. In this way, they establish an appropriate mechanism for program governance.

A program control framework

To establish a framework for program control, Darren and Margaret Greger decide which tools they are going to use to track and measure the progress of the software development. They also decide how they are going to test the software to establish whether it meets the client's expectations and specifications.

Facilities and required infrastructure

The program office must ensure that facilities and required infrastructure such as office space, all needed equipment, and mechanisms for communicating program information are available to the program team.

IT systems and communication technologies

The program office must make sure that the necessary communication and IT systems, such as telephones, Internet, and relevant portals, are available to the team.

Once MyBudget Software has put a supporting infrastructure in place for its software development program and all the key results for the third life-cycle phase have been achieved, the program can proceed through a phase gate review and then move into the delivering benefits phase.

Question Set

Color and Style is a company that manufactures clothes for chain department stores. A new client has just asked Color and Style to manufacture a range of clothes.

The assignment has already been approved, and has reached the establishing program management and technical infrastructure program life-cycle phase.

Question 1 of 2

The establishing program management and technical infrastructure phase is the third phase in a program's life cycle.

What are some of the key results that Color and Style must achieve during this phase?

Options:

1. The appointment of a program director, program manager, program team, and project managers

2. The establishment of a program office

3. Specific procedures, an approval system, and a review tool to ensure that the clothes are of a high quality

4. A set of clearly defined projects for including in the program

5. A report detailing all tangible benefits of completed program work

Answer

Option 1: This is a correct option. Staffing of an organizational structure for the program is one of the key expected results of the third program life-cycle phase.

Option 2: This is a correct option. In the third life-cycle phase, a program office must be assembled to support the program. This office oversees program tasks and puts supporting infrastructure in place.

Option 3: This is a correct option. A program governance mechanism is one of the expected outcomes of the third program life-cycle phase.

Option 4: This is an incorrect option. Identifying the projects that a program will include should occur during the program setup phase, which must be completed before appropriate program infrastructure can be established.

Option 5: This is an incorrect option. The appropriate infrastructure must be established before actual program benefits can be realized, in the next phase of the program's life cycle.

Question 2 of 2

What additional key results must Color and Style produce in the establishing program management and technical infrastructure life-cycle phase?

Options:

1. A scoring system so that the seamstresses can be paid per clothing item they manufacture

2. A system for measuring the quality of the new clothing range

3. The provision of enough machines and seating space for seamstresses

4. Installed telephones and a computer system so that everyone who is involved in the program can communicate efficiently

5. A training course to prepare employees for their next program

Answer

Option 1: This is an incorrect option. Developing a system to determine payment of employees doesn't relate to providing the needed infrastructure for a program. Instead, the company must establish a system to measure and track progress in reaching the program's targets.

Option 2: This is a correct option. Establishing a program control framework is an expected result of the third life-cycle phase.

Option 3: This is a correct option. Securing facilities and the required infrastructure is one of the expected outcomes of the third program life-cycle phase.

Option 4: This is a correct option. Providing needed IT systems and communication technologies is one of the expected results of the third program life-cycle phase.

Option 5: This is an incorrect option. Program-specific procedures – rather than steps designed to ease the transition into a new program – must be put in place in the third life-cycle phase.

x

Delivering benefits

The deliver the benefits phase in a program's life cycle is the phase in which projects are initiated and benefits are generated incrementally.

The program management team needs to manage the group of related projects and ongoing work to generate incremental benefits that could not be generated if the projects were not managed as a program.

If the program's establish program management and technical infrastructure phase passes the third phase gate review, the program moves into the deliver the benefits phase of its life cycle.

This phase ends with the fourth phase gate review, after which the program moves on to the closing phase.

The deliver the benefits phase can last indefinitely and only ends if the program is closed down. The processes in this phase are iterative, following the patterns of the program's component projects.

To manage benefits effectively during the deliver the benefits phase, you need to:

initiate projects to meet program objectives
The program management team needs to initiate

Sorin Dumitrascu

projects to meet program objectives.

The scheduling of projects should facilitate the delivery of program benefits quickly and effectively. So each project needs to be reviewed in terms of how it contributes to program benefits and where it fits in to the program.

manage transition to the program's target state

To manage the transition to the program's target state, the program team needs to ensure that project governance structures are in place.

Using these structures, the team ensures that project managers use approved methodologies. They monitor progress against the program and project plans, and they ensure that resource use is carefully coordinated.

identify changes that impact benefits and risks

The program management team needs to identify changes that impact benefits and risks. The program needs to be flexible enough to respond to new challenges and opportunities.

Risk mitigation plans should address identified risks and should be altered to reflect any changes in the environment that may affect the program or its projects.

Program Management

The Easy Nomad Travel agency has initiated a new program focusing on travel packages to Eastern Europe. Amrit Khan is the program manager.

The program components include a research project, a training project for improving customer relations, a development of strategic relationships project, a marketing project, and a sales project.

The identified benefits of the program include increased revenue, increased market share, improved customer relations, and improved strategic relations with Eastern European tourism departments.

During the deliver the benefits phase of the program, Amrit and her team need to initiate the various projects so that they deliver benefits incrementally for the program.

To do this, Amrit maps program benefits to project deliverables and structures the projects so that training and the development of strategic relationships both begin once the research project is complete. Both of these projects can then begin generating benefits simultaneously.

Amrit explains her strategy for managing the transition from the agency's current state to that of the program's end goal to Gina – the program sponsor for the Eastern Europe program.

Gina: Now that we're getting started with the research project, I'd like you to fill me in on the strategies that you intend to use to govern the projects and their managers.

Amrit: Well, the PMO will forward all policies and procedures to the project managers. I will be meeting with each of them on a regular basis and I have put a responsibility matrix up on the intranet to ensure that each person knows what they are responsible for. I've also placed the templates for project plans and reports on the intranet so that everyone can use the same format.

Gina: That sounds great! And will this link up with how you intend to coordinate the resources between projects too?

Amrit: Yes, the program site has a list of resources that can be checked out in real time. Also, I have special procedures and checks in place for shared resources that were identified in the resource management plan and the interface management plan.

Gina: You seem to have that under control. Well done. What I am still worried about is how you will be able to track and monitor progress to ensure we reach those targets. There is a large budget that I have to justify to the board.

Amrit: I have set a series of meetings at critical

points in the projects' life cycles and will check our measures of linked benefits to their targets at each stage. This should pick up any developing problems. I have also instigated a direct line of response if any of the program or project teams pick up a problem that could be serious. So any changes can be responded to as quickly as possible.

Amrit's conversation shows that she has a clear understanding of how to manage the transition to a program's target state. She uses and builds on the infrastructure put in place during the previous life-cycle phase of the program to guide and oversee ongoing program work.

Amrit uses the agency intranet to help coordinate resource use and prioritizes shared resources.

She also has measures and procedures in place to analyze progress, checking benefit delivery targets against actual measures. For example, if the program benefit of increased market share has a set target of 15% in the first quarter, Amrit can measure market share at this point and compare it to the 15% target.

Eastern Europe is experiencing unusually cold and snowy weather beyond the typical winter period. This weather affected the benefits and the needed risk mitigation strategies for Easy Nomad

Travel's program.

Benefits

The inclement weather affects benefits in terms of reducing the number of winter sales packages that the agency could sell. In response to this, the schedule to meet benefits targets for increased sales revenue was extended by two months.

Risks

The inclement weather affected risk mitigation strategies because the team had to ensure that there were sufficient hotels available near airports to accommodate travelers whose flights had been delayed.

For rail and bus services that were slowed or canceled due to the weather, the risk plans added a budget for gifts of woolly hats with the slogan "Snow Survivor" as well as a list of discounted accommodation locations to placate clients who had been inconvenienced by the weather.

Easy Nomad Travel's program management team has identified the need for its program to change due to the bad weather. The program is flexible enough to accommodate an extension to the benefits targets and a risk mitigation plan that takes care of stranded or disgruntled passengers.

Program Management

Question

Match examples of activities to each of the key steps in the deliver the benefits phase of a program.

Options:

A. Launch a training project to generate skills to increase customer satisfaction

B. Ask the PMO to generate procedures for a specific project

C. Reschedule benefit delivery in response to the release of a competitor's product

D. Plan a new project to create a product geared toward a different demographic

E. Write a report detailing current benefit delivery against the benefit delivery targets

Targets:

1. Initiate projects to meet program objectives

2. Manage the transition to the target state

3. Identify changes impacting on the program

Answer

Initiating the projects required to achieve program goals involves mapping project deliverables to program benefits and then launching and overseeing appropriate projects. In this case, the program objective to which a project maps is to increase customer satisfaction by improving employees' skills.

Managing the transition to the program target state involves ensuring project governance is in place – for example through available procedures – and analyzing progress in terms of incremental benefit delivery.

Identifying changes that impact the program's benefits and risks involves altering benefits targets or creating new risk mitigation strategies in response to changed conditions. In this case, the benefits delivery target is extended and a new project is initiated to spread the risk.

How you run a program during the deliver the benefits phase differs according to each program's needs. However, activities for initiating projects, managing the transition to the program's target state, and identifying changes impacting program benefits and risks are common to all programs.

Closing the program

The close the program phase is the final phase of a program's life cycle. It ensures that the program is terminated through a controlled and carefully managed process.

A program closes when its targeted benefits are met or when other external factors dictate that it should close.

For example, the Eastern Europe program, developed to increase the sale of travel packages to destinations in key Eastern European countries, reached its benefits targets within its three-year schedule.

Because the benefits were realized and there was a high level of awareness about travel options in the region, the program was ready to close and have its resources integrated into the ongoing activities of the travel agency.

Not all programs are closed because they've achieved their goals, however. For example, a program run by a charity might have to close due to lack of funding.

Activities that are carried out during the close the program phase include:

compiling the benefits status review

Compiling the benefits status review entails reviewing the measures for each of the program's actual, delivered benefits against the benefit targets.

disbanding the program

Disbanding the program involves dismantling the program infrastructure and disbanding the program organization and program team. Once the program infrastructure is dismantled, the physical resources used by the program must be redeployed across the organization. Similarly, program resources and staff need to be redeployed.

providing customer support

Providing customer support involves providing guidance and ensuring that maintenance occurs so that any issues that arise after the release of the program's products and services are addressed. Typically, this type of support is documented in a contract between the organization and the customer.

detailing lessons learned

Detailing lessons learned entails documenting best practices, program successes, and program weaknesses for managers and other members of future programs to learn from.

During the close the program phase, you may provide feedback on identified changes that are beyond the program's scope, store and index all documentation, and manage transitions across the organization.

The Easy Nomad Travel agency is closing its Eastern Europe program. During this phase of the program's life cycle, the program team carries out the following tasks:

compiling the benefits status review

In compiling the benefits status review, the program team notes that the program is 8% beyond its target of a 20% rise in sales revenue. It also notes that the rise in customer satisfaction is below its target due to mismanaging customers' expectations regarding rural infrastructure in Eastern Europe.

disbanding the program

When disbanding the program, the team ensures that both physical and human resources are redeployed across the agency when it dismantles the program infrastructure and disbands the teams.

providing customer support

In providing customer support, the team ensures that people with knowledge of the area are identified and can be used in the future to help other travel agents with inquiries for customers hoping to travel in the region.

detailing lessons learned

In detailing lessons learned, the program team outlines the best practices for marketing and networking. It also documents how the team's weakness in managing customer expectations affected customer satisfaction.

Question

Match each example of an activity to the step it represents in the close the program phase of a program.

Options:

A. Report that customer satisfaction levels exceeded the target by 5%

B. Redeploy web developers to a new web project for another program

C. Write procedures for handling product faults

D. Document best practices for creating and marketing a product

Targets:

1. Compiling a benefits status review
2. Disbanding the program
3. Providing customer support
4. Detailing lessons learned

Answer

The benefits status review outlines current benefit measures and compares them with the program's targets. So it reports where benefits such as customer satisfaction meet, exceed, or miss their targets.

Disbanding a program involves ensuring that human and physical resources are redeployed, so sending web developers to a new program is an aspect of disbanding a program.

To ensure continued customer support after a program closes, the program manager needs to provide resources to support internal or external customers. So writing product fault procedures is an aspect of providing customer support when closing a program.

Detailing lessons learned includes documenting best practices, as well as successes, weaknesses, and any problems experienced during the program. Future programs can then benefit from this information.

CHAPTER 3 - Program Management Processes and the Initiating Process Group

Business is increasingly operated on a project-by-project basis as organizations aim to streamline their business objectives using clearly-defined components.

In this environment, process management plays an important role. It enables program managers to use a synergistic approach, coordinate functional groups, resolve issues between projects, and ensure good program governance.

With so many business demands and a highly competitive business environment, organizations are increasingly resorting to program management to achieve the business goals they set for themselves.

To achieve the benefits that the organization expects, managers can use a results chain model to link core components that underlay all business programs.

Program processes are performed by people and, much like program phases, interrelate and depend on one another to get the best possible end result delivered to an expectant customer.

There are five process groups that perform tasks at the program level, or at a program's composite projects level: Initiating, Planning, Executing,

Monitoring and Controlling, and Closing.

The Initiating process group should be used to ensure organizational authorization and to identify the conditions for program success.

The group is also useful for identifying program stakeholders and for creating and finalizing reporting requirements.

In this lesson you will learn about using the Initiating process group processes. You will also learn about the inputs, outputs, and controls that are common across processes and process groups.

Program management is the management of a number of related processes. Recognizing how the processes interact is key to successful management.

The common inputs and outputs of processes in program management provide a basis for recognizing commonality between the program processes.

Using common inputs and outputs is a best practice that highlights important considerations when dealing with any process.

The Initiating Process group processes are used to initiate a program in alignment with a strategic plan. The group consists of three processes.

The Initiate Program process is used to define the scope and benefits of the program and to authorize funds for it after it is shown to be linked to

Sorin Dumitrascu

the company strategic priorities.

The Authorize Projects process is used to initiate components of the program, such as projects. The process creates charters and approves funding for projects.

The Initiate Team process is used to recruit employees to work on the program and to formalize the appointment of the program manager.

Processes in program management

Program and project management competencies are essential skills in almost any modern organization. While the project management culture is maturing, an increasing number of business units are forming their own program management offices.

Although similar, there are a few differences between the two, with the most obvious difference being the fact that program management operates at a higher organizational level, with a broader scope, and involves the coordinating of projects to achieve certain beneficial outcomes.

More and more organizations are organizing their work on a project-by-project basis in order to achieve their business objectives most economically. And as with any project, the work consists of various processes.

For instance, whether you plan to overhaul your organization's internal network, or host extensive management training – these projects involve various processes. Such processes, if seen from an organizational perspective, guide and coordinate your efforts toward achieving a strategic outcome.

The Project Management Institute (PMI®) defines such a process as a "set of interrelated actions and activities performed to achieve a specified set of products, results, or services."

Processes are important to a program manager, as they:

- • help resolve issues between projects,
- enable the use of a synergistic approach,
- enable the coordination of functional groups,
- help ensure successful program governance.

Processes help resolve issues between projects by enabling the program manager to look at a failed process and prevent the problem from recurring elsewhere as the program progresses.

For instance, if preliminary studies leading up to a restaurant launch show that the proposed venue does not have a broad enough customer base to satisfy the profit needs of the restaurant, an efficient program manager needs to suggest alternative locations in advance, or otherwise change the program plan accordingly.

Program processes make a synergistic approach possible, in which a program's various project processes cooperate to achieve a program outcome that is greater than any of its individual components.

When overhauling the company's internal network, for example, the IT coordinator's careful planning, support from technical staff, and the input of security analysts together contribute to the program's eventual success, more than any of these inputs do individually.

Using processes, program managers coordinate functional groups and efforts between projects to enable processes to overlap and interrelate as necessary.

This grouping together of processes is done because processes typically execute more than once at various stages of a program's progression anyway. Also, dealing with related issues together is more effective than dealing with them one at a time.

Say a program manager identifies and deals with an issue that crops up at the program level. This saves the effort, time, and money of having to resolve the problem each time it occurs at the individual project levels.

Program management processes help ensure that program managers, program teams, committees, and other program support structures can ensure successful program governance.

A strong program governance structure defines roles, responsibilities, and an organization's strategic activities clearly. This definition enables managers, committees, and other executives to focus their energies on the required outcomes.

There are several groups of processes:

Initiating

The Initiating process group authorizes and defines a program, or project within a program, and produces the program's benefit realization plan. This plan structures, monitors, and tracks benefit delivery at the program level.

Planning

The Planning process group plans the best alternative course of action to deliver the benefits and scope that the program intends to address. This group of processes also defines the metrics and systems used to track and deliver benefits.

Executing

The Executing process group integrates people, projects, and other resources that carry out a program. Processes within this group acquire and use the resources needed to accomplish program benefits.

Monitoring and Controlling

The Monitoring and Controlling process group measures a program and its component projects against expected results to identify deviations from the program's plan and to form a clear idea of the program's expected benefits.

Closing

The Closing process group formally accepts a service, product, or result to close a program in an orderly and controlled manner. This group of processes demonstrates that all expected program benefits have been delivered.

Consider Darren, a program manager at an architectural firm that is designing an office building in the city. As program manager, Darren should be aware of the general activities that occur in the various design projects, just as you'd expect a program manager in your industry to be familiar with project activities that constitute a program completed at your organization.

For example, if a design team at Darren's firm encounters height restrictions for the area in which they're planning to build, he'll need to determine if the restrictions affect the program's completion, or not. Alternatively, he'll need to apply to the City Planning Department for special permission to exceed the limit, and warn project managers at other design teams to look out for restrictions during their initial planning.

Question

Why are processes important to any program manager?

Options:

1. They enable the coordination of functional groups

2. They enable the use of a synergistic approach

3. They provide historical information about a project

4. They provide solutions to similar problems experienced across multiple projects

5. They remove the need for changes during the program development

6. They facilitate successful program governance

Answer

Option 1: This is a correct option. With the use of program management processes, a program manager can coordinate the functional groups that constitute a program.

Option 2: This is a correct option. With a synergistic approach, program management processes align to deliver an end result that surpasses the effects of its individual components.

Option 3: This is an incorrect option. Although historical information can be a relevant component of a program management process, the process does not convey information about a project's history.

Option 4: This is a correct option. With program management processes, the program manager can oversee the processes to identify problems as they occur and stop them from repeating elsewhere.

Option 5: This is an incorrect option. Although some program processes may facilitate the ease with which changes in the program's development are addressed, they do not stop changes from happening.

Option 6: This is a correct option. With program management processes, project managers can ensure that program governance proceeds as planned and that activities deliver the most effective results.

x

The results chain and initiatives

All organizations invest time and resources on programs in order to achieve beneficial outcomes. After all, if an organization doesn't draw any benefit from running a program, then why bother doing it?

To assist program managers in realizing the intended benefits of a program in a controlled and coordinated manner, program managers rely on the program life cycle.

Just as every project has a beginning and an end, the program's life cycle spans all stages of the individual projects that constitute a program – from initial phases through to eventual outcomes.

But how do you ensure that you have the appropriate projects running to achieve the benefits you want?

Using a specially developed benefits management approach, you can establish the appropriate processes and measures through which to track and assess the benefits you want to maintain throughout a program's life cycle.

In fact, benefits management is a vital theme in the program life cycle of any business hoping to succeed in the business environment. Without effective benefits management, a program has little hope of actually realizing its benefits.

Apart from benefits management, the other themes prevalent in a program's life cycle are:
- • stakeholder management,
- • program governance.

Processes that support benefits realization in the program life cycle include:

defining each benefit and how it can be realized

By defining each benefit and how it can be realized, program managers and stakeholders understand the context of benefits, how to support, track, and process benefits, and how to deliver good results.

mapping benefits to program outcomes

By mapping benefits to program outcomes, managers can define the expected program benefits in terms of the project outcomes and the results the program intends to deliver within the organization.

defining metrics and procedures to measure benefits

Metrics and procedures to measure benefits are defined to help assess the strategic effect that program and project outcomes will have within an organization.

defining roles and responsibilities for benefit management

Defining roles and responsibilities for benefit

management ensures that certain strategic projects deliver the expected program outcomes that benefit the organization.

transitioning the program into ongoing operation and sustained benefits

Unless program managers transition the program into an ongoing operation with sustained benefits, the program is unlikely to be operational enough to deliver its intended benefits, because changes in the strategic plan could throw a program off course.

Through extensive interviews and workshops with business stakeholders, a program was developed to create a shared understanding of the links between components and processes and to use these to realize benefits.

This program of linked components, known as the results chain model, is aimed at making program benefits a reality by acting as a practical "road map" that indicates how components that produce benefits are interrelated.

The results chain model links core elements of the benefits realization process to show the desired outcomes and the possible paths that can be taken to reach intended outcomes, no matter how many variables and elements of change are present in a program's life cycle.

Program Management

There are four interrelated components that comprise the results chain.

Initiatives

Initiatives refer to the actions that contribute to making one or more of a program's outcomes a reality, and the decisions regarding what these actions will be.

Assumptions

Hypotheses that describe the conditions needed to make results or initiatives a reality are known as assumptions. The organization usually has little or no control over these conditions. Assumptions also represent the risks that might prevent outcomes from being realized.

Contributions

The roles that elements of the results chain model play in contributing to other initiatives or outcomes (either initiatives or intermediate outcomes), are referred to as contributions.

Outcomes

Outcomes refer to the desired results, including intermediate outcomes, outcomes that are necessary but insufficient in themselves to achieve an end benefit, and ultimate benefits that need to be achieved.

When compiling a strategic program, how do you know what processes and actions to use to get the benefits that your organization requires?

To come up with the initiative – the strategic actions and measures you need to take to realize results – a good idea is to have the proposed benefit or program result in mind, and then work backward from there to initiate the program.

For example, if you're a sales consultant deciding to bid for a contract from an external customer, you already know the outcome you want: the contract.

Agreeing on the processes and steps you need to implement to get the contract helps you create the strategic initiative.

Question

A pharmaceutical manufacturing company had to recall one of its products from the market. The firm had trouble recalling the drug because there were no processes in place to track products in the supply chain after leaving the manufacturer.

The company's management decided to use a benefits realization approach to assess the viability of implementing an electronic tracking system to track products through the supply chain to the point where it was dispensed to a consumer.

In this scenario, what is the initiative in terms of the results chain approach?

Options:

1. The decision to implement an electronic tracking system

2. Control over the progression of all drugs throughout the supply chain

3. Electronic tracking devices that monitor a drug's shelf life and retail venue

4. Barcoded drugs that comply with strict industry standards for supply chain visibility

Answer

Option 1: This is a correct option. The company's management took the initiative of implementing electronic tracking to help realize its benefits.

Option 2: This is an incorrect option. Gaining better control over drugs in the supply chain is an outcome, and not an initiative that makes the outcome a reality.

Option 3: This is an incorrect option. How tracking devices monitor various aspects of a drug is an aspect that contributes to outcomes, and not the initiative.

Option 4: This is an incorrect option. Having drugs comply with strict industry standards is an assumption, and not the initiative to make benefits a

Sorin Dumitrascu

reality.

Outcomes of benefits realization

Using a results chain model, business executives undertake initiatives to create and implement programs that deliver beneficial results. But how do you decide on the right approach?

First ask yourself what you would like the results of the program to be. By defining the outcomes, you can decide on an approach that will make your intended benefit a reality.

Outcomes in a benefits realization approach take various forms, such as cost savings, new business opportunities, a reduced employee turnover rate, or revenue growth. Some outcomes are intermediate in that they are necessary but insufficient to achieve an end benefit in themselves. Others are ultimate outcomes.

Consider a company that provides copy, scanning, and mailing facilities to consumers. Due to low sales figures and customer complaints about the length of time it takes to deliver orders, the company's management has to solve the problem. The goal is simple: to implement an order-processing system that will deliver good service to customers – fast.

By implementing a new order-entry system, the firm's lengthy ordering process can be reduced –

thereby achieving an intermediate outcome.

The ultimate outcome, however, is often achieved long term, and not necessarily as a direct result of a change that was made in the organization's strategic functioning.

For example, if a company benefits from using a high tech new access control system – an intermediate outcome – the ultimate outcome is only achieved later on when sales figures improve, customer service is enhanced, or other tangible results are achieved that are not directly linked to the short-term investments that were made.

Sally, a program manager, talks to a stakeholder in the organization, Michael, about his proposal for a program to upgrade the company's security system.

Sally: Hi Michael, did you get the report I sent you last week in reply to your proposal to upgrade the company's security?

Michael: Yes, thanks Sally. I'd like to ask you a few questions about that when you have a moment.

Sally: Sure, go ahead. What's bothering you?

Michael: Well, I didn't expect it to be turned down. What happened with that? I mean, I thought everyone would be in favor of having better security around here.

Program Management

Sally: Yes you're right, Michael. However, your proposal got turned down in favor of another approach that aims to resolve the same issue, but with better long-term benefits.

Michael: And to think that my proposal wasn't even that expensive. So the long-term outcomes really made the other proposal that much more appealing?

Sally: Yes, like it said in the report. However, I would like to thank you for your input. It really gave perspective on what is important to the company's stakeholders.

Michael: Oh, I understand. As long as it's best for the company, that's what really matters.

Sally: Alright. But feel free to discuss it in more detail with me later, if you feel you'd like to.

As Michael found out, long-term benefits are as important – if not more important – than short-term benefits and cost savings. What benefits the organization in the long run is what matters most.

Question
A medical insurance company recently received complaints from customers that payments for prescriptions and medical transactions took too long to process.

The company's management decided that it would be useful to implement a benefits realization approach to cut back on the time it took to process these and other transactions.

Identify the outcome in this scenario.

Options:

1. Providing customer service training to personnel that interact with customers

2. Reducing the time it takes to process customers' transactions

3. Implementing a new computer system that can process transactions fast

4. Having customers wait as long as necessary until their transactions complete

Answer

Option 1: This is an incorrect option. Providing customer service training is a contributing aspect of the results chain in this case, and not an outcome.

Option 2: This is a correct option. Reducing the time it takes to process orders and transactions is an outcome, as the company benefits from having transactions completed fast enough to please customers.

Option 3: This is an incorrect option. Implementing the new IT system is an initiative to make one or more outcomes a reality in this benefits realization model, and not one of the outcomes itself.

Option 4: This is an incorrect option. Having customers wait for their transactions to be processed is one of the assumptions of this benefits realization approach, and not a desired outcome.

Assumptions and contributions

Many organizations mistakenly attempt to achieve benefits using an approach that is focused too much on short-term costs and intermediate results instead of the targeted benefits.

By identifying the actions and conditions that contribute to the eventual outcome of a benefits realization program, management ensures that not only intermediate outcomes are realized, but the eventual tangible benefits as well.

But what makes benefit realization tricky is that a business program isn't static. It needs to change and adapt to reflect changes in market conditions, organizational priorities, and business trends that affect organizations.

So in order to stay current and achieve the planned benefits, an organization's approach to benefits realization needs to be flexible enough to take into account any changes in the business environment.

A good way of ensuring that your benefits management approach is resilient enough to withstand industry change is through the results chain model.

With the results chain approach to benefits realization, assumptions and contributing factors are linked to the eventual outcomes that a program aims to achieve, thereby enabling management to handle any risks or obstacles that come between a program and its planned outcome.

Two components that ensure a flexible results chain model are assumptions and contributions.

Assumptions

In order to achieve specified benefits in an often tumultuous business environment, assumptions in the results chain help assess the possible risks that could prevent the realization of benefits.

Assumptions also state which processes and components are ideally needed to make benefits possible.

Contributions

Contributions include factors that contribute and affect other initiatives and outcomes in a benefits realization approach.

These contributions can be aspects that are influential in making eventual outcomes a reality, or aspects that affect how the program progresses through various project stages.

For example, consider a stationery supply company whose management decides to improve customer loyalty by enhancing the company's value

Sorin Dumitrascu

chain, creating a more customer-driven environment.

As part of the value chain enhancement strategy, the company implements an electronic customer relationship management (e-CRM) system. The new system works on the assumption that a growing, Internet-driven consumer culture can contribute to systems, such as inventory and access control, by creating a free exchange of information – an intermediate outcome.

Company management needs to realize that the initial capital spent on some benefits realization approaches – although substantial – are likely to deliver benefits that far outweigh these initial costs. By thinking long term, you can ensure that the benefits achieved are long term too.

Using a benefits realization approach, such as the results chain model, your company can develop and apply a strategic vision, evaluate existing operational processes, and align technological infrastructure requirements, not only to address short-term needs but to ensure that long-term tangible results are realized too.

Question
Officials at a regional airport want to implement new technology to control and track travelers'

luggage.

They plan to use a results chain model to ensure that the benefits realization strategy for the implementation pays off. The new RFID system will enable officials to track every piece of luggage from check-in counter to its destination.

What assumptions and contributions are applicable in this situation?

Options:

1. Lost luggage is a major concern for airport officials and airports throughout the country

2. New technology that ensures more revenue is generated

3. People not minding having their luggage tracked, as long as their privacy is respected

4. Airport officials who cannot be blamed or be held responsible for lost luggage

Answer

Option 1: This is a correct option. One of the major factors that contributed to management's need to realize benefits and have better control over luggage, was concern over travelers' lost personal belongings.

Option 2: This is an incorrect option. Generating more revenue, although desirable, is an outcome of the benefits realization approach and not one of the assumptions or contributing factors.

Option 3: This is a correct option. The benefits realization approach operates on the assumption that people prize the safety of their possessions over concerns about their privacy.

Option 4: This is an incorrect option. Airport officials cannot be excluded from the benefits realization process, as they may well be held responsible for lost luggage, especially in the eyes of travelers.

Program management process groups

All organizations need an infrastructure in place that provides them with the knowledge, tools, skills, and techniques necessary to support their programs. Without knowing what results, quality level, or capability a program is expected to provide, such a program will be difficult to plan, execute, or conclude.

Processes enable organizations to conduct projects in a consistent and well-managed manner, thereby creating quality products on time and within budget.

Program managers coordinate the processes of each of the projects that constitute a program's successful execution. In this way, program-level processes interact with project-level processes during all stages of a program's life cycle to ensure successful completion. Moreover, processes aren't bound to a program's life cycle.

Program processes are independent of application areas or industry focus. Processes are organized into five groups:
1.   1. Initiating
2.   Planning
3.   Executing
4.   Monitoring and Controlling

5. Closing

Initiating processes are performed to authorize and define the scope of a new program or program phase, or to continue a program that was stopped at some point. This ensures that a program does not contradict the organization's ongoing work and strategic priorities once it is implemented.

Because the start of a program is critical for program success, the basic processes within this group are important. The program's stakeholders also need to formally accept the proposed program's scope, usually by having each stakeholder sign off on the scope document.

Consider the case of Callinsure, an insurance firm in which management decided to implement a new billing system to speed up the rate at which their billing transactions were processed.

During initiating phases to install Callinsure's new system, program managers neglected to involve all stakeholders, including certain customer groups.

This was a mistake, because without stakeholder involvement, program and project managers didn't have adequate access to information, and based subsequent planning on inaccurate information. The system was a failure when implementation was eventually completed.

Program Management

The Planning process group helps to draw up the processes that are necessary to lay the foundation for a program's successful completion. Included in this are activities that assess the program's feasibility, identifying benefits that will satisfy the program's goal and achieve its benefits, and creating the management plan that defines the tactical means by which the program will eventually be executed.

During program planning, you need to verify that project goals and objectives are defined, that the project is aligned with the strategic goals of the program, and you need to decide how the cost and risk factors should be managed, not only at the program level, but also for each project.

Once planning is in place, the Executing process group integrates projects, people, and other resources to carry out the plan for a program and deliver the program's benefits.

After execution, the group of processes responsible for monitoring and controlling a program's components checks that a program is on course to produce the benefits it is expected to deliver.

Also, a program's progress is measured regularly to ascertain whether it aligns with the program management plan, and if not, to make the necessary corrections to achieve the benefits in time.

Finally, the Closing process group formalizes acceptance of a product, service, or benefit; thereby bringing a program or program component (such as a project) to an orderly end.

Like program processes, project processes are also divided into five groups. However, project processes differ from those of programs in a number of ways.

Initiating group

At the project level, initiating processes occur at the start of a project, and at the start of each project phase for larger projects. Initiating confirms that a project, or the next project phase of a program, should start.

At the program level, initiating processes assist in ensuring that projects are in place. For example, checking that a project manager has been assigned, that project teams are functional, and that individual project objectives are valid.

Planning group

During planning at the project level, a project's goals are defined, and a breakdown of the work and risks that need to be considered are provided. This process group also specifies the project's expectations and identifies the stakeholders.

This differs slightly from program level planning, during which a program's scope is defined, and projects are checked to ensure they align to the program's objectives.

Executing group

At the project and program level, the executing group of processes involves putting the relevant management plans into action.

Within the executing group of processes at the project level, project work produces outcomes called deliverables. At the program level, the outcomes that are achieved are known as benefits.

Monitoring and Controlling group

When monitoring and controlling at the project level, the project's status is reviewed. All changes to the project's scope, timing, cost, and quality need to be aligned to the broader program.

At the program level, the processes in this group measure and monitor project execution so that corrective action can be taken, if necessary.

Closing group

During closing at the project level, performance measurements are taken to review whether stated deliverables were realized by the various projects. Accounting and financial files are also closed.

At the program level, closing processes terminate all activities of a program or phase, transfer the completed product to the customer, or close a canceled program in an official manner.

Question

Identify the program and project process groups.

Options:

1. Project Plan Development, Initiation, Scope Planning, Change Control, and Closing

2. Initiating, Planning, Execution, Monitoring and Controlling, and Closing

3. Project Plan Development, Initiation, Scope Planning, Execution, and Closing

4. Initiation, Project Plan Development, Integrated Change Control, Scope planning, and Closing

Answer

Option 1: This is an incorrect option. Although the Initiating and Planning processes in the process groups may contain some of these activities, these are not the five process groups.

Option 2: This is the correct option. The process groups at the project and the program level are Initiating, Planning, Execution, Monitoring and Controlling, and Closing.

Option 3: This is an incorrect option. Project plan development and scope planning are activities performed as part of some of the processes in the five process groups, rather than the names of the actual groups.

Option 4: This is an incorrect option. Activities such as scope planning and change control are performed as part of the processes in the process groups, but differ from the five process groups themselves.

The tasks of program process groups

Each of the five process groups fulfills a specific task in a program's successful completion. Instead of being discrete, one-time events, the overlapping tasks of process group activities occur at varying levels of intensity throughout each phase of a program's completion.

For example, planning processes may repeat several times during each program phase to help keep projects aligned with the program's goals.

During a program's early phases, information flows from the program to the projects (initiating and planning) and then flows from the projects to the program in the later phases of executing, controlling, and closing a program.

The Initiating process group helps define the scope and benefits that are expected of a program, thereby ensuring that a program's strategic intent is authorized with its stakeholders, as well as configuring and grouping proposed (and existing) projects into a program.

For example, as part of a program's initiating phase, program managers can assign a project manager and project team, help to review and approve the project charter document, and convene with other stakeholders to authorize and provide funding for a program's completion.

It is the task of the Planning group of processes to draw up the processes necessary to lay the groundwork of a program's successful execution. These activities include identifying deliverables that will satisfy the program goal and achieve its outcomes, and creating the program management plan.

Once the earlier tasks for a program's successful execution are in place, three remaining process groups help realize a program's benefits:

Executing

Executing processes drive a program according to its management plan. In this way, program managers ensure that processes are executed in accordance with stakeholder plans and established policies. Executing processes also help ensure that program communication is administered correctly to provide strategic information and feedback.

Monitoring and Controlling

The Monitoring and Controlling process group is responsible for obtaining and consolidating statistical data from individual projects to program packages. Activities in this group also interface with the program governance structure, and report on any corrective actions needed to achieve the planned benefits.

Closing

As part of a program's Closing activities, processes in this group formalize the acceptance of products, services, or results that complete a program.

Activities of the Closing process group help demonstrate:

- • all program benefits that were delivered and the scope that was fulfilled,
- contractual obligations with sellers and customers,
- that all required documentation has been archived,
- that all intellectual property gathered during the program has been captured.

Remember Callinsure? During initiating phases to install its new billing system, program managers neglected to involve all stakeholders and give them shared ownership of the proposed program. This was a big mistake, because without the involvement of stakeholders, program and project managers didn't have adequate access to information, and based subsequent planning on inaccurate information.

At the planning stage, management had trouble

defining the project activities that needed to be performed. Without the proper program schedule, financial planners had no idea how much to budget for the various projects.

Without proper initiating or planning, the executing, monitoring and controlling, and closing tasks may all be problematic or riddled with unforeseen errors. At worst, a program's benefits may never be realized.

For Callinsure, inadequate initiating and planning resulted in a newly implemented billing system that could not deliver the benefits that management expected of it.

Not only was the system poorly scoped, but due to numerous unforeseen errors that cropped up, the extra cost of hiring external software developers to fix problems put Callinsure in the red.

Question

A government health department recently decided to implement programs to improve emergency services and disease surveillance capabilities. The programs need to ensure appropriate training for employees.

Match the descriptions to the process groups involved in the implementation of the programs.

Options:

Sorin Dumitrascu

A. Getting authorization from the Health
Department

B. Defining a preliminary scope for the
emergency services program

C. Assessing service quality and surveillance
measures

D. Distributing program information and
providing training for the team

E. Delivering adequate disease surveillance, and
improved emergency services

Targets:

1. Initiating
2. Planning
3. Monitoring and Controlling
4. Executing
5. Closing

Answer

When initiating a program, getting the program's
stakeholders to provide proper authorization is
important.

In planning, program managers need to state
what the scope of the program is and what
characterizes the program.

Monitoring and controlling processes perform
quality assessments to ensure the program delivers
what is expected of it.

Executing processes ensure that information is

Program Management

distributed and that the program team is developed to prepare them for upcoming tasks.

Closing processes ensure that beneficial outcomes are delivered to the expectations of customers.

The Initiating process group

Century Solutions provides services and products to organizations seeking to manage the identities of their customers or employees.

The company wants to expand its sales so it decides to convert the security products project into a program with a number of projects under it - biometric security systems, customer marketing, and customer satisfaction. The program has a mission to increase market share by 5%.

The newly-appointed program manager, Ayana Bardon, is wondering where to start.

Program management is the coordination of a number of projects with some commonality in their business outcomes.

It involves three themes: benefits management, stakeholder management, and program governance.

Program managers differ from project managers in that they delegate authority for the day-to-day management of the activities within their program.

In order to effectively manage project and program benefits, and provide program governance, program managers can use a number of processes specified in the Standard for Program Management.

The Standard for Program Management divides program management processes into groups – the first of which is the Initiating process group.

The Initiating group involves processes performed to authorize and define the scope of a new phase or program, or that can result in the continuation of halted program work.

This group is important for linking program activities to the strategic business objectives of the company. It supports the three broad program management themes:

benefits management

A program manager can forecast an end state of a program and show the potential benefits to the company with the Initiating process group. The manager can use this information to ensure that the program has organizational authorization. This fulfills the benefits management role of the program manager.

The benefits management outputs are indicated: Program charter, Program benefits statement, and the Benefits realization plan.

stakeholder management

A manager identifies the stakeholders affected by and involved in the program during the Initiating process group to facilitate stakeholder management.

The stakeholder management outputs are indicated: Project manager identification, Core program team assignment, and Program sponsor identification.

program governance

The Initiating process group allows the creation and authorization of reporting requirements that support the program governance theme.

The Program governance output, namely the Reporting requirements, is highlighted.

How might program managers benefit from completing the processes within the Initiating process group? They will be able to

- • ensure the program has organizational authorization,
- illuminate the desired organizational end state of program success,
- identify the core program team members,
- finalize reporting requirements.

During the life cycle of the security products program, a number of the Initiating process group processes are used to facilitate the three program management themes:

benefits management

The Initiate Program process is used to manage benefits by using the strategic business objectives to create a program charter and a preliminary program scope statement. Based on the strategic alignment of the program's charter, the steering committee approves the program.

program governance

The Authorize Projects process uses the scope statement, project selection criteria, and the strategic plan to select projects, such as the voice identification design project. During this process, program governance reporting procedures for project managers, program managers, and the steering committee, are developed.

stakeholder management

During the Initiate Team process, the program manager is assigned to the program, and the rest of the program management team is selected. This is an early stakeholder management activity.

Ayana, the program manager, benefits from the Initiating process group being used because the program has official authorization from top management based on the clear program charter.

A specific reporting procedure is already in place to facilitate in monitoring the projects to ensure that they align to the business objectives.

And a list of the team members and all stakeholders is already developed, so the manager can begin to manage their roles and expectations as the program begins.

Question

When managing a program, what are the benefits of using processes of the Initiating process group?

Options:

1. Organizational authorization can be ensured
2. The conditions for program success can be identified
3. Core team members can be identified
4. Reporting procedures can be created
5. Alternative courses of action can be planned
6. The program's benefits can be delivered

Answer

Option 1: This is a correct option. The program manager can expect organizational authorization when using processes in the Initiating processes group, such as the Initiate Program process.

Option 2: This is a correct option. The Initiate Program process is also used to create a program charter, which identifies an expected outcome or goal for the program.

Option 3: This is a correct option. The program manager will be able to manage the stakeholders' roles and expectations using an early indication of the team membership. The team membership is identified in the Initiate Team process, a part of the

Initiating process group.

Option 4: This is a correct option. During implementation of the Initiating process group processes, reporting requirements for projects are planned to assist in program governance.

Option 5: This is an incorrect option. Another process group is responsible for planning alternative courses of action.

Option 6: This is an incorrect option. Another process group is responsible for delivering the program's benefits.

Common inputs and outputs

Many program management processes have elements that are common to other individual processes.

The common elements relate the processes to the specific business environment of the organization and the program.

The common elements may be inputs, outputs, or controls. Some elements can be inputs for one process or outputs for another.

There are three inputs that can be common to program management processes:

constraints

Factors that limit the flexibility of a process are known as constraints. They tend to be associated with resources or the schedule.

historical information

Historical information is a source of lessons learned from previous programs. Information that is pertinent to a current program could be artifacts, estimations, or a description of the failures experienced in previous programs.

organizational process assets

Organizational process assets are formal and informal practices that are institutionalized in the organization. They can include procedures and guidelines, and sometimes historical information as well.

There are three common outputs in program management processes:

lessons learned

Lessons learned are similar to historical information and organizational process assets. Any process provides lessons to be learned, and they should be formalized as an output to transfer the information to other processes.

supporting details

Supporting details are artifacts that are not included in the formal program documentation but are important factors for the success of the process.

information requests

Information requests are outputs of processes that are sent to Information Distribution processes as inputs.

Assumptions can be common inputs or outputs. They are factors or conditions that affect a process and that are considered to be true without having to be proven.

The third common element, after inputs and

outputs, is controls.

Controls are used to standardize the program management processes so that they are predictable.

Controls can be standards specific to that industry or to a specific contract. Organizational policies act as controls as they specify procedures and methods for the work that a program seeks to achieve.

Another control is the strategy plan of the organization, which is reflected in the program management plan.

Government regulations, as well as review and audit findings, also provide control factors for a program. A real estate consultancy is branching out into land and building development.

The executives charter a program called Land and Building Development. They aim to have the land development service available within one year and the building development service available six months later.

The program involves a number of projects including, for example, the Property Acquisition project. A review of the program documents reveals the following common inputs:

constraints

A constraint is that the resources required for the

program initiation are small – they include the time taken for executive employees to deliver a program charter and approve projects.

organizational process assets

An organizational process asset is that the company has many years of experience in property management, and the data collected during normal operations will prove useful. For example, the employees are familiar with local building codes and a contact list of government officials has already been established.

historical information

Data from the commercial leasing program is historical information. It lists the reasons why clients chose to allow their commercial property leases to expire. For example, a large number of clients required better road infrastructure for expansions, such as the installation of a weigh bridge or a fuel station.

A Lessons Learned document is created that highlights a case where the land owner failed to perform a Phase One Environmental Site Assessment (ESA), which resulted in the landowner and lending body being held legally responsible for cleaning the site.

In order to avoid this responsibility, a control is

introduced to the program.

It specifies the completion of environmental site assessments that meet the American Society for Testing and Materials (ASTM) standards.

An assumption is noted in the program documents that a normal Phase One ESA takes an average of nine days to complete.

A Phase One ESA template and instructions are created and included in the program documentation as supporting details.

A currently open item in the documentation is a request for information by the project manager, who has asked the program manager to clarify who would be responsible for financing an ESA.

Case Study: Question 1 of 2

Scenario

For your convenience, the case study is repeated with each question.

SunSide Food is a food and beverage company based in Washington State that is initiating a new program.

Answer the questions in the given order.

Question

Match each of the following common input factors to their examples.

Options:

Program Management

A. Constraints

B. Historical information

C. Organizational process assets

D. Assumptions

Targets:

1. The program budget is $500,000

2. A similar program was postponed because of an E. coli outbreak

3. There are established processes that can help ensure food safety

4. The average project duration will be ten weeks

Answer

Cost limitations are constraints, as they limit the flexibility of the process.

Historical information from a previous program can be a good source of lessons learned.

Existing processes and capabilities are organizational process assets.

Estimations of the schedule components are assumptions if they are expected to remain the same.

Case Study: Question 2 of 2

Now match the common outputs to their examples.

Options:

A. Lessons learned

B. Supporting details

C. Information requests

Targets:

1. Suppliers alone cannot be responsible for E. coli testing

2. A document that explains how to comply with industry regulations and that provides forms for doing so is developed

3. A program office employee e-mails the program director for approval to use a specific public health consultant

Answer

Corrective action taken in light of a previous error is a lesson learned.

Artifacts that are needed for program success are supporting details.

Requests for information should be collected and analyzed so that they can be included in future programs.

Initiating process group components

Program management differs from project management in a number of ways. The most obvious of these is that program management operates at a higher organizational level, with a broader scope, and it involves the management of projects.

Program management defines criteria for project selection and is responsible for coordinating project benefits.

There are some similarities between project and program management, such as the process group names.

The process elements, however, are different. They have different inputs, functions, controls, tools, and outputs.

The life cycle of a program is longer than that of a project. A long life cycle makes it more difficult to maintain focus and deliver results near the end of the program life cycle than a project life cycle.

As the life cycle is longer, programs are more likely to require maintenance or adjustment of the program focus.

Programs are more able to adjust in response to the lessons learned during their life cycle than projects because of the longer life cycle.

Sorin Dumitrascu

Many of the activities in the Initiating process group for project management are performed outside the scope of the project. They exist in the role of program or portfolio management.

For example, funding and authorization of projects is handled at the program management level.

There are three processes that make up the Initiating process group in the Standard for Program Management:

Initiate Program

The Initiate Program process helps to define the scope and expected benefits of a program. It links the program to an organizational strategic objective or future state and it contextualizes the program within the current organizational state.

Authorize Projects

The Authorize Projects process helps to initiate components of the program, such as projects. This process interfaces with project management processes closely as project managers and sponsors are identified, reporting requirements are set, funding is allocated, and project charters are authorized.

Initiate Team

The Initiate Team process is used to assign a

Program Management

program manager and recruit the other human
resources required to work on the program.

The Initiate Program process

The Initiate Program process is the starting point for a program. Before this process an organization has only strategic goals and objectives but no method for achieving them.

The function of the Initiate Program process is to use a strategic objective to help develop the tactical practices that will assist in achieving the objective.

It aligns tactical management at the project level with top-level management goals. A number of inputs are required for the Initiate Program process.

Business case

A business case is a formal proposal for a program. It attempts to justify the program by pointing out potential benefits when compared to alternative programs or inaction. The business case shows the alignment of the proposed program with the current and future-state strategic business objectives. The business case is usually developed outside the domain of program management.

Investment analysis

An investment analysis is a forecast of the required resources necessary to achieve the goals relative to the expected benefits of the program. A common calculation is the return on investment

(ROI) for a program. The investment analysis is usually developed outside the program management domain.

Funding for initial phases

The process requires funding for the initial phases of the program. This funding should carry the program through the initiation and planning phases, after which the cost and budgeting estimates come into play.

Organizational strategic and tactical plans

The process uses the organizational strategic and tactical plans, which are normally included in the business case and investment analysis, to develop the process outputs.

The Initiate Program process generates a number of outputs.

Documentation required for a contract or statement of work

The documents required for a contract or statement of work are developed in the Initiate Program process. The details provide a high-level statement of the work that will be undertaken and a price associated with the work.

Program charter

The program charter is a high-level document

that contains the vision statement for the program. It highlights the potential benefits or end state of the program, and it shows the alignment of the program to the strategic business objectives. It is the primary driver for program authorization.

Program manager identification

The Initiate Program process identifies a number of potential program managers. The program manager is assigned during the Initiate Team process.

Program scope statement

A preliminary program scope statement is developed in the Initiate Program process to be used as an input in the Authorize Projects process. The scope statement is reviewed when the program is being considered for authorization.

Program benefits statement

The program benefits statement is often included in the program charter. It describes the expected benefits of the program.

Project selection criteria

The Initiate Program process generates the criteria for selecting appropriate projects within the program. The criteria ensure that the projects align with the strategic objectives of the organization.

Benefits realization plan

The benefits realization plan focuses on how the

benefits will be achieved. The benefits realization plan is maintained through all phases of a program. It includes a definition of each benefit mapped to program outcomes, along with further benefits management information.

Program sponsor identification

A program sponsor, or the person responsible for approving resources for the program, is identified in the Initiate Program process.

Brocadero is an electronics manufacturer that specializes in sound equipment. It aims to reduce costs associated with the manufacturing of its core line, portable music players.

The business leaders and the program management office develop a business case for a program to reduce the costs associated with the transportation of materials in response to the strategic business objective.

It shows the current performance of the supply chain and contrasts it with the potential benefits of the program.

The business leaders have the Finance Department provide an investment analysis of the program to forecast the resources that will be required, and to estimate the benefits of the program.

The executives use the Finance Department report and the business case to create a program charter. It includes a scope statement as well as a benefits statement and realization plan.

The program enters the first phase of its life cycle with a meeting for the identification of a program sponsor and manager.

A supply-chain director is elected as the sponsor and she identifies Sara Wang as a potential program manager.

Sara meets with the program team and they create the criteria for project selection.

Question

What are some of the outputs of the Initiate Program process?

Options:

1. Program charter
2. Project selection criteria
3. Preliminary program scope statement
4. Project charter
5. Business case

Answer

Option 1: This is a correct option. A program charter is developed during the Initiate Program process.

Option 2: This is a correct option. Project

selection criteria are developed during this process to act as inputs for the Authorize Projects process.

Option 3: This is a correct option. An initial estimate of the scope of the program is developed in the Initiate Program Process. It is further developed in the Authorize Projects process.

Option 4: This is an incorrect option. Project charters are developed in the Authorize Projects program management process and in the project management Develop Project Charter process.

Option 5: This is an incorrect option. A business case is an input for the Initiate Program process.

Question

Match the Initiating Program process inputs and outputs to their appropriate examples.

Options:

A. Input

B. Output

Targets:

1. A document outlining the program's expected benefits and their alignment with company goals

2. A forecast of the return on investment for a program

3. A high level statement of the work that will be undertaken

4. The document that contains the vision

statement for the program

5. An employee is earmarked as a potential manager

6. The person responsible for approving program resources is identified

Answer

The type of document described is an example of a business case. A business case is an input.

This is an example of an investment analysis that forecasts a financial goal of a program. An investment analysis is an input.

This is an example of a document that contains a statement of work. A statement of work outlines the types of work of a program and the costs, and is an output.

The program charter is an output that contains the vision statement of a program. It illustrates how a program aligns to the strategic business objectives.

Program manager identification is a process in which potential program managers are selected. It is an output.

Program sponsor identification is a process in which the person responsible for approving program resources is identified. It is an output.

Question

Identify the Initiating Program process inputs

and outputs from the examples.

Options:

A. Input

B. Output

Targets:

1. The business leader approves resources for initiating the program

2. The program is expected to increase market share by 15%

3. The organization aims to improve its personal electronics market share

4. Success in the IT project and training project will increase market share by 15%

5. The projects must contribute to the tactical plan

6. The program includes IT and marketing business areas

Answer

Funding for the initial phases of the program is an input.

A program benefits statement is an output.

Organizational strategic and tactical plans are an input.

A benefits realization plan is an output.

The project selection criteria are an output.

The preliminary program scope statement is an output.

The Authorize Projects process

Remember Sara Wang, the Brocadero program manager?

Having met with the program team and created the criteria for project selection, Sara is ready to begin the process of initiating the program components and projects.

The Authorize Projects process takes the preliminary program scope statement, project selection criteria, and the organization's strategic plan, and initiates appropriate projects within the program.

Projects can be initiated at any time in the program life cycle, other than at the program closing phase. The Authorize Projects process generates a number of outputs.

Program reporting requirements

The program reporting requirements are developed. Channels for project managers to report to the PMO are defined.

Project charters

Project charters are developed in this process. The project charter is used as an input in the develop-the-preliminary-project-scope-statement project management process.

Project manager assignment

During project manager assignment, the employees who will manage the projects in the program are assigned.

Project sponsor identification

Project sponsor identification occurs in this process. The sponsor is usually an executive such as a program director.

Project funding approval

Project funding approval, necessary to complete the individual projects within the program, occurs in this process.

Recall the Brocadero program initiation. The program management office (PMO) waits for the preliminary program scope statement and the project selection criteria from the Initiate Program process.

When these outputs are ready, the office uses them and the strategic plan to begin the process of authorizing projects. The PMO uses the process to develop program reporting requirements.

The process specifies the reporting channels and a schedule for regular reports by project managers to the PMO. The requirements also specify regular reports by the program manager to the oversight committee.

The PMO creates charters for each of the projects that are required to deliver the benefits of the program. One of the projects is the Transportation project.

The Transportation project charter also identifies potential project sponsors and assigns a project manager to the project.

The project aims to develop transport contracts with optimal delivery frequency and routes to deliver the best transport performance.

When the project sponsor is assigned, the PMO will approve the funding required for the Transportation project.

Question

What are examples of the inputs of the Authorize Projects process?

Options:

1. The program includes transport but not storage
2. The projects must all be associated with the portable music player
3. The company aims to reduce costs associated with the portable music player line
4. The formal proposal for the program that justifies the focus on the portable music players

5. The transportation project will reduce delivery time by 30%

Answer

Option 1: This is a correct option. This is an example of the type of information you would find in a preliminary scope statement. A preliminary scope statement is an output from the Initiate Program process, which serves as an input to the Authorize Projects process.

Option 2: This is a correct option. This is an example of the criteria used for project selection. The project selection criteria from the Initiate Program process is used as an input in the Authorize Projects process.

Option 3: This is a correct option. This is an example of the information found in a strategic plan. The strategic plan, which is developed outside the scope of the program, is needed to create the Authorize Projects process outputs to ensure that they are strategically aligned.

Option 4: This is an incorrect option. This is an example of information found in a business case, which is an input for the Initiate Program process.

Option 5: This is an incorrect option. This is an example of the information found in a project charter, which is an output of the Authorize Team process.

Sorin Dumitrascu

Question

What are some of the outputs of the Authorize
Projects process?

Options:

1. The vehicle communications project will
improve the delivery time of raw materials

2. The project sponsor approves resources for
the Transportation project based on its charter

3. The Transport project manager will make
weekly presentations to the PMO

4. A plan for each project benefit is mapped to a
program outcome

5. A plan to improve sales of personal music
players

Answer

Option 1: This is a correct option. This is an
example of the information found in a project
charter. The Authorize Projects process develops
project charters, which are inputs in the develop-
the-preliminary-project-scope-statement project
management process.

Option 2: This is a correct option. This is an
example of project funding approval. The Authorize
Projects process is used to approve funding for all
the projects and components in the program.

Option 3: This is a correct option. This is an

example of program reporting requirements. The Authorize Projects process is used to develop program reporting requirements, such as channels for project managers to report to the PMO.

Option 4: This is an incorrect option. This is an example of the information found in a benefits realization plan, which is an output of the Initiating Program process.

Option 5: This is an incorrect option. This is an example of the information found in a strategic plan, which is an input of the Authorize Projects process.

The Initiate Team process

The Initiate Team process uses the organization's established recruitment practices, as well as the staffing pool description to develop the human resources required for the program.

The program sponsor is responsible for assigning a program manager during the Initiate Team process.

The other outputs are the assignment of the core program team and a directory of all the program team members.

Recall the Brocadero Program. The Initiate Team process has already been used a number of times.

It was used to help identify a program manager and sponsor in the Initiate Program process. It also helped identify project sponsors and approve project managers in the Authorize Projects process.

The process uses the standard recruitment practices, as used by the Brocadero Human Resources Department, and a description of the staffing pool required to work on the program to initiate the team.

The program manager and sponsor, who have been identified in the Initiate Program process, are now finalized in the Initiate Team process. It also concludes the appointment of the core program management team.

The process also results in a Brocadero program team directory so that all employees can find and contact the appropriate program management staff.

Question

What are the outputs of the Initiate Team process?

Options:

1. Core program team assignments
2. Program manager assignment
3. Program team directory
4. Recruitment practices
5. Documentation required for a contract or statement of work

Answer

Option 1: This is a correct option. The Initiate Team process is used to assign employees to the program.

Option 2: This is a correct option. The program manager is assigned using the Initiate Team process.

Option 3: This is a correct option. A program team directory is developed in the Initiate Team process.

Option 4: This is an incorrect option. Recruitment practices are inputs of the Initiate Team process.

Option 5: This is an incorrect option. Documentation required for a contract or statement of work is an output of the Initiate Team process.

Lena Lang is a large fashion brand that is initiating a new program to enter a large and potentially lucrative market.

The executives at Lena Lang used the three processes in the Initiating process:

Initiate Program

In the Initiate Program process, the Lena Lang executives used the business case, the market gap analysis, the strategic and tactical plans, and some initial funding to develop the program charter. They also created a benefits statement and realization plan, project selection criteria, and documentation needed for contracts. Finally, a program manager and sponsor were identified.

Authorize Projects

In the Authorize Projects process, the executives used the strategic plan, the program scope statement, and the project selection criteria to create project charters. They developed reporting channels for the projects to report to the PMO, and once the project manager and sponsor were assigned, funding for the projects was approved.

Initiate Team

The executives used the Initiate Team process to select employees to work on the program. They used the standard Lena Lang recruiting practices and a description of the program staffing pool to assign the program manager and to create the team directory.

CHAPTER 4 - Program Planning

The program planning team is responsible for developing the program management plan, which incorporates plans for many aspects of the program. Careful planning is crucial to ensuring a program's success.

This lesson takes a closer look at the inputs and outputs of the Develop Program Management Plan process and reviews the Interface Planning, Transition Planning, Resource Planning, and Creating a Program Work Breakdown Structure (PWBS) processes.

A program management plan and program benefit statements are the outputs of the Develop Program Management Plan process. Inputs for the process include a range of subsidiary plans, each of which is consolidated into the program management plan to create a comprehensive guide to program execution and control.

Although much planning occurs at the beginning of the program, the Develop Program Management Plan process is iterative and continues throughout the program life cycle.

The Interface Planning process identifies and evaluates program interfaces. It then assesses interface management strategies that enable information to be communicated between interfaces in a way that is accurate, succinct, timely, and pertinent.

Inputs into the Interface Planning process include the staffing management plan, the Stakeholder Analysis chart, the communications management plan, the risk register, the Program Work Breakdown Structure (PWBS), and the schedule management plan. Its outputs are the interface management plan, a list of program interfaces, program schedule updates, and requirements for planning individual project communications.

The Transition Planning process involves planning how program and project deliverables must be handed over to receiving stakeholders to ensure that the benefits of the deliverables are sustained. Steps in this process include identifying receiving stakeholders and including them in planning, clarifying the deliverable and the scope of each transition, and planning the transfer of all necessary resources to stakeholders.

Steps in the Resource Planning process include prioritizing critical external skills or needed resources that are missing, identifying candidates to fill skill gaps, allocating shared resources to optimize their use, and using historical information to identify appropriate resource strategies.

A Program Work Breakdown Structure (PWBS) provides an overview of a program and shows how each project fits into it. Its inputs are the benefits realization plan, the program scope statement, and the scope management plan.

The PWBS clarifies the scope of a program, logically groups work components, and lists all program artifacts and deliverables. These include program benefits and project deliverables such as services and products.

Planning is one of the most important aspects of program management. Different types of planning are used in program management, including schedule planning, cost planning, and quality planning.

Schedule planning uses the Program Work Breakdown Structure (PWBS) as a starting point for developing a program timeline, which specifies resource availability and use, and provides a common goal for teams.

Cost planning is used to forecast total expenditure for a program and helps to improve the use of program capital. It allows program managers to stick within a specific budget and coordinate spending across different segments of a program.

Quality planning involves identifying quality

standards and how to achieve them within a program. It ensures that high standards are achieved early on and then sustained in a program.

Each activity in a program is examined and placed in sequence during the Schedule Development process. The starting point for the process is the Program Work Breakdown Structure (PWBS). This basic outline is fleshed out to include all details of the program, including duration estimates and the expected completion date.

Once a program schedule has been completed, the program manager estimates the costs involved in each part of the program and budgets for these costs. There are a number of tools and techniques, such as analogous estimating and parametric estimating, which can assist with cost estimation.

The starting point for budgeting is also the PWBS. During this process, program managers allocate the available funding to the different program packages outlined in the PWBS.

The success of a program relies on the effective organization of human resources. Within program management, human resources planning involves the process of identifying, documenting, and assigning program roles, responsibilities, and reporting structures.

The success of a program also relies on the

successful provision of quality services or products. The effective implementation of relevant quality control methodologies and standards ensures that a program maintains high quality.

For a quality plan to be successful, it needs to outline what needs to be checked, the appropriate way to check it, when it should be checked, who should check it, and what quality assurance tools should be used.

During the Communications Planning process the information and communication needs of a program's stakeholders are identified. The program manager is the link between all stakeholders and is in a position to set up and manage clear communication channels.

Program managers need to consider the Stakeholder Analysis chart, communication requirements, program reporting requirements, program charter, program scope statement, and Program Work Breakdown Structure (PWBS). These result in a communications management plan and the communication technology requirements plan.

The Risk Management Planning process is the stage in program planning at which program managers identify the probability of undesired events occurring and the impact they may have on a program. The four steps in the process are risk identification, qualitative analysis, quantitative analysis, and risk response planning. The outputs of the process are a list of identified and prioritized risks and the risk management plan.

The Program Purchases and Acquisitions process is the stage in program planning at which the program manager decides what services and goods to buy, when, and what strategy to use to acquire them. The outputs of this process are the contract statement of work, make or buy decisions, a procurement management plan, and a qualified vendor list. The procurement management plan is the basis for the Program Contracting process.

Why develop a program plan?

"Every minute you spend in planning saves ten minutes in execution." – Brian Tracy, author

Like Brian Tracy, PMI® stresses the importance of planning for effective program management.

Much of this planning occurs in the early phases of the program. However, plans need to be revisited at significant program milestones – such as project initiation and closure, year-end budgets, and when unplanned organizational changes occur.

The program planning team performs several iterative functions – planning and revisiting earlier plans – throughout the program life cycle.

Its purpose is to create a program management plan that includes scope, schedule, costs, resources, quality, and communication plans.

This process provides an infrastructure and a roadmap for the program to follow.

Thorough planning can help mitigate risks and increases the chances of realizing sustained benefits from a program.

The benefits of developing a program management plan for a program manager include:

realistic benefits and objectives

A program plan helps to establish realistic benefits and objectives. It ensures that the program benefits are consistent with the company mission or objective in a defined time frame.

ownership

The work that goes into program planning helps to foster a sense of ownership of the program among program employees. This increases intrinsic motivation for those working on the program.

efficient resource use

Careful program planning helps to ensure the most efficient use of resources across numerous projects and ongoing program activities.

a baseline for measurement

Program planning provides a base against which progress can be measured. It sets targets against which program stakeholders can evaluate the progress and relative success of the program.

A program management plan incorporates the outputs – or planning documents – that result from the following planning processes:

- • Develop Program Management Plan process
- Interface Planning process
- Transition Planning process
- Resource Planning process

- Scope Definition process
- Creating a Program Work Breakdown Structure (PWBS) process
- Schedule Development process

Other outputs that are incorporated in the program management plan include those from the Cost Estimating and Budgeting, Quality Planning, Human Resource Planning, Communications Planning, Risk Management Planning and Analysis, Program Purchases and Acquisitions, and Program Contracting processes.

Question

Adam is a program manager at a cereal manufacturing firm. He is in charge of a program to improve quality standards in the shipping section.

How can developing a program plan benefit Adam?

Options:

1. It helps to establish realistic benefits and objectives

2. It encourages a sense of ownership of the program

3. It allows him to ensure the most efficient use of resources

4. It provides a base against which progress can be measured

5. It helps him to guarantee stakeholder buy-in

6. It reduces the need for program documentation

Answer

Option 1: This is a correct option. Planning helps to ensure that the established benefits of a program are realistic and that they align with company objectives within a given time frame.

Option 2: This is a correct option. The work involved in planning helps to ensure that program employees develop a sense of ownership of the program.

Option 3: This is a correct option. Through careful planning, the planning team can ensure that resources are assigned efficiently across projects and ongoing program activities.

Option 4: This is a correct option. Planning provides baseline measures and targets against which the program's progress can be measured.

Option 5: This is an incorrect option. Although careful planning can help to sell a program to its stakeholders, effective stakeholder management is the main factor in ensuring stakeholder buy-in.

Option 6: This is an incorrect option. Creating a program plan involves producing a set of documents, and doesn't reduce the documentation required once program activity begins. All program

Sorin Dumitrascu

phases should be documented to help with program evaluation and to distribute learning throughout an organization.

Program management plan components

An environmental agency, Fresh Earth, wants to create a program management plan to ensure that its strategic objective of building environmental awareness among the public is achieved in a timely and cost-effective manner.

What should such a plan contain?

The program management plan is created by the program planning team. This plan consolidates other subsidiary planning documents to create a comprehensive guide to program execution and control.

Components of the program management plan include the following subsidiary plans:

resource management plan

The resource management plan specifies the people, equipment, and other resources that are needed to perform program activities, and it states how these resources should be spread across the program.

schedule management plan

The schedule management plan defines the program components needed to produce program deliverables. It identifies the order in which the components must be executed and estimates the amount of time required for each component.

cost management plan

The cost management plan aggregates all costs for a program using an estimate made by the program team or an aggregate based on individual estimates of projects and work packages. It establishes budgets and identifies any financial constraints.

staffing management plan

The staffing management plan documents and assigns program roles, responsibilities, and the reporting relationships of individuals and groups, both within the organization and outside of it.

contracts and procurement management plans

The procurement management plan determines what to procure for the program and when. The contracts management plan identifies potential contracting sources and creates formal contracting documents for implementing contracts with suppliers, either external to or within the organization.

Some subsidiary plans may simply be incorporated into the program management plan rather than generated first as separate plans.

Program Management

Question

Match descriptions to the subsidiary plans developed by the planning team.

Options:

A. Determines the order in which program components should be executed

B. Aggregates all costs for a program using estimates

C. Assigns program roles, responsibilities, and reporting relationships

D. Prioritizes skill gaps and identifies candidates for open positions

E. Identifies potential contracting sources and creates formal contracting documents

Targets:

1. Schedule management plan
2. Cost management plan
3. Staffing management plan
4. Resource management plan
5. Contracts management plan

Answer

The schedule management plan determines the order in which the program components that are needed to produce deliverables should be executed.

The cost management plan aggregates all costs using estimates. It establishes budgets for the program based on the budgets for its individual

317

projects and for ongoing program activity, and identifies any financial constraints on the budget.

The staffing management plan documents and assigns program roles, responsibilities, and the reporting relationships of individuals and groups, both within the organization and external to it.

The resource management plan ensures that there are sufficient resources – including staff with appropriate skills – for the program. It therefore prioritizes skill gaps and identifies candidates for open positions.

The contracts management plan documents potential contracting sources and creates formal contracting documents. The procurement management plan identifies what must be acquired – or purchased – for the program and when.

Each of the following plans may be added as subsidiary plans to the program management plan:

scope management plan

The scope management plan clarifies the boundaries of the program and specifies how the program scope should be managed throughout the program.

benefits management plan

The benefits management plan includes benefit descriptions, measures, and strategies for managing benefits across the program.

interface management plan

The interface management plan identifies and maps interrelationships within the program and between the program and other organizational activities.

communications management plan

The communications management plan determines the information and communication needs of the program stakeholders. It specifies who needs what information, when they need it, and how it will be communicated.

quality management plan

The quality management plan identifies standards relevant to the program and specifies how to comply with them.

risk management plan

The risk management plan identifies risks and provides quantitative and qualitative analyses of these risks. It also provides risk response strategies.

Depending on the specific characteristics of a program, some of the subsidiary plans may not be used. You need to review each program to assess which plans are necessary.

Question

Sorin Dumitrascu

Match the descriptions of functions to the subsidiary plans with which they are associated.

Options:

A. Maps interrelationships within the program

B. Clarifies the boundaries of the program

C. Identifies standards relevant to the program

D. Determines the information needs of the program stakeholders

E. Analyzes factors and events that could compromise a program

Targets:

1. Interface management plan

2. Scope management plan

3. Quality management plan

4. Communications management plan

5. Risk management plan

Answer

The interface management plan identifies and maps interrelationships within the program and between the program and other organizational activities.

The scope management plan clarifies the boundaries of the program and specifies how the program scope should be managed throughout the program.

The quality management plan identifies standards relevant to the program and specifies how to comply with them. This process must occur early in the program to ensure that the required competencies are available throughout the planning of critical program activities and processes.

The communications management plan determines the information and communication needs of the program stakeholders. It specifies who needs what information, when they need it, and how it will be communicated.

The risk management plan specifies ways to minimize risk for a program and its individual components. It identifies and prioritizes risks, as well as specifying plans for minimizing or avoiding them.

Process inputs and outputs

Subsidiary plans and project planning process outputs serve as inputs to the Develop Program Management Plan process.

As plans are developed for each project, this information is fed into the subsidiary plans, which are then updated and added to the program management plan.

This process is iterative, and occurs when changes to plans or projects occur. The program plans depend on information generated at the project level.

The outputs of the Develop Program Management Plan process include the program management plan itself and program benefit statements.

Program benefit statements list the program's benefits, their measurements, and how they are to be managed.

These outputs guide program execution and control throughout the life cycle of the program.

Fresh Earth, the environmental agency, has a total of six main programs and now wants to create a seventh program to focus on promoting environmental awareness among the general public.

Program Management

The program planning team for the Fresh Earth environmental awareness program develops the following subsidiary plans:

scope management plan

The team develops the scope management plan to clarify the boundaries of the environmental awareness program. The benefits realization plan informs this planning process by helping to differentiate between this program's benefits and those of the other programs. This clarifies what tasks the team for each program should undertake to deliver the identified benefits.

interface management plan

The interface management plan is created to identify interfaces between the environmental awareness program and the other six programs in the company's portfolio, and between the program and external customers and suppliers. It also identifies interfaces within the program itself. Identifying interfaces helps to clarify how program role players should communicate and with whom they should be communicating.

staffing management plan

The staffing management plan specifies who is on the program team, the skills that the different players need to bring, and the reporting relationships that must exist to ensure smooth management of the teams.

contracts management plan

The contracts management plan identifies consultants and other contractors that need to be brought into the program. These contracts fill skill gaps in the program.

communications management plan

The communications management plan specifies how communication should take place, when it should take place, and which players should be involved in communicating. With clear communication, the program has a far greater chance of success.

The program planning team for Fresh Earth's environmental awareness program develops a quality management plan to take advantage of existing quality expertise and methodologies, such as Six Sigma, within the program domain.

The program planning team needs to develop a risk management plan to assess the risks facing the environmental awareness program and to develop strategies to respond to potential crises.

In addition to other plans, the program planning team needs to generate the following subsidiary plans and add them to the program management plan:

resource management plan

The planning team develops the resource management plan to ensure that resources are not duplicated and that all resources are used efficiently. Examples of resources include employees for each project, equipment, contractors, and funds.

procurement management plan

The planning team develops the procurement management plan to specify which major purchases must be made for the program. This includes major software purchases to generate the various print and electronic media required for the program.

cost management plan

The planning team develops the cost management plan to ensure that the program runs within budget and to help allocate budgets for individual projects.

schedule management plan

The planning team develops the schedule management plan to ensure that projects run and deliver required results at the optimal times within the program. For example, running the print and broadcast projects concurrently ensures that a wide audience is reached as quickly as possible.

When the team completes each subsidiary plan,

it adds it to the program management plan.

Question

Categorize each of the following as inputs or outputs of the Develop Program Management Plan process.

Options:

A. Benefits management plan

B. Procurement management plan

C. Program management plan

D. Program benefit statements

Targets:

1. Inputs for program planning

2. Outputs of program planning

Answer

Inputs for the Develop Program Management Plan process include information gathered and compiled into several subsidiary plans, each addressing considerations that must affect program execution. So the benefits management and procurement management plans are examples of the subsidiary plans that form inputs for the development of the program management plan.

The end products or outputs of the Develop Program Management Plan process are the program management plan itself and program benefits statements. These outputs are then used to execute

Program Management

and control the program throughout the rest of the program life cycle.

Interface planning overview

The Interface Planning process is a process through which the boundaries and relationships between individuals, groups, and organizations associated with a program are identified.

This planning also outlines how problems and communication between the identified entities should be managed.

So interface planning serves two purposes – identifying interdependencies and supporting the communications management plan.

Effective interface planning helps to ensure that:

- • roles, responsibilities, and reporting relationships are clarified,
- processes, policies, and procedures are consistent,
- resources are used effectively.

If interface management is not planned properly, program teams or project teams within a single program may not have vital information before making decisions.

For example, the team for the new devices program of an electronics company needed to create a component for a new product it was developing. However, it was not aware that the team for the video products program was working on a similar component. If the interface management between the two programs had been maintained, development of the component could have been shared, resulting in significant savings.

Poor planning of interface management affects processes, policies, and procedures because the interrelationships between related program components are not mapped.

In the case of the electronics company, designing two versions of the same component resulted in inconsistencies between the final versions of the components in the company's portfolio.

Poor planning of interface management may result in ineffective use of resources because the overlap and relations between programs aren't monitored.

In the example of the electronics company, poor interface planning between two program teams led to duplicated efforts and wasted resources.

Some of the common interfaces that require identification in a program are:

interfaces within the program

Common interfaces within a program occur between individual program team members, between program team members and project team members, and between program office and project team members. They also occur between program managers and the program board, their teams, and their project managers.

interfaces external to the program

Common interfaces external to a program include interfaces between portfolio managers and program managers, program managers of different programs, program teams, and program management office (PMO) members or administration staff.

interfaces external to the organization

Common interfaces external to the organization include interfaces with suppliers, customers, regulatory boards, contractors, consultants, and competitors.

There are several reports and plans that the program planning team can use to develop an interface plan. Two of these inputs are the staffing management plan and the Stakeholder Analysis chart.

The staffing management plan and the Stakeholder Analysis chart help the team to identify who is involved with the program and what their respective roles are. This information helps them to map interfaces.

A matrix comprising information senders and

receivers helps to identify interfaces and show critical areas.

The remaining inputs for the Interface Planning process include the:

communications management plan

The communications management plan helps the team assess reporting relationships and the types of communication available to help them complete the communication aspect of the interface management plan. These are assessed against risk and critical interface areas to ensure they meet all requirements.

risk register

The risk register helps the team to focus on potential problem areas and how communication between various interfaces may be able to mitigate any negative effects. It also helps the team to rate interfaces in terms of risk, so those that are prioritized can be closely managed.

Program Work Breakdown Structure (PWBS)

The Program Work Breakdown Structure (PWBS) helps the team to formalize the program scope in terms of program benefits and the work needed in each project to produce those benefits. This informs interface planning in that it highlights formal communications and reports that the interface planning team can assess.

schedule management plan

The schedule management plan establishes the timeline for program milestones and the delivery of benefits. Interfaces at these milestones need to share information, and the interface planning team needs to ensure that communication between the key interfaces occurs at each milestone.

The outputs of the Interface Planning process are the interface management plan, a list of program interfaces, program schedule updates, and requirements for planning communications for individual projects.

Program schedule updates specify meetings and processes for relaying critical information between key interfaces.

The planning team sets requirements for individual project communications. Project managers then have to set up their processes to accommodate the communications and risk management issues highlighted through the process.

Interface planning should be adapted to the specific needs of the program. However, the key to good interface planning is good communication.

All good communication is:

- •   • reliable

- succinct
- timely
- frequent

Question

What are the inputs for the Interface Planning process?

Options:

1. The communications management plan
2. The staffing management plan
3. The schedule management plan
4. The PWBS
5. The risk register
6. The program schedule updates
7. The requirements for planning individual project communications

Answer

Option 1: This is a correct option. The communications management plan helps the team assess reporting relationships and provides information to help them complete the communication aspect of the interface management plan.

Option 2: This is a correct option. The staffing management plan helps the team to identify who is involved with the program and what their respective roles are.

Option 3: This is a correct option. The schedule management plan identifies program milestones. The planning team can use these to ensure that communication occurs between the key interfaces at each milestone.

Option 4: This is a correct option. The PWBS informs interface planning by highlighting formal communications and reports that the interface planning team can assess.

Option 5: This is a correct option. The risk register helps the team to focus on potential problem areas and to rate the risk associated with interfaces. This assists the team in prioritizing interfaces for management.

Option 6: This is an incorrect option. Program schedule updates are an output of this process.

Option 7: This is an incorrect option. The requirements for individual project communications planning are an output of this process.

Each Interface Planning process needs to follow three basic steps:
- • identify and evaluate interfaces,
- determine whether current interface management practices for each interface are sufficient,
- complete action plans to improve interfaces

Program Management

and their management.

The Fresh Earth environmental agency is embarking on an environmental awareness program that will be implemented across all of its other programs. Therefore, interface planning for the new program will have to occur with every other program. Representatives from each program need to be available to talk about their programs and to identify and evaluate interrelationships.

Once the interfaces have been identified and evaluated, the planning team can assess current interface management practices and develop action plans to improve these processes.

Question

What are the outputs of the Interface Planning process?

Options:

1. The interface management plan
2. A list of program interfaces
3. Program schedule updates
4. Requirements for individual project communications planning
5. The communications management plan
6. The risk register

Answer

Option 1: This is a correct option. The interface

management plan is the primary output of this process. It details what interfaces should be managed, as well as how and when.

Option 2: This is a correct option. The Interface Planning process includes identifying program interfaces and documenting these in a list.

Option 3: This is a correct option. The Interface Planning process specifies interface meetings and information-sharing sessions that impact the program schedule.

Option 4: This is a correct option. The Interface Planning process identifies interfaces that need to be managed. This generates requirements that individual project managers and project teams need to meet in terms of their planned communications.

Option 5: This is an incorrect option. The communications management plan is used to help develop the interface management plan and, as such, it is an input into the Interface Planning process.

Option 6: This is an incorrect option. The risk register assists the planning team in rating the risks of identified interfaces while developing the interface management plan. The risk register is an input of the Interface Planning process.

Interface management assessment

Once the program's planning team has identified and evaluated program interfaces, it needs to assess interface management strategies and draw up action plans based on these assessments.

When determining whether or not current interface management practices for each interface are sufficient, you assess the interface management strategy by asking:

what?

Your what questions should cover what information is required to meet goals and what comprises the critical content of this information.

why?

Your why questions need to focus on why specific information is important or critical. This can be determined by exploring how this information will be used and the consequences of it.

who?

Your who questions need to focus on who will use this information and who is authorized to provide it. Those who are not authorized to give information need to be informed of this.

how?

Your how questions need to focus on what the

mode and style of communication is. For example, is the communication one-way or two-way? You also need to focus on how the information is documented and whether or not a record of occurrence must be made.

when?

Your when questions need to focus on when the communication will be required, whether the communications should be scheduled regularly, or whether they should be triggered by particular events.

The planning team at Fresh Earth recognizes that the interface between the program managers of the environmental awareness and the pollution prevention programs needs to be formalized.

For this interface, the planning team identifies research information as critical because this information needs to be gathered to complete all the media projects that have been planned.

The program manager, Catherine Barden, is accountable for giving the research and information requirements to the pollution prevention research team. The plan specifies that she is the only person authorized to do this. This ensures that the team does not receive conflicting requirements.

The information regarding the environmental

awareness program's pollution prevention research should be two-way. This allows the research team to clarify issues and make suggestions if critical pollution prevention areas are not covered.

The planning team specifies that the information must be organized into a report and then discussed with the group in scheduled bi-weekly meetings during the initial implementation phase of the program.

Consider a manufacturing plant that has initiated a new safety program. To assess critical interfaces, the program planning team needs to:

identify what information is critical

The team notes that the program goal for the safety program is to improve safety practices at a manufacturing plant. Critical information for the program includes current practices, industry regulations, and current risks.

explain why the information is critical

The team explains why specific information is critical. It needs to fully understand current practices on the shop floor to be able to identify which of these are unsafe and what new practices need to be taught.

specify reporting relationships

The team specifies reporting relationships by

indicating who should give information to a safety training team. In this case, shop floor workers and line managers should provide information on current practices to the training team. Legal representatives and industry policy experts should give the training team information regarding industry regulations and best practices.

specify communication processes

The team specifies the communication processes for passing critical information across the program interfaces. The plan should include two-way communication between a training team and employees. It should also specify how the information should be documented – in minuted meetings and in a report on current practices.

specify when and how often information must be communicated between interfaces

When specifying when and how often information must be communicated between program interfaces, the team schedules a series of meetings and workshops for early in the program. After this, meetings should be held only if there is a change in regulations or if a change in the tools used at the plant occurs.

In the manufacturing plant scenario, the planning team goes through each of the required steps by focusing on what, why, who, how, and when communication should happen within a specified interface.

Case Study: Question 1 of 2
Scenario

A health product company is running a program to identify and produce a range of products based on African plants that have healing properties. The program planning team is currently drawing up the interface management plan.

Access the learning aid Health Product Company to help you to answer this question. Answer the questions in the order in which they are presented.

Question

The team has answered some of the questions related to planning management of the interface between the program's research and marketing projects.

What critical questions does the team still need to ask and answer while creating an interface management plan?

Options:

1. What information is critical to this interface?

2. Why is this information critical to this interface?

3. Who should be involved in communication for this interface?

4. How should the communication be handled?

5. When and how often should the information be shared?

Answer

Option 1: This is an incorrect option. The team has identified plant properties and traditional uses of the plants as critical information for the interface between marketing and research projects within the program.

Option 2: This is an incorrect option. The team has asked this question because it explores the reasons why plant properties and traditional uses are critical information and specifies that this information can strategically increase the market share for the company.

Option 3: This is a correct option. The team needs to identify who will use the information identified as critical and who is authorized to provide it. Those who are not authorized to give information need to be informed of this.

Option 4: This is a correct option. The team needs to focus on what the required mode and style of communication is. It also needs to specify how the information must be documented and whether a record of occurrences of communication must be kept.

Option 5: This is an incorrect option. The team has considered when the communications will be required, and specified a schedule for them. The team has also specified conditions under which an ad hoc meeting should be called.

Case Study: Question 2 of 2

How should communication be handled for this interface?

Options:

1. Communication should be two-way between the research team and the marketing team

2. Minutes should be taken at each meeting

3. Reports detailing agreements should be written up and signed off by the program manager

4. The research team should provide the information and direction for the marketing team

5. All developed processes should be sent directly to the program management office (PMO)

Answer

Option 1: This is a correct option. Both groups need to share information. The marketing team needs to specify what types of properties are saleable and the research team needs to be able to provide plant information for the marketing team to use in campaigns.

Sorin Dumitrascu

Option 2: This is a correct option. The information generated in meetings between the marketing and research teams will be vital for the company, so careful records should be taken.

Option 3: This is a correct option. Agreements made at this stage will impact the entire program, so all decisions and directions taken should be clearly outlined and approved by the program manager.

Option 4: This is an incorrect option. The marketing team also needs to provide information on the plant properties that potential customers will be interested in.

Option 5: This is an incorrect option. The marketing and research teams are unlikely to develop processes, and even if they did, the information generated would first need to be approved by the program manager.

Transition planning

A web development project was completed and handed over to the Public Relations Department of a large retail store. Within a week, content on the site needed to be updated, but no one had the password to edit the site.

With careful transition planning, this type of problem can be avoided.

The Transition Planning process involves identifying transitions within the program and planning for the transition from the program team to the recipients of benefits and ongoing activities that result from the program.

For example, once a research project in a program is complete, the findings of the research are passed on to customers, other projects, and the organization. These findings help with further activities, projects, and ongoing work.

The function of the Transition Planning process is to provide a formal mechanism for handing over the control of activities associated with the benefit or deliverable that is transferred from a program to the organization. This helps to ensure that the benefits the program generates are sustained.

A smooth transition requires a clear understanding of what needs to be handed over and a formal acceptance of the change in responsibility for the ongoing monitoring and control of the transferred deliverable.

The program planning team uses the Stakeholder Analysis chart to identify the receiving organizations, functions, and other stakeholders for the program. They can then contact these stakeholders and include them in the Transition Planning process.

The planning team uses the program schedule to identify key transition points – for example, when a project ends, the product that is created is handed over to a different project or team to process further.

When planning a transition, the planning team uses the program scope statement to identify program scope and responsibilities. The statement helps the team identify when to transfer program work to a receiving stakeholder. For example, when a project delivers a software solution, the software is transferred to customers and to the company's After-sales Service Department.

The Transition Planning process is characterized by:

formal contract-based activities
Transitions are often for formal contract-based activities. For example, a manufacturing company

outsources trainers to train key groups about safety practices. Once the trainers have fulfilled their contractual requirements, the benefits – safety processes and practices – are handed over to the appropriate departments of the company.

benefit transferal

Transitions often result in the transferal of benefits – for example, the program benefit of improved safety practices can be transferred to all departments and branches of an organization. This transferal ensures that best practices for safety are implemented and monitored across the organization.

receiving stakeholders

Transitions require clearly defined receiving stakeholders. These stakeholders are the group of people that receive the benefit or component. For example, a company selects employees to receive training material on safety practices. These employees are the receiving stakeholders for the development of training material project.

transition scope

Setting the transition scope allows you to manage the expectations of those receiving the benefit or component. For example, when receiving a demonstration version of online training, the receiving stakeholder should not expect the package to cover all training areas and training features. The client and the development team must negotiate what should be included.

resource transferal

Transitions require a transferal of resources such as documentation and personnel. For example, the program should transfer training documentation, safety procedures, and trained personnel from a training project to the organization's manufacturing departments. The departments can use these resources to ensure that the benefit of improved safety practices is sustained.

The receiving stakeholders need to carry out transition planning that mirrors the program's transition planning.

The receiving stakeholders' planning should accommodate preparation for the deliverable so that they are able to sustain any benefits that the program generates.

For example, the team that receives training in safety practices should plan the rollout of the training to the rest of the company's employees. The team of trained employees should also set up controls and procedures to ensure that the safety practices become embedded in how employees carry out their ongoing work.

Consider the transition planning for handing

over press kits to a project developing consumer literature and web sites for Fresh Earth's environmental awareness program.

During the Transition Planning process, the program team should cover these steps:

identify and include receiving stakeholders

Stakeholders in the receiving function or organization must be properly identified and should participate in the transition planning.

In this case, the consumer literature and web site project manager and project team are the receiving stakeholders of this particular transition. These stakeholders are then included in the planning process.

clarify the deliverable

The transition planners need to clarify the deliverable. To do this, they need a clear understanding of what they are handing off to the receiving stakeholders - in this case, the completed press kits for all six of Fresh Earth's programs.

The receiving stakeholders can expect the kits to be edited, correctly researched, accurate, and ready for distribution.

deliver resources

Transition planning must accommodate the delivery of resources – such as documents, training, materials, personnel, and supporting systems – to the receiving agency. In this case, project team members who will join the new project, research documents, and the press kits themselves should be delivered to the consumer literature and web site project team.

A transition plan should include benefits statements. For example, the benefits that Fresh Earth's new project needs to deliver are "increased environmental awareness" and "improved skills for employees."

The planning for the other transitions for the company's environmental awareness program should also cover all three of the planning steps.

Question

A software development company is planning a transition in which a demonstration version of its product is handed over to the customer, Easy Nomad Travel Agency, for testing and review.

What steps should the planning team take to plan this transition effectively?

Options:

1. Identify Easy Nomad Travel employees and managers who will be involved in the review of the software, and include them in planning meetings

2. Create a list of working and non-working components

3. Identify personnel, documentation, and support systems that the team needs to provide to Easy Nomad Travel

4. Request a testing plan from Easy Nomad Travel and provide input on the handling of testing and reviews

5. Provide Easy Nomad Travel with a full schedule for the completion of the software and details of its rollout plan

Answer

Option 1: This is a correct option. Stakeholders in the receiving organization must be properly identified and need to participate in the Transition Planning process.

Option 2: This is a correct option. Transition planners need to have a clear understanding of what exactly it is that they must hand over to the receiving stakeholders. In this case, the team needs to define the scope of the transition and clarify the deliverable.

Option 3: This is a correct option. Transition planning should accommodate the delivery of resources – such as documents, training, materials, personnel, supporting systems, benefits measurements, and maintenance plans – to receiving stakeholders.

Option 4: This is an incorrect option. Easy Nomad Travel needs to perform its own planning for the transition, which is likely to include plans for testing the software. The company that provides the software should not be involved in this unless it is asked to assist.

Option 5: This is an incorrect option. The completion schedules and rollout plans are outside of the scope of this particular transition.

Resource planning

The Resource Planning process determines the equipment, people, and other resources that a program needs to meet its objectives.

It focuses on resources across projects and ongoing work rather than on the finer details of project resource management.

The planning documents that result from the process cover who should provide resources for individual program projects, how resources will be funded, and the details of contracts or service-level agreements that are associated with contracted resources.

Resource planning outlines what is needed to gain program benefits, and it specifies how much of each resource is needed. This results in the resource requirements list.

The main output of the Resource Planning process is the resource management plan, which specifies how resources should be managed at a program level and includes the details of any contracts for resources.

The Resource Planning process uses several inputs.

Program schedule

The planning team uses the program schedule to review when particular resources will be needed and when they will be available.

Resource pools

The planning team uses resource pools to review what resources and skills are available within the organization and to highlight any skill gaps that need to be filled for the program to succeed.

Program scope statement

The planning team uses the program scope statement to ensure that program resources are not assigned to work that is outside of the program's scope.

Program Work Breakdown Structure (PWBS)

The planning team uses the PWBS to ensure that resources are grouped effectively, to note any common resources, and to ensure that the resources are allocated only to tasks listed in the PWBS.

To optimize resource use for programs, the planning team should take the following steps during the Resource Planning process:

prioritize critical external skills

When planning resources, it is essential that you prioritize critical external skills.

For example, a project needs to develop a video

advertisement and the performing agency does not have directing skills or video camera equipment. The planning team needs to prioritize these missing resources.

identify candidates

Planning teams should enlist the opinions of operational teams and experts to help them to identify candidates to fill any skill gaps in the program's resources.

focus on shared resources

The Resource Planning process should focus on shared resources to ensure that they are used optimally and to ensure that the resources are available when needed during the course of program implementation.

use historical information

If any historical information on resource use is available, the planning team should use it to guide its current resource allocation and scheduling plans.

Historical documents list problems, strengths, schedules, and other important information that can guide the team in generating the best possible solutions for resource use and management.

When planning the resource management for Fresh Earth's environmental awareness program, the planning team identified web development as a skill that the agency did not have and an Internet host server as equipment that the company would need to outsource.

The team discussed the gaps with program teams and identified experts. As a result of these discussions, the team recruited two skilled web developers and a web designer. It also created a contract with a respected Internet host provider.

In these ways, the team prioritized critical external skills and found suitable candidates to fill skill gaps.

Fresh Earth's planning team noted that press kits, consumer information, and web content were shared resources across the press kit project and the consumer literature and web site projects.

They reviewed documentation on media drives that the agency had undertaken before to identify key employees and to assess how the resources should be shared.

After considering the pros and cons of timing, integration, and the content of the various media projects, the team decided that the press kits should be developed first and then handed over to the consumer literature and web site projects.

In these ways, the planning team focused on shared resources and benefited from using historical information.

Question

A software development company specializing in C+ and Perl coding is creating custom software for its customer, Easy Nomad Travel, as part of its travel industry program. The company typically outsources any facilitation or documentation tasks. The planning team is currently updating its resource management plan.

Which steps does it need to follow?

Options:

1. Review coding components shared across projects and create a database of completed coding

2. Review the resource management plan of a project that was completed for another travel agency

3. Prioritize C+ and Perl coding skills among the company's existing programmers

4. Discuss Easy Nomad Travel's end-user requirements and hardware limitations

5. Prioritize the recruitment or outsourcing of facilitators and documentation companies

6. Discuss with the R&D team and with industry experts which candidates to use for facilitation and documentation

Answer

Option 1: This is a correct option. Completed coding is a shared resource. The planning team needs to ensure that it is used optimally and that software developers don't duplicate work.

Option 2: This is a correct option. Historical information on resource use is helpful in guiding current resource allocation and scheduling plans.

Option 3: This is an incorrect option. C+ and Perl are coding skills the company already has. The planning team needs to prioritize skill gaps.

Option 4: This is an incorrect option. This level of detail is an aspect of project implementation and not of program resource planning.

Option 5: This is a correct option. The planning team needs to prioritize skill gaps. Because facilitation and documentation need to be outsourced, these are skills that the company does not have available for the program and that the planning team must prioritize.

Option 6: This is a correct option. The planning team should enlist the opinions of operational teams and experts to help identify candidates to fill any skill gaps in the program's resources.

PWBS basics

A Program Work Breakdown Structure (PWBS) details the deliverables that program components will produce, the total scope of the program, and its major milestones.

It provides an overview of the program and shows how each project fits into it.

Before creating a PWBS, the program planning team must complete the Program Scope Definition process, which generates a program scope statement and the scope management plan.

The program scope statement provides the basis for program decisions and specifies the boundaries of the program, while the scope management plan details how the program scope should be managed.

The benefits realization plan should also be available before drawing up a PWBS. The PWBS fulfills four major functions:

clarifying the scope of the program

The PWBS clarifies the scope of the program by listing everything that falls within its scope. Anything that is not listed in the PWBS is outside of the program scope.

identifying logical groupings of work components

The PWBS groups work components into a logical structure. Because the PWBS provides a full outline for the program, it requires that you group work components according to benefits, schedules, teams, or other logical categories.

identifying the interface between operations and products

The PWBS ensures that you identify the interface between operations and products,because all deliverables and ongoing work are listed in the document.

clarifying the program conclusion

The PWBS clarifies the program conclusion by specifying its scope and by clarifying program and work component termination points. It specifies where the program ends.

In addition to the PWBS, a project Work Breakdown Structure (WBS) needs to be created. This is set at a lower level than the PWBS and considers project deliverables rather than program deliverables.

The Creating a PWBS process generates updates to the program management plan. The updates typically include changes to the controls and management of projects and other work components.

Program Management

The PWBS also includes a PWBS dictionary that provides a full description of each of the PWBS components.

Question

What functions does a PWBS need to fulfill?

Options:

1. Clarify the scope of the program
2. Group work components logically
3. Identify interfaces with operations
4. Clarify the program conclusion
5. Identify shared program resources
6. Identify program stakeholders

Answer

Option 1: This is a correct option. Any work component not listed in the PWBS is outside of the program scope.

Option 2: This is a correct option. The PWBS organizes work components into groups according to specific logical categories to provide an overview of the program and its deliverables.

Option 3: This is a correct option. All types of work included in a program are listed and grouped logically to show how they fit into the program as a whole. As a result, the interfaces between operations and products become clear.

Option 4: This is a correct option. The PWBS

provides a detailed definition of program scope and clarifies the end points of the program and of all its work components.

Option 5: This is an incorrect option. The PWBS may help to identify concurrently running projects but does not provide enough detail to identify all shared resources.

Option 6: This is an incorrect option. Program stakeholders are identified in the stakeholder management plan rather than in the PWBS.

PWBS contents

How you structure or lay out a PWBS depends on your own preferences and the contents of the program itself.

You can organize the PWBS according to the life cycle of the program, or group it according to the different deliverables for a program.

You can create the PWBS in an outline mode that includes numbered lists, program components, and subcategories, or you can create a graphical PWBS that shows program hierarchies and connections between components.

A PWBS should include:

- • program management deliverables,
- component deliverables,
- program management artifacts,
- major milestones for the program,
- program office support deliverables,
- program projects and ongoing work,
- contracting plans for the program.

A PWBS should only detail work components and deliverables that are at the level of control required by the program manager. Generally, this means that the top two levels of each project WBS are included in the PWBS.

Sorin Dumitrascu

The PWBS for Fresh Earth's environmental awareness program groups information in these broad categories:

program deliverables

In a PWBS, program deliverables are the benefits that the program generates. Fresh Earth's program's benefits are the promotion of environmental awareness, the broadening of the employee skill base, and the provision of information services to the general public.

program management artifacts

The program management artifacts that a PWBS typically contains include all program planning documents and program management office (PMO) deliverables or artifacts – such as procedures, standards, and processes that the program should follow.

projects

The PWBS lists each of the program's projects. The PWBS structure outlines how each project fits into the program. Fresh Earth's environmental awareness projects are listed as subcategories of the benefits that they contribute toward. So the media training project is listed as a subcategory of the broaden employees' skill base benefit.

project deliverables

The PWBS lists all project deliverables. This can include technical objectives, products, services, or other results. For example, the production of video advertisement project should deliver five 30-second advertisements for public broadcast.

ongoing work

In addition to detailing project work, the PWBS lists the program's ongoing work. For example, ongoing staff assessment, program administration, environmental research, and customer interactions that promote the program deliverables or benefits are non-project work for which the program is responsible.

The environmental awareness PWBS groups program components according to three broad categories – program management artifacts (planning), PMO artifacts (policies and procedures), and deliverables (benefits).

The policies and procedures section includes both PMO artifacts – such as policies – and ongoing work – such as administration.

The benefits section lists three program deliverables or benefits – promote environmental awareness among the general public, broaden employee skill base, and provide ongoing information services to the public.

Sorin Dumitrascu

The environmental awareness program projects are listed with the benefits to which they are most closely associated. For example, the consumer hotline project is listed as a subcategory of the "provide ongoing information services to the public" benefit.

Ongoing work such as recruitment is listed as a separate deliverable within the "broaden employee skill base" benefit category.

Various training projects are listed as part of the training strategy for broadening the employee skill base. Each project has a specific or implied end product or service – such as press kits, video advertisements, or media training.

Case Study: Question 1 of 2
Scenario
Lisbeck Films has recently initiated a program for a series of documentaries on ocean life.

Access the learning aid Ocean Series PWBS to review the program's PWBS so that you can answer the questions that follow.

Answer the questions in order.
Question
Match the PWBS program work components to the categories to which they belong. Not all work components listed match a category and categories

may have more than one associated component.

Options:

A. Episode 1

B. Customer relations

C. Marketing

D. Print marketing

Targets:

1. Projects

2. Ongoing work

Answer

The program has a project for each episode in the Ocean Life Series, as well as a marketing project and two sales projects. Print marketing is listed one level below marketing, so it is a subcategory of marketing and not a full-fledged project.

Customer relations and administration are aspects of the program's ongoing or nonproject work. These are listed at the same level as project work.

Case Study: Question 2 of 2

Match the deliverables and artifacts to the categories to which they belong. One deliverable or artifact won't be used.

Options:

A. Increased awareness of ocean-related conservation issues

B. Interface management plan

C. Radio advertisement

D. Filming procedures

E. Administration

Targets:

1. Program deliverables

2. Program management artifacts

3. Project deliverables

4. PMO artifacts

Answer

Program deliverables are program benefits. These include increased awareness of ocean-related conservation issues, staff development, and increased sales.

Program management artifacts include program plans such as the interface management plan, phase gate reports, and other documentation specific to program management tasks.

Project deliverables are the end products, services, or results that a project is created to achieve. In this case, project results include the 30-minute documentaries, radio advertisement, print adverts, and so on.

PMO artifacts include specific policies, procedures, and legislation that program and project teams need to follow.

Schedule, cost, and quality planning

"Good fortune is what happens when opportunity meets with planning." Thomas Edison, 1847-1931

This statement from the American inventor and businessman is as true today as it was a century ago. Recognizing a good opportunity is often not enough to succeed in the current business environment – good planning is also essential for success.

Planning is one of the most important elements of program management because it enables the program manager to properly initiate, develop, and close a program. Without good planning, a program manager may execute a program badly and program outcomes may be invalid.

A program manager implements different types of program planning for specific functions, including:

- • schedule planning and development,
- cost planning,
- quality planning.

Program managers use schedule planning and development to ensure that the best methods are used to achieve program goals, organize resources, and obtain the full benefits of a program.

Whereas resource planning helps the program

manager determine the type and quantity of the needed resources, schedule planning helps determine how to use the chosen resources within given deadlines.

During schedule planning and development, a plan is created to outline the preferred sequence of events for the program. Following this plan closely allows the program manager to ensure that the program goals are achieved.

The Program Work Breakdown Structure (PWBS) provides a basic framework and context for the program. It is usually the starting point for schedule planning.

Program managers extend the PWBS during schedule planning by including details of all the program's projects and the work that lies outside the scope of individual projects. This gives program managers better control over the interactions and dependencies between projects and provides a context for monitoring the progress of an entire program.

In addition to providing a detailed framework for a program, schedule planning:

- • gives teams a common goal,
- is a strong tool for achieving program goals.

An industrial paper products company plans to expand into the commercial paper products market.

The program manager uses the PWBS to plan a schedule for the program, and sets regular deadlines that the project teams must meet if the program is to achieve its goals.

After the first month of the program, the team that organizes the construction of the new production plant must have decided on the plant's location. The plantation management team must have identified the source of additional paper pulp. Each team works toward a common deadline and common goals, giving the program manager and project managers specific markers for checking program progress.

Program managers use cost planning to forecast total expected expenditure for a program and to comply with a specified budget.

Cost planning consists of two activities:

cost estimating
Program managers use cost estimating to calculate the expected total cost for the program. They estimate cost by adding the average costs for all individual projects or by estimating the cost of an entire program.

cost budgeting
Program managers use cost budgeting to establish a budget for the entire program. When

calculating the budgets for individual projects, they consider projects' time frames, as established during schedule planning, and available funds.

Cost planning benefits the Program Planning process by helping managers achieve program goals, coordinate segments within an organization, and control available capital.

For example, the program manager from the paper manufacturer uses the cost estimates from each project to anticipate the total cost of the commercial paper products program. This helps the program manager to ensure the best use of the available capital and to ensure that the program achieves its goals within the specified budget.

Program managers use quality planning to identify goals and standards, and the ways in which they can achieve them both within projects and within a total program.

Program managers need to implement quality planning early in the Program Planning process so that standards can be maintained throughout the program.

Program managers should use a company's existing quality systems and expertise to ensure that they implement quality planning in the most efficient way possible. If such systems don't exist, it may be necessary to implement them throughout the company, as well as for a program.

Quality planning is an important consideration not only for program managers, but for everyone in an organization. Good quality planning ensures that high-quality products or services are produced. Customers support organizations for their high quality by returning with repeat business.

Several internationally recognized quality management systems are available. There are two popular examples.

ISO 9000

The International Organization for Standardization (ISO) developed the ISO 9000 quality

standard. The goal of this standard is to manage system effectiveness.

ISO 9000 provides a method of meeting customer needs and improving quality tracking and measurement. It can also be used as a marketing tool because the ISO accreditation informs customers of the level of quality that they can expect from a company's products or services.

Six Sigma

Six Sigma is a quality management system that uses data and statistical analyses to reduce the number of errors and waste in processes for delivering services and products. It provides program managers with tools to improve operational performance and increase customer satisfaction.

The Six Sigma philosophy states that if you are able to quantify the number of errors in a process, you can systematically eliminate them and get the process as near to perfect as possible. A process that complies with Six Sigma cannot have more than 3.4 defects per million opportunities (DPMO). An opportunity is defined as a chance for error.

The paper products company decided to implement Six Sigma throughout its operations two years ago. By applying the philosophy, the company increased overall profits by 6% and improved customer satisfaction.

The program manager applies the same principles to the new commercial paper products program. The company gains access to the lucrative commercial paper products market by marketing the high quality of its products to potential customers.

This course will help you to manage programs effectively by providing instruction on how to:
- • schedule and budget for a program,
- plan for program quality and realize the benefits of this type of planning,

- apply Communications Planning processes to a program.

Question
Program schedule, cost, and quality planning are important aspects of program management.

Match the benefits to the types of planning that produce them. Each benefit may match to more than one type of planning and each type of planning may have more than one benefit.

Options:
A. A team is united by common goals

B. Desired goals are easily achieved and managed

C. Appropriate standards and processes are identified

D. Capital is better allocated

E. High program standards are assured

Targets:
1. Schedule planning
2. Cost planning
3. Quality planning

Answer
Schedule planning allows managers to set deadlines throughout a program and to unite all employees within the different teams working on a program. Managing the program timeline keeps the

program on track.

Cost planning is a useful tool for ensuring that a program achieves the desired outcomes. Whereas schedule planning ensures that a program is completed on time, cost planning ensures that it is completed within budget. Cost planning also coordinates different segments of an organization by providing a single, unifying budget.

Quality planning allows program managers to identify appropriate standards and processes, and to implement them across a program. This type of planning also provides benchmarks for checking that a program is of a consistently high standard.

Schedule Development process

Timing is everything when managing a program. Poor time management can result in profit loss, missed opportunities, and disappointed clients.

The program schedule is a vital program management tool. Program managers use it to deliver a program's expected outcomes on time and within the limitations of a set budget.

The main aim of the Schedule Development process is to develop a program schedule. The process also leads to the development of an updated resource requirements plan and the schedule management plan, which helps program managers maintain the program schedule throughout a program's lifespan.

To schedule a program effectively, program managers need to consider:

- • the Program Work Breakdown Structure (PWBS),
- interdependencies between constituent projects,
- timelines for various program packages significant milestones,
- a plan to manage the schedule.

Program managers need to examine each component of a program, so they begin the Schedule

Sorin Dumitrascu

Development process by examining the PWBS.

Program managers develop a successful program schedule when they provide enough detail for every part of the program within the PWBS. A part of a program is also known as a program package.

The information that program managers enter into a PWBS is the basis for a program schedule. Program managers flesh out the PWBS framework with details of the program packages during the Schedule Development process. This provides a comprehensive overview of all work that they need to manage during the course of a program.

Using the PWBS as the starting point for schedule development ensures that details of every program package and work item are included in the program schedule.

In addition to providing the framework for the program schedule, the PWBS:

- • identifies program objectives and the anticipated end products or results,
- illustrates how each project fits into a program,
- details any interdependencies between projects,
- helps to make the best use of available resources.

Program Management

An important aspect of the PWBS is that it details how projects relate to one another. So program managers use the PWBS when developing a program schedule to identify interdependencies between constituent projects.

Interdependencies occur when one project relies on another. For example, when building a football stadium, the type and placement of irrigation pipes depends on the type of field covering – either seeded or synthetic grass. The irrigation project manager relies on the actions of the field design team to run the irrigation project.

Effective scheduling takes interdependencies into account because they can have a significant effect on the duration and timing of projects.

For example, the irrigation project is scheduled to begin once the field design project manager has delivered a report detailing field specifications. The report is then handed to the irrigation manager so that the irrigation team can begin its work.

To schedule a program effectively, managers need to consider timelines, significant milestones, and calendars.

Timelines for various program packages

Program managers sequence all activities within a program on a timeline. The sequence depends on

379

the estimated duration of each activity, the resources it requires, and its interdependencies.

Changes to a program's timeline can have an effect on resources. For example, when a supplier delivers tofu two weeks before it is required by an event management company that produces tofu ice cream, the company will bear additional storage costs. The management team may not be able to store the food properly and it will go to waste, incurring additional program costs.

Milestones

Milestones are significant points or events in the program schedule. They are included in the schedule to keep the program on track for the estimated completion date. A milestone typically marks the completion date for a major component of a program.

Calendars

Calendars ensure that all projects are running according to the same schedule. If projects run in different countries or states, a common schedule is critical to the success of an entire program. For example, during a critical period in a program, a US project team may work five days in a row. The team will need to know that its European counterpart enjoys a midweek break because of a public holiday. All deliverables will need to be scheduled around this holiday.

In addition to well-defined deadlines, a program schedule includes:

estimates

A program schedule includes duration estimates, as well as cost estimates. Program managers provide reasons for these estimates so that they can update them if a condition of an estimate changes.

For example, if duration estimates depend on the availability of a certain building item at a certain time, the reason for this must be justified in the program schedule – perhaps it is an imported material that arrives only by shipment at a specific date.

resource capabilities and availability

The program schedule indicates which resources are available and when. This helps both project and program managers make the most effective use of available resources, including human resources.

internal and external dependencies

Internal and external dependencies are listed in the program schedule to prevent scheduling clashes and the overuse of resources.

Program managers need to develop a plan for

managing the program schedule to ensure that the schedule is updated when necessary and that those affected by the schedule are informed of changes in a timely manner.

As a program develops through its stages, problems may occur that cause the project to deviate from the original plan. For example, a shortage of ink for packaging printing could slow down the production of a new product.

Individual components of a program, such as the design of packaging, may also take longer than expected to complete. When one component fails to meet a deadline, dependant components may not reach their deadlines and a program's final completion date may be under threat.

For example, late finalization of the packaging for a product may impact on the expected date of shipment to retail outlets and cause deliveries to run late.

An environmental agency, Fresh Earth, has decided to initiate a new program that promotes environmental awareness. The Planning process group for the new program is nearing completion, and the planning team is now starting the Schedule Development process.

Follow along as Catherine, the program manager

for Fresh Earth's new program, and the managers of the program's projects develop the program schedule.

Catherine: The planning process for our newest program is nearing completion. It's time we start thinking about the program schedule. The PWBS shows that the program will take two years to complete. Sally - any comments?

Catherine is happy.

Sally: Yes, I think that to keep the program fresh, we will need regular cycles of new public relations campaigns. My team's video advertisements can be ready for initial release in six months.

Sally is thinking.

Catherine: Good. We'll also need similar cycles of marketing communications. Perhaps we could follow the advertisements with press release kits in another six months? Rick?

Catherine is happy.

Rick: I'll plan my project around those release dates. My team will have them ready on time.

Rick is paying attention.

Catherine: Great! With regard to resources - we'll require the services of the two environmental engineers only for the first six months. They'll help us initiate the projects, so please coordinate between yourselves when you want them to work on your projects. Any other scheduling issues can be dealt with as they occur. As long as we stick to the timeline, the program will stay on track.

Catherine is smiling.

Catherine knows that a good starting point for creating a program schedule is the PWBS. She uses the PWBS to set deadlines for component projects, and to ensure that interdependencies between the projects are accurately reflected.

She also develops a plan to manage changes to the established program schedule, which allows her to keep all project managers informed.

Question

Jack is a program manager who is scheduling a program of language software projects aimed at children. His last program went way over schedule, resulting in financial penalties for his company. He needs to ensure that this program comes in on time for the marketing launch.

How can Jack schedule for the program effectively?

Options:

1. Use the description of all work in the program as a starting point for the schedule

2. Check what programmers and resources are available

3. Include a clear sequence of events in the schedule

4. Include dates for handovers between scripting and design

5. Outline how he intends to manage the schedule

6. Ensure each language project is scheduled separately

7. Provide project managers with a single common deadline

Answer

Option 1: This is a correct option. By using the PWBS as the starting point, program managers can examine all work that needs to be scheduled and make sure that nothing is forgotten.

Option 2: This is a correct option. The program schedule needs to indicate any interdependencies between projects, including shared resources. If this is not done, time and money may be wasted when one project is held up by another that it depends on.

Option 3: This is a correct option. Effective program scheduling means that all program packages are logically sequenced into a timeline of events. The program manager can then easily manage program packages and ensure that they are delivered on time.

Option 4: This is a correct option. An effective program schedule includes timelines and significant milestones, such as handover dates. Milestones act as interim deadlines, allowing the program manager to check that the program stays on track for the final deadline.

Option 5: This is a correct option. A program is a dynamic entity, and a management plan is essential for ensuring that any changes to the schedule are quickly passed to the relevant people. This ensures that all projects run smoothly and on time, and that effort and resources aren't wasted.

Option 6: This is an incorrect option. Scheduling must consider interdependencies between projects. By scheduling each project separately, any interdependencies would be ignored, which may result in scheduling clashes or overuse of resources.

Option 7: This is an incorrect option. Scheduling must include dates of significant milestones that help program managers to monitor progress toward the final deadline. These milestones are interim deadlines that differ between program packages.

Cost Estimating process

So how much is it going to cost?

Program managers use the Cost Estimating process to answer this question.

The Cost Estimating process provides program managers with estimates for each of the program packages that are identified in the PWBS. The estimates are added together to get an estimated cost for the entire program.

There are eight tools and techniques available to assist program managers in getting the most accurate cost estimates possible:

1. analogous estimating
2. bottom-up estimating
3. parametric estimating
4. program management software
5. vendor bid analysis
6. reserve analysis
7. cost of quality
8. resource rates determination

The first four tools and techniques are used to predict cost estimates:

analogous estimating

Analogous estimating, also called top-down estimating, uses cost estimates from previous

Sorin Dumitrascu

programs or projects to predict costs of future programs.

For example, when estimating the cost to produce a batch of 10,000 promotional brochures, the program manager uses the production cost for a batch of similar brochures recently used in another program as the basis for the estimate.

bottom-up estimating

In bottom-up estimating, cost estimates for each activity in the program are combined to get a total program cost estimate. This type of estimating can be used later in a program when the program schedule and work breakdown are in place.

For example, the program manager takes cost estimates for each process in the production of a batch of promotional brochures – designing, paper purchase, and printing – and adds them together to get a total production cost estimate.

parametric estimating

Parametric estimating is a quantitative method that involves estimating cost by multiplying the number of times an activity is performed by the cost for the activity.

For example, the program manager takes the cost to produce a single promotional brochure – including design, paper, and printing. The estimate is then multiplied by 10,000 to reach a cost estimate for a batch of 10,000 brochures.

program management software

Sometimes program management software can be used to provide relatively accurate cost estimates. The cost of this software itself must be included in the total cost estimation for a program.

Program managers develop a cost management plan during the Cost Estimating process. This plan gives an estimated cost for the entire program, including all program packages mentioned in the PWBS, and is essential for budgeting and monitoring spending.

The program manager can also use historical information, such as existing estimates and management plans for similar programs, as a reference when developing cost estimates.

When calculating the total program cost, program managers must take varying costs over the entire duration of the program into account. For example, the cost of hiring specialist equipment for spray-painting signs may be payable annually. If the program runs over several years, the program manager

must not forget to add the estimated hiring costs for each year.

Program managers need to substantiate the cost

estimates because the basis of estimates may change. This is important if the cost estimates are to be as accurate as possible.

Program managers also need to include any assumptions they made in developing the cost estimates - assumptions can be incorrect.

A large pesticides manufacturer wants to produce a range of household pesticide sprays. The program manager begins development of cost estimates for the new program by examining the PWBS. The PWBS gives a good overview of each part of the process and of the work that needs to be included in the cost estimate.

The program manager reviews an existing cost management plan that includes estimates for several procedures that are used in the new program. She uses analogous estimating to calculate all other costs involved in the entire program.

Finally, the program manager produces a detailed cost management plan that includes cost estimates for the program and its components, and a description of how she arrived at those estimates. These estimates are used in the Cost Budgeting process.

Question
Andrew is a program manager for a leading

manufacturer of party decorations. The last program he worked on was underfunded due to inaccurate cost estimates.

How can Andrew ensure that costs for the new program to manufacture Halloween decorations are estimated accurately?

Options:

1. Examine the cost estimates made for a Christmas decorations program developed last year

2. Include cost estimates for production, manufacturing, and shipment

3. Monitor any changes in the basis of estimates

4. Start by examining all program packages

5. Include costs for a Thanksgiving decorations program that follows the current program

6. Base estimates on estimates made for a lighting program he was previously involved in

Answer

Option 1: This is a correct option. The program manager should take the cost estimates for similar programs that are already running or have been completed into account. Using historical information also helps in forming a more accurate estimate of the actual costs involved in the current program.

Option 2: This is a correct option. Programs may run over several years, and all costs over the duration of the program need to be included in the cost estimate. This is to ensure that the program doesn't run over budget or incur unexpected expenses in the future. In this case, Andrew needs to think about all costs throughout the program. For example, he needs to estimate the cost of shipping, even though the product hasn't actually been created yet.

Option 3: This is a correct option. The reasoning behind estimates may change, and program cost estimates need to reflect these changes. The program manager uses the cost management plan to update program estimates and ensure that they remain accurate.

Option 4: This is a correct option. The PWBS details all parts of the program, including all program packages. By using the PWBS as the starting point for developing cost estimates, Andrew can ensure that he has not left any estimates out of the final estimation.

Option 5: This is an incorrect option. The final program cost estimate should include estimates for all program packages. Work outside the scope of the program, such as follow-up programs, should not form part of the final cost estimate.

Option 6: This is an incorrect option. Considering estimates from previous programs is an effective way of estimating costs. However, any previous cost estimates that are considered must be from similar programs if they are to be comparable.

Cost Budgeting process

Once program costs have been estimated, program managers develop a budget to illustrate how much funding is needed for each part of the program. Budgeting must take any financial constraints, such as funding limits, into account.

The main aim of the Cost Budgeting process is to allocate funding for each program package, ensuring that the total budget doesn't exceed the available funds.

A good starting point, as with cost estimating, is the PWBS. The PWBS provides a detailed breakdown of all program packages that need to have funding allocated. It provides an easy reference for ensuring that each part of the program receives adequate funding.

To create an effective budget, the program manager needs to consider the availability of funds, as specified in the resource management plan. Often cost estimates are too high and the budget is exceeded. So the manager needs to be aware of the limitations of the budget and make adjustments to the estimates accordingly.

Consider the pesticides manufacturer that wants to produce a range of sprays for household use. The program manager begins the budgeting process by examining the PWBS and the cost estimates for each component it includes, as outlined by the cost management plan.

If the total estimated cost exceeds available funds, the program manager needs to determine how best to allocate the actual funds. This involves providing each program package with as close to the estimated amount as possible, but with reductions made where most appropriate.

As with estimating costs, there are several tools and techniques that a program manager may use to develop a budget:

cost aggregation

Cost aggregation is the process of adding cost estimates for scheduled work packages and then combining these to get a total cost for higher-level components such as individual projects. This is useful when budgeting because it illustrates which parts of the program the funding should go into, and how the funds need to be allocated among the program packages for the program to stick to schedule.

reserve analysis

Reserve analysis is used to allocate a reserve amount to the budget to cover unforeseen costs. This differs from the Cost Estimating process, in which reserve analysis establishes the accuracy of cost estimates.

parametric estimating

Parametric estimating is done in the same way during the Budget Planning process as during cost estimating. However, it is used only to calculate the amount that should be budgeted for each activity in the program schedule, rather than the amount that each activity will cost.

funding limit reconciliation

Funding limit reconciliation is part of managing the budget, and occurs during the execution of the program. It involves linking the amount budgeted with the amount actually spent per activity. The budget must be adjusted to reflect these differences to give an accurate reflection of funds used. This is particularly important if there are financial constraints to the budget, such as funding running out at the end of a fiscal year.

Poor budgeting can spell disaster for programs – in the worst case, it can mean that a program must be abandoned before completion, and at best that a program is completed but costs more than anticipated. This can hurt a company's reputation and lead to poor performance in other, related projects.

Program Management

It is better to extend the planning time for a program than to rush into a program and suffer the consequences later.

Question

Anna is the program manager at an IT company. The company has initiated a new program to provide documentation services for the company's IT products.

How can Anna ensure that an appropriate budget is drawn up for the new program?

Options:

1. Start by examining the outline of the program packages

2. Check which writers are available and when

3. Include writing, designing, and printing costs in the budget

4. Allocate funding for a marketing program for documentation services

5. Ensure that each team has its own budget

Answer

Option 1: This is a correct option. Using the PWBS, which includes an outline of all program packages and all work in the program, as the starting point is an effective method of budgeting. It provides program managers with an overview of the program, and shows which program packages need

Sorin Dumitrascu

to be allocated funding from the budgeted amount.

Option 2: This is a correct option. The program manager needs to ensure that available funds and resources, including writers in this case, are allocated appropriately across program packages. The resource management plan informs program managers of the limits of available funding and resources.

Option 3: This is a correct option. The budget needs to include cost estimates for all work and to specify how much funding each program package will receive.

Option 4: This is an incorrect option. Costs that are outside the scope of the program do not need to be budgeted for. Costs for the entire program do, however.

Option 5: This is an incorrect option. The budget needs to include estimates for all work in the program. Separate budgets are confusing and make it easy to overspend, especially because teams within a program are likely to need to share specific resources.

Human Resource Planning process

Program managers know that the people they work with are the greatest asset of a program. Program managers develop a human resource plan to identify the human resource needs of a program.

The human resource plan is formed with close attention to the program's financial and business plans, to ensure that the human resource plan is achievable.

Program managers use the Human Resource Planning process to identify and assign roles and responsibilities to the most appropriate staff members and to document all staffing decisions.

The Human Resource Planning process also helps program managers identify and document reporting structures within a program.

Andrea, the human resources manager at a national financial company, is working on the human resource plan for a large real estate program. While planning, she:

identifies program roles and responsibilities

Andrea identifies the program roles and responsibilities for the program's legal team. For example, she identifies the need for a senior legal adviser to coordinate the use of legal documents directly with the program manager. The program manager communicates with project managers on all legal matters and relays their requirements to the senior legal adviser.

assigns program roles and responsibilities

Once Andrea has established the roles and responsibilities of a legal team, she assigns the program roles and responsibilities to the most appropriate candidates. She asks Mike to take on the position of senior legal adviser and assigns him the responsibility of consulting with Sam, the program manager, on legal issues that the project managers raise.

documents roles and responsibilities

Andrea documents the roles and responsibilities of the legal team. She formulates job descriptions and lists the responsibilities for each employee. She also constructs a staff management plan to monitor staff members and their roles.

documents the employee reporting structure

Andrea documents the employee reporting structure. She uses an organizational chart and Program Work Breakdown Structure (PWBS) to illustrate the reporting structures within the program. Mike, the senior legal adviser, and Sam, the program manager, will report back to each other on a regular basis to ensure that the program doesn't experience any legal pitfalls.

The success of the Human Resource Planning process often depends on external factors and influences such as:

- • external end users who may use the new product or service that a program develops, such as real estate sellers and buyers who expect sound legal documentation,
- organizations with a stake in the program's success, such as investors or shareholders in a real estate company.

There are a number of inputs to the Human Resource Planning process:

core program team assignments

Core program team assignments are the key roles and objectives that each team is expected to fill within the program.

program interfaces

Program interfaces include all formal and informal relationships among people, departments, organizations, and functions within the program.

resource management plan

The resource management plan contains goals, strategies, and objectives that relate to needed and available program resources, including human resources.

staffing requirement plan

The staffing requirement plan outlines the recommended number of employees needed to support a program.

Stakeholder Analysis chart

The Stakeholder Analysis chart summarizes the program's key role players, their perspectives, and their likely impact on the program.

The outputs from the Human Resource Planning process are:

organizational chart

An organizational chart illustrates the distribution of authority and responsibility within a program.

assignment of roles and responsibilities

Assignment of roles and responsibilities includes a detailed breakdown of job descriptions, reporting structures, and employee tasks.

staffing management plan

The staffing management plan documents how project team members will be brought onto and removed from projects.

An environmental agency, Fresh Earth, has

decided to initiate a new program that promotes environmental awareness. The Planning process group for the program is nearing completion of its tasks and the planning team is now starting to develop the human resource plan.

In the resource planning stage, Catherine determines which human resources are needed. Ten employees will be assigned to the new program from the existing programs – two project managers, three graphic artists, two technical writers, one marketing director, and two environmental engineers.

Follow along as the program manager, Catherine, and the managers of the various projects, start the Human Resource Planning process. Catherine asks Sally what the core team assignments are.

Sally: My team will develop consumer literature and web sites, so I need at least two writers and one designer who knows HTML on a full-time basis over the first month of the project. Who will my team members report to?

Sally is looking concerned.

Catherine: Your team members will report directly to you, the project manager. I will leave it up to you and Rick to negotiate how much time each employee spends on each of your projects. What do you think about that, Rick?

Catherine is looking confident and friendly.

Rick: I am fine with that. The media tracking, reporting, and analysis work that my team's involved in won't require any writers or designers at first. I do need researchers. However, we should discuss allocating a writer and possibly a designer to my team when the research is complete and we start to write up the results.

Rick is looking serious but happy.

Sally: We'll also need the support of an environmental engineer to help us compile the literature.

Sally is looking serious but happy.

Catherine: Sounds like you're both well organized. Let's meet early next week to discuss the details of the work we need to get done.

Catherine is looking happy.

Catherine is responsible for overseeing the program. She decides that the projects will share human resources, so Sally and Rick need to negotiate who they require, at what time, and for how long.

Catherine proceeds to document the roles and responsibilities of each of the staff members working on the projects to ensure that available human resources are deployed effectively.

Question Set
The human resource plan offers staffing solutions for a program.

Question 1 of 2
Categorize each item as either an input or output of the Human Resource Planning process.
Options:
A. Input
B. Output
Targets:
1. Core program team assignments
2. Stakeholder Analysis chart
3. Role and responsibility assignments
Answer
The core program team assignments are an input that outlines the key roles and objectives that each team is expected to fill within the program.

The Stakeholder Analysis chart is an input of the Human Resource Planning process. It summarizes the program's key role players, their perspectives, and their likely impact on the program.

Role and responsibility assignments include a detailed breakdown of job descriptions, reporting structures, and employee tasks. These are an output of the process.

Question 2 of 2

Now label each remaining component as an input or output.

Options:

A. Input

B. Output

Targets:

1. Organizational chart
2. Program interfaces
3. Resource management plan
4. Staffing requirement plan

Answer

The organizational chart is an output of the Human Resource Planning process. It illustrates the distribution of authority and responsibility within a program.

The program interfaces are an input to the Human Resource Planning process that identify all formal and informal relationships among people, departments, organizations, and functions.

The resource management plan is an input to the Human Resources Planning process. It contains the goals, strategies, and objectives that relate to available human resources.

Program Management

The staffing requirement plan is an input to the Human Resources Planning process. It documents how project team members will be brought onto and removed from projects.

Program Quality Planning process

David T. Kearns, former Chairman of XEROX, wrote, "In the race for quality, there is no finish line."

Program managers need to take heed of the fact that assuring program quality is an ongoing process. The success of a program relies heavily on a program manager's ability to implement and maintain relevant quality standards, and to ensure that each project in a program meets the same standards.

Quality planning involves identifying relevant quality standards and applying methods to ensure that those standards are met.

The inputs to the Quality Planning process include:

environmental and health legislation

Program managers need to adhere to existing local and national environmental and health legislation. For example, a multinational company that manufactures various cleaning agents needs to apply the worker health and safety legislation that is particular to each country in which operations occur.

product description

Program managers need to develop a detailed product description that complies with a program's quality standards. A product description may outline the quantity, manufacturing time, and materials used in a program.

program scope statement

Program managers develop a program scope statement that outlines the boundaries of a program to secure a program's quality. These boundaries can include, but are not limited to, program deliverables, life cycle, data sources, organizations, and key functionality.

The outputs of the Quality Planning process are:

operational definitions

Operational definitions are descriptions of variables, terms, or objects that are relevant to a program. According to W. E. Deming, a statistician and quality control expert, operational definitions translate concepts into measurements.

For example, a program manager needs to clarify which event signifies the end of a component's production process – when the component leaves the production line, is packaged, or leaves the factory.

program cost of quality

The program cost of quality describes how much

it will cost to implement a program's quality planning, control, assurance, and needed reworking.

For example, the costs of product quality reviews at various stages of the manufacturing process need to be detailed.

quality checklists

Quality checklists include all aspects of a program's product or service that need to be monitored to ensure that quality levels remain high.

For example, the program manager formulates a checklist that lineworkers will use to ensure that finished products comply with quality standards set by management.

a quality improvement plan and objectives

A quality improvement plan and objectives include all goals and targets that relate to quality within a program. The plan outlines how the program aims to achieve the quality objectives.

For a program that aims to improve educational outcomes at different educational institutions, for example, a quality improvement plan specifies the number of institutions it wants to target and what improvements the program must bring.

a quality management plan

Program managers develop a quality management plan to ensure that programs create services or products of the highest quality at the lowest possible cost. The plan incorporates the concepts of quality assurance, quality control, and quality improvement.

For example, a quality management plan for a program dealing with the production of sensitive electronic components focuses on continuous improvement, process control, and product failure analysis.

quality metrics

Quality metrics form the foundation of quality assessments. Program managers use quality metrics as a standard for assessing the level of quality that the program achieves.

For example, a manager for a program that aims to raise the pass rate at different educational institutions assesses the program's success by the number of targeted institutions that record a 20% increase in the pass rate six months after the program's inception.

At the start of a program, management needs to choose the quality assurance approach that best suits a program and the organization. The two most popular approaches to quality control are the International Organization for Standardization (ISO) 9000 standard and the Six Sigma methodology.

If no suitable quality control standard or

methodology is available, management needs to
formulate a new one for the program.

The ISO 9000 standard, initially published in
1987, was the first international quality control
standard designed to cover all industries. To date,
over 343,643 organizations in over 150 countries
hold ISO 9000 certificates.

The ISO 9000 standard is a total quality
management approach to product and service
quality. It addresses quality concerns by
standardizing workplace practices and ensuring that
these standards are maintained through a system of
external and internal audits.

Organizations use ISO 9000 to:

- • satisfy customer needs and demands,
- improve quality monitoring, measurement,
  and approval,
- satisfy marketing requirements.

In the 1980's, Motorola began to lose market
dominance in nearly every market in which it was
present. Management decided to establish a new
vision for Motorola using the Six Sigma
methodology.

Six Sigma is based on a multi-faceted approach
that uses tools such as benchmarking, cost-benefit
analysis, and cost of quality to ensure that high
levels of quality are achieved. A fundamental idea

of Six Sigma is the continual improvement of processes.

Six Sigma is now used in many successful organizations:

- • to maintain their success
- create performance goals for all involved,
- improve value to customers
- increase the rate of improvements,
- encourage learning and more radical thinking,
- implement strategic changes.

During the Quality Planning process, the program manager develops a quality plan. This plan outlines the methods that an organization can apply to develop quality policies, achieve quality objectives, and meet quality system requirements.

The quality plan includes all major deliverables, quality standards, quality tools, roles and control activities, and quality assurance activities.

The key elements of a quality plan include details of:

items that need to be checked for quality

Program managers need to identify items that need to be checked for quality. Program deliverables are the most common items that need to be checked. However, it is critical that all important deliverables of a program, such as requirement documents, be subjected to some form of quality checking. For certain projects, it may be appropriate to review the quality of certain management practices as well.

the best way to check for quality

The quality plan must outline the best way to check for quality. The method used depends entirely on the required end result. If quality needs to achieve a required standard, compliance with that particular standard is measured. Managers need to ensure that the methods outlined in their quality plans are comprehensive but simple to implement.

when quality should be checked

Program managers need to decide when quality should be checked. Quality checks are often carried out just before a deliverable is completed. For deliverables with extensive lead times, it may be wise to schedule regular quality checks during the development period. This will reduce costly revisions and wasted effort.

who should be involved in checking quality

The quality plan must specify who should be involved in checking quality. The producers of deliverables are the key role players that need to be involved in quality planning. Depending on the type of project, receivers of items such as deliverables can be included to ensure that they understand the contents of the material and are not excluded by the use of jargon.

the tools that should be used to ensure quality standards are met

The quality plan must outline the tools that should be used to ensure quality standards are met. One role of these tools is as a form of reminder to ensure that quality reviewers check for all possible flaws. The most common quality tools are checklists based on quality standards. Quality reviewers often rely on these checklists as a form of quick reference instead of using more cumbersome forms of standards.

Sally, a project manager at Fresh Earth, meets with Tom, an environmental engineer, to develop a quality plan for a new recycling program. These are the elements of the plan:

deliverables

Sally and Tom need to write up the program's deliverables in a manner that ensures they meet Fresh Earth's quality standards. The affected deliverables include the material requirement documents and management practices.

methodology

Sally and Tom decide on the most appropriate methodology for ensuring the program's quality. They work backward and establish that the required result is the program's compliance with Fresh Earth's environmental policies and procedures. Sally and Tom instigate a number of standard audits to ensure that the program is compliant.

quality inspections

Due to the relatively long duration of the program, Sally and Tom decide to implement a number of on-site quality inspections prior to completion of the program instead of one inspection at its end. The increased frequency of quality checking will help ensure that the program meets all quality standards.

producers and receivers

Sally and Tom ensure that all producers and receivers of deliverables in the program are included in the Quality Planning process. They do this to ensure that the receivers understand the terminology the producers use.

checklists

Sally and Tom summarize Fresh Earth's environmental policies into a checklist and distribute it to all project managers. The checklist forms a handy and abridged summary of all Fresh

Program Management
Earth's environmental policies and quality
standards.

Communications Planning process

Have you ever been part of a team where communication was poor or nonexistent? Do you remember how frustrating it was? Nothing seems to get done, because everyone is trying to find out what needs to be done rather than getting on with the job.

Time and resources are wasted when instructions are miscommunicated or given to the wrong people at the wrong time.

Communication is key to the success of any program. Timely, accurate, and relevant communication keeps programs running smoothly and program stakeholders informed and focused on the task ahead.

The Communications Planning process is a vital part of program management during which the program manager develops a communication plan.

A good communication plan addresses the communication and information needs of a program's stakeholders. The program manager establishes who needs what type of information at what time.

The program manager is the link between all stakeholders - portfolio managers, project managers, customers, and external parties such as contractors and investors. A program manager is also in the best position to coordinate information flow.

There are various inputs to the planning process that assist the program manager to develop an efficient communication plan:

Stakeholder Analysis chart,

- •   communication requirements,
- program reporting channels,
- program charter,
- program scope statement,
- Program Work Breakdown Structure (PWBS).

The first step in the Communications Planning process is to develop a Stakeholder Analysis chart. This chart lays out the complex relationships among stakeholders using flowcharts or relational diagrams.

The Stakeholder Analysis chart helps program managers ensure that the communication expectations of the stakeholders are met and that communication channels are maintained.

Consider Erika, the program manager at a medical equipment manufacturer, who creates a chart mapping the relationships between all stakeholders involved in a new program for developing an antimalaria drug - from the laboratory staff at the research facility to the external investors. This helps her determine who needs what information.

For example, Margaret, the manufacture and supply project manager, needs to meet regularly with Julio, the research and development (R&D) project manager, so that she can ensure that the factory is ready to begin production as soon as research is completed.

Once the stakeholders have been identified, program managers need to establish communication requirements. Three questions help identify the communication requirements of different stakeholders:

1. What information do different stakeholders expect from the program manager?

2. How often do stakeholders expect to communicate with management and each other?

3. What communication methods, such as e-mail or meetings, do stakeholders prefer?

Erika is compiling a report detailing the communications requirements for the company's program to produce an antimalaria drug. She asks Julio, the R&D project manager, about his requirements.

Program Management

Julio: Well, I will need to be kept informed of any changes in financial backing, as well as of updates to the budget and program schedule.

Julio is thoughtful.

Erika: Yes. I will be holding weekly meetings for all project managers to discuss scheduling issues. I'll also send out e-mails detailing any changes to the budget.

Erika is explaining.

Julio: That's a good idea, but the investors providing financial backing for the research project also need to be kept updated with progress reports.

Julio is thoughtful.

Erika: OK, we will set up quarterly meetings, supplemented by reports for the investors, which I'd like you to sit in on. That's the minimum they will need. You'll also need to keep in touch with our manufacture and supply project manager. She's expecting an outline of the latest product requirements. I'll schedule a handover meeting to discuss production times based on your project's progress. In the meantime though, just e-mail her your progress reports every week.

Erika is pleased.

Julio: Right. I'll do that. I'll also hold team meetings twice a month with my scientists to communicate any changes that are relevant to them.

Maybe more often, as the case requires.
Julio is pleased.

Erika has identified the communication requirements of different stakeholders in the company's drug program using three questions:

What information do program stakeholders require?

The R&D project manager needs to be kept informed of changes to the budget and program schedule. Investors need to be kept updated of the progress of the R&D project, and the manufacture and supply project manager needs to be kept informed of scheduling and the results of the R&D project.

How often do stakeholders expect to communicate with management and each other?

Erika will communicate scheduling updates to her project managers in weekly meetings. The R&D project manager also expects to be informed whenever budget changes are announced. The manufacture and supply project manager expects a formal handover meeting with the R&D project manager once research is completed, as well as weekly updates on the progress of research. The investors are expecting to be updated in quarterly meetings.

What type of communication do stakeholders prefer?

Erika established the type of communication that stakeholders prefer. Different stakeholders may prefer to be notified or updated via e-mail, conference or video calls, or through memos. For example, the R&D project manager prefers meetings, while the manufacture and supply project manager prefers e-mails. The investors prefer hard copy reports of the program's progress.

Communication requirements are often complex because several links may exist between different stakeholders. The program manager needs to make sure that all needed communication channels are identified and maintained.

Communication requirements may also change unexpectedly. Program managers need to manage changing requirements and inform stakeholders of a change when it directly affects decisions or actions that they may need to take.

For example, Erika, the program manager, needs to inform Julio, the R&D project manager, of any changes to the budget. However, he doesn't need to raise the issue with his laboratory staff unless the budget changes affect the procedures and equipment they use in researching the new drug. Similarly, changes in the research budget do not need to be communicated to the manufacture and supply project manager, because they will have no effect on her project.

Program managers need to outline program reporting channels to ensure that information flows unhindered from sender to the intended receiver. Well-managed reporting channels prevent miscommunication.

Program managers also need to inform everyone working on a program of their communication responsibilities. For example, a program manager may need to inform the R&D project manager when he is expected to submit a progress report to the program manager and other program stakeholders.

Investors have decided that they expect progress updates on a monthly basis. Follow along as Erika and Julio discuss the reporting requirements for the R&D project, before production begins.

Erika: I want to give a presentation to investors, who'd like a monthly update so they can get an overall view of how things are going throughout the program. I will need progress reports at the end of each month.

Erika is confident.

Julio: OK. I'll ask our head researcher to provide me with the relevant information so that I can give you a good overview of the drug's progress.

Julio is smiling.

Erika: That's good. I really want everyone to know where they stand, and what is expected of them. You should also let your employees know that you will be their communication link with me and the head office. I don't want them bothering the head office with queries.

Erika is smiling.

Julio: OK. I'm sure it won't be a problem if we establish the correct channels right from the start of the project.

Julio is pleased.

Erika has established the reporting requirements for the investors and R&D project of the antimalaria drug program.

She still needs to repeat the steps of establishing what information stakeholders need, how often they expect communication, and in what form, until she has established a clear reporting network that includes all stakeholders. This can get complicated, which is why a good communication plan is needed if she wants to avoid a communication breakdown.

Program managers draw up a program charter,

which is a document containing a description of the program and its expected outcomes. It illustrates the link that exists between the program and other programs that one organization manages.

Program managers need to communicate the program charter to all stakeholders so that they work toward a common goal.

The program scope statement describes the work that everyone working on the program is responsible for, the expected outcomes, and program constraints, assumptions, deliverables, and objectives. This information is presented in a document which is made available to all program stakeholders.

Program managers work with the statement throughout the duration of the program because it allows them to keep track of everything.

The Program Work Breakdown Structure (PWBS) details the work that needs to be done. It provides details of how the program is going to produce the expected benefits.

The program manager uses the PWBS to control the timeline and framework of the program, keep track of who is doing what work, and track how different stakeholders relate to one another. This is useful for ensuring that the right people get the information they need on time.,

Erika used the PWBS to work out exact dates for when a stakeholder needs to receive information.

For example, a program is due to begin in March. The PWBS indicates that the research component of the program is scheduled for completion by October. The manufacturing manager needs to know the production start dates for each production line. He will also need to know the exact components of each product line so that he can order everything in time.

Once a program manager has completed the Communications Planning process, he will have created the following outputs:

communications management plan

The communications management plan is a complete set of documentation that outlines how the communication needs of all stakeholders will be met.

The document includes details of the required information, who will communicate it and who will receive it, the method of communication, and the frequency and format of communication. The plan must also include details of how to update communication channels to accommodate the changing needs of stakeholders.

communication technology requirements plan

The communication technology requirements plan documents how stakeholders will communicate with one another, and the equipment that is needed for them to do this.

When deciding on types of communication, the program manager needs to take the existing equipment, such as fax machines and telephones, into account and note what needs to be installed or upgraded.

Erika collates all documents she prepared during the Communications Planning process into the final communications management plan.

Erika also compiles a communication technology requirements plan. Erika plans to use the existing intranet system and e-mail to communicate with her project managers. However, for presenting progress reports to foreign investors, she will set up videoconferencing facilities.

Case Study: Question 1 of 3
Scenario

Spartan Gear is a large sports equipment manufacturer. The company's management has recently initiated a program to produce a line of sports clothing to complement existing product lines. The program will include two projects – clothing manufacture and brand marketing. You have been appointed as program manager.

Answer the questions in order.

Question

A vital part of the Program Planning process is communications planning.

What is the first step you would take to plan communications for the new program?

Options:

1. Identify who is involved in the program
2. Call a meeting with the project managers
3. Find out what communication technology is available for use

Answer

Option 1: This is the correct option. The first step in planning communication channels is identifying who is involved in the program and what their level of involvement is. This information can be presented visually in a Stakeholder Analysis chart to make the relationships among stakeholders clear.

Option 2: This is an incorrect option. Before you can call a meeting with the relevant parties, you need to identify exactly who is involved in the program. This means identifying all stakeholders and presenting the relationships among them in a Stakeholder Analysis chart.

Option 3: This is an incorrect option. The first step is identifying who is involved in the program, and who you need to plan communication for. You should plan technology to suit stakeholders' needs, rather than planning methods of communication around existing systems. Often new technology will need to be installed.

Case Study: Question 2 of 3

After compiling a Stakeholder Analysis chart, you can easily recognize who is involved in the program and the relationships among them.

What is the next step you would take when planning communication?

Options:

1. Call a meeting with the project managers to find out their expectations

2. Outline a reporting system for each stakeholder and send them a memo about it

3. Continue planning the technical requirements of communication

Answer

Option 1: This is the correct option. By meeting with the project managers, you will be able to find out what communication they are expecting and what the preferred format is. Some managers may prefer hard copy reports, and others may prefer e-mail. Meeting stakeholders' expectations is a large part of good communication.

Option 2: This is an incorrect option. You need to find out what stakeholders' communication requirements are before devising reporting systems. This means meeting with them and determining their needs and preferences. Forcing people to use systems they don't like can result in poor communication.

Option 3: This is an incorrect option. It is important to find out the expectations of stakeholders before continuing with the development of a communication plan. This allows you to create communication channels that meet stakeholders' particular needs. You need to find out what each stakeholder prefers before deciding what the technological requirements of the program are.

Case Study: Question 3 of 3
Now that you know how stakeholders prefer to communicate, how would you ensure that they receive relevant information when they need it?
Options:
1. Use the PWBS and the Stakeholder Analysis chart

2. Use the Stakeholder Analysis chart and the communication technology requirements plan

3. Use the PWBS and the communication technology requirements plan

Answer

Option 1: This is the correct option. The Stakeholder Analysis chart provides an easy reference to the requirements of stakeholders, detailing what they need to know. The PWBS provides a time frame, including anticipated completion dates for individual sections of work. These two documents together give a reference of who needs what and when, allowing you to provide information on time.

Option 2: This is an incorrect option. The Stakeholder Analysis chart will tell you who needs what information, and the communication technology requirements plan will tell you how they will receive it. These two items will not tell you when stakeholders need the information. You need to use the PWBS for this.

Option 3: This is an incorrect option. The communication technology requirements plan will tell you what technology is available for communicating, and the PWBS provides a time frame, including anticipated completion dates for individual sections. Neither of these will tell you what information each stakeholder needs to know. For this you need to use the Stakeholder Analysis chart.

Risk Management Planning process

During the Risk Management Planning process, program managers calculate the probability of undesired events and the impact these may have on a program, should they occur. They do this so that they can minimize or eliminate potential risks which may have a significant negative effect on a program's objectives or benefits.

The four steps in the Risk Management Planning process are:
1. risk identification
2. qualitative risk analysis
3. quantitative risk analysis
4. risk response planning

Expert consultants conduct risk identification to recognize and document potential risks. They conduct a program analysis or they examine previous programs.

After risks are identified, two types of analysis are carried out:

qualitative risk analysis

Qualitative risk analysis determines the impact of identified potential risks. For example, how will a power failure at a manufacturing plant affect the delivery schedule?

quantitative risk analysis

Quantitative risk analysis determines the probability of a risk occurring and assigns a priority to each one.

For example, a power failure at a manufacturing plant may be given a lower priority than mechanical failure of parts of the production line. Both will have negative effects on production, but mechanical failure will take longer to repair and have a greater impact than a power failure.

During risk response planning, program managers decide what actions to take to reduce the threat posed by prioritized risks.

As with other planning processes, the Risk Management Planning process has several inputs:

- • program schedule,
- program budget,
- PWBS,
- risk categories,
- stakeholder risk tolerance threshold.

The program manager uses the program schedule, budget, and PWBS developed in previous planning processes to identify potential risks.

These risks are placed into broad risk categories to make it easier to develop a risk response plan. Risk categories may include external, technical, financial, and schedule-related risks, and many more depending on the individual situation.

The stakeholder risk tolerance threshold indicates how willing stakeholders are to take risks. The threshold is based on an evaluation of positive and negative aspects of each risk. At what point is the risk not worth the gain? The program manager answers this question to decide what action to take to minimize the impacts of risks.

The outputs of the Risk Management Planning process are:

- • a list of identified and prioritized risks,
- a risk response plan.

The four steps of the Risk Management Planning process involve several program-specific activities:

reviewing risk response plans

Previous programs may have experienced similar risks, so reviewing risk response plans previously used to reduce risk impact gives insight into effective risk management.

determining root causes

Program managers need to dig deeper to determine the root causes of risks. For example, a shortage of raw materials at an automobile manufacturing plant may be caused by late shipments. However, the late shipments may be caused by a heavy snowfall. The heavy snowfall is therefore the cause of halted production at the manufacturing plant.

proposing solutions to risks

Program managers must propose solutions to risks, especially high-priority risks. For example, if heavy snowfalls delay the shipment of raw materials, the program manager could allow additional time for shipments during winter, or find an additional source as a backup when the main supplier is unable to deliver.

implementing response mechanisms

Implementing response mechanisms is important to minimize risks. The risk response plan must clearly state what must be done if an event identified as a risk occurs. The program manager is responsible for ensuring that these actions are carried out.

managing a contingency reserve

Some risks can be eliminated by allocating a reserve amount, called a contingency reserve, of funds or time. Program managers must manage the contingency reserve so that it is available for when events identified as potential risks actually occur.

A good risk response plan can help program

managers to achieve program benefits easily. Without a good plan, unexpected events can start a chain of negative consequences which may lead to the failure of a program.

Question

Which of the following are program-specific risk activities?

Options:

1. Reviewing risk response plans
2. Determining root causes
3. Proposing solutions to risks
4. Implementing response mechanisms
5. Managing a contingency reserve
6. Identifying who is involved in the program
7. Examining resource analysis plans

Answer

Option 1: This is a correct option. By reviewing previous risk response plans, program managers can identify what responses worked in the past. This is vital in creating an effective plan for minimizing risks.

Option 2: This is a correct option. Program managers need to find the origin of each risk if they are to plan an effective response for it. This means investigating the risks initially identified to find their underlying causes.

Option 3: This is a correct option. It is not enough just to identify potential risks. Program managers must propose solutions to overcome them. These solutions are the main method of reducing or eliminating the negative effects of risks.

Option 4: This is a correct option. Program managers must actively initiate methods for overcoming risks, if their negative effects are to be minimized.

Option 5: This is a correct option. Additional time and funds can be set aside for dealing with events identified as risks when they occur. This reserve must be managed by the program manager.

Option 6: This is an incorrect option. This is not a risk management activity. Rather, it is used for communications planning.

Option 7: This is an incorrect option. This activity is a step in developing a program budget. The program budget is used but not analyzed or developed during risk management planning.

Program Purchases and Acquisitions

During the Program Purchases and Acquisitions process, the program manager decides what services and goods to buy, when, and what strategy to use to acquire them.

Program managers also use this process to determine which items can be made with internal resources, and which must be acquired from outside suppliers or contractors.

Inputs to the Program Purchases and Acquisitions process are the:

- • program scope statement,
- program charter,
- PWBS,
- resource management plan,
- Stakeholder Analysis chart.

Program managers use the program scope statement and the program charter to identify the deliverables of the program.

The PWBS and the Stakeholder Analysis chart provide a detailed breakdown of the work and people involved in achieving the program's objectives and deliverables. This information is used to determine what resources are needed by whom, and how much of each will be needed.

The resource management plan documents any

organizational policies that could affect purchasing. Deviations from the protocol could jeopardize the program's success.

For example, a protocol may specify that an application for funds must be made before purchases can be authorized. If the correct forms are not completed, the funds may not be released, resulting in a lack of funds for the purchase of services or goods vital to the program.

The outputs of the Program Purchases and Acquisitions process include:

the contract statement of work

The contract statement of work contains details of any goods or services to be purchased. It includes a detailed description of each needed item or service, the reason for purchase, and a description of how it will be used in the program.

make or buy decisions

Make or buy decisions indicate which items are more cost effective to produce using internal resources and which are cheaper to source from external suppliers. This information is passed on to the Program Contracting process, in which external suppliers are identified and formal contracts are issued.

the procurement management plan

Sorin Dumitrascu

The procurement management plan details how purchases are managed. It includes details of the type of contracts, the services and goods needed, and how the purchasing process must be coordinated. The plan must also detail how many external suppliers are involved and how they will be managed.

the qualified vendor list

A qualified vendor list supplies program managers with details of preferred external suppliers. These may be suppliers that have provided services to previous organizational programs or that the organization has special agreements with, such as bulk order discounts.

The program manager uses the procurement management plan as an input to the Program Contracting process. It details which goods or services must be externally sourced through contracts with preferred vendors.

A leading manufacturer of clothing recently initiated a new line of baby clothes. The procurement management plan indicates that the fabric for the new line will be manufactured in one of the company's factories. It also states that trimmings for the new line must be sourced externally.

The program manager contacts the preferred vendors indicated in the plan to bid on the contract to supply the company with fasteners and trimmings. Once all bids are submitted, the program manager chooses the supplier with the most cost-effective bid, and the process of finalizing the contract is started.

Question

How do the Program Purchases and Acquisitions process and the Program Contracting process relate to each other?

Options:

1. The procurement management plan is an output of the Program Purchases and Acquisitions process and an input to the Program Contracting process

2. The contract statement of work is used to solicit external vendors in the Program Contracting process

3. The Program Purchases and Acquisitions process formalizes the agreements with internal suppliers initiated during the Program Contracting process

Answer

Option 1: This is the correct option. The procurement management plan created during the

Program Purchases and Acquisitions process details the type of contracts, services and goods needed, as well as how the purchase process will be coordinated. This is vital information when drawing up official contracts with external vendors during the Program Contracting process.

Option 2: This is an incorrect option. During the Program Contracting process, program managers invite external vendors to bid for contracts based on the information in the procurement management plan. The contract statement of work details the types of purchases and the reasons for them.

Option 3: This is an incorrect option. The Program Contracting process procures contracts for goods and services supplied by external vendors. These contracts are based on the information supplied in the procurement management plan, which is an output of the Program Purchases and Acquisitions process.

CHAPTER 5 - The Executing Process Group

In this lesson, you'll learn how the Executing process group supports the three themes of program management, which are managing benefits, managing stakeholders, and active program governance according to established plans.

It is important to understand the Executing process group because it ensures that the resources needed for a program are acquired, that change requests and communications with stakeholders are managed effectively, and that program governance proceeds according to the established governance plan.

The Direct and Manage Program Execution (DMPE) process is used to integrate the outputs of the other processes in the Executing process group. The four main activities it integrates are the management of human resources, communication, procurement, and quality.

Human resource management involves balancing the skills needs of the program with the need for internal employee development. Communications management ensures that information is distributed to the appropriate stakeholders in a timely and appropriate manner. Procurement management involves managing the risks and costs associated with procurement. Quality management involves ensuring that program outputs meet quality requirements.

The Perform Quality Assurance process ensures that the program meets planned quality expectations. During quality assurance, an audit is performed on the quality systems of the program, including manufacturing and business systems.

Repeatability and reproducibility (R&R) tests are performed on the quality performance metrics, and a root cause analysis is performed if the quality performance is low.

The employees are interviewed to gain insight into the functioning of the systems, which may lead to quality performance failures.

Information that is distributed using the Information Distribution process can be status information, notification of change requests and change approval, filings with regulatory bodies, or public announcements.

For the process to be effective, it must deliver information that is relevant to the recipient, is accurate and received on time, and is in an appropriate format.

As part of the Executing process group, the Develop Program Team process aims to improve the skills of individuals in a program team, as well as the skills of the team as a whole. It also aims to improve cooperation between team members, to enable the team to effectively complete a program.

This involves building the individual competencies and skills of team members in accordance with their current and possible future roles in program execution.

The program team consists of those individuals carrying out the program's activities, under the supervision of the program manager.

The program manager is responsible for acquiring and developing a team of individuals that make up the program team. To do this in a structured and formal manner, program managers follow the activities and tasks laid out in the Acquire Program Team and Develop Program Team processes, as part of Executing process group activities.

As part of a program's execution, a program's management is responsible for following the Request Seller Responses process and the Select Sellers process.

During the Request Seller Responses process, program managers obtain information from prospective sellers through requests for information

(RFIs), requests for proposals (RFPs), and requests for quotations (RFQs).

During the Select Sellers process, program managers review all proposals from prospective sellers, select the most suitable seller, and negotiate the terms of a contract.

The Executing process group

"OK, so we finally have our plans drawn up. It's time to get this aircraft built - but I'm worried about getting the right resources. Also, what if there are changes to plans? And how will we manage to make decisions, given the number of people with a vested interest?"

Processes in the Executing process group enable you to complete the tasks set out in a program management plan, in order to accomplish a program's objectives.

Program management operates at a higher organizational level than project management and with a much broader scope – it involves the coordinated management of a group of projects.

Processes in the project management Executing process group have the same names as those in the program management Executing process group. However, they have different inputs, functions, controls, tools, and outputs.

Many of the processes in the Executing process group for project management are performed at the program or portfolio management level. For example, requests for changes at the project level are assessed and authorized at the program level.

The Executing process group consists of seven

processes.

Direct and Manage Program Execution

The Direct and Manage Program Execution process executes the program plan to deliver the benefits of individual program components or projects.

Perform Quality Assurance

Perform Quality Assurance is the process of ensuring the quality of the program outputs across all projects.

Acquire Program Team

Acquire Program Team is the process of getting the necessary human resources working on the program execution.

Develop Program Team

Develop Program Team is a process that deals with training the program team to meet the ongoing competency requirements of the program.

Information Distribution

The Information Distribution process provides accurate and appropriate information to the stakeholders of a program. It administers communication with clients, sponsors, and project or component managers.

Request Seller Responses

Request Seller Responses is a process that is

used to request information, proposals, or quotations from vendors.

Select Sellers

The Select Sellers process is used to evaluate seller responses, select sellers, and negotiate contracts.

It is important to understand the processes in the Executing process group because they enable you to ensure that:

- • resources needed to accomplish program benefits are acquired,
- change requests are managed effectively,
- stakeholders receive and give information in a timely manner,
- the program is governed according to an established governance plan.

Quito Air is involved in developing a low-cost, mid-range aircraft. Quito Air executives are collaborating with other companies to develop various components, which will be shipped to a central assembly line.

Vendor proposals are reviewed and suppliers of components such as the engines are added to a selected vendors list.

During development, a project to develop an avionics architecture is found to be behind schedule and over budget.

A review of the project is initiated in accordance with the program governance plan, and a report that highlights the availability of a commercial off-the-shelf (COTS) avionics architecture is forwarded to the program management office (PMO).

The PMO arranges a meeting with the component manager and the sponsor of the avionics architecture team. They decide that buying the COTS product will meet program cost, schedule, and quality requirements better than developing an in-house product.

The PMO authorizes the change request and makes funds available to buy the COTS product, and the avionics project team is charged with integrating the product in the aircraft design.

Thom, the program manager at Quito Air, benefited from using the processes in the Executing process group.

The processes enabled him to:

ensure the acquisition of resources needed to accomplish the program goals
The PMO was able to allocate resources for purchasing the COTS product. effectively manage
change requests, such as the decision to buy the COTS product

Program Management

The change request for the COTS product was managed when the PMO facilitated a meeting with the component manager and the project sponsor to decide whether to approve the change.

allow stakeholders to receive and give information in a timely manner

Information about the avionics architecture project – which was behind schedule and over budget – was delivered to the stakeholders in a timely and appropriate manner.

ensure that program governance proceeded according to the established governance plan

The PMO authorized the change request only after the planned program governance procedures – such as an official change request posting, the meeting with the component manager and the project sponsor, and an official change request authorization – had been executed.

Question

Why is it important for program managers to understand the processes in the Executing process group?

Options:

1. It allows them to ensure the resources needed to accomplish a program's goals will be acquired

2. It allows them to effectively manage change

requests

3. It allows them to ensure stakeholders receive and give information in a timely manner

4. It allows them to ensure a program is governed according to the established governance plan

5. It allows them to initiate new projects or program components

6. It allows them to plan the management of risks and costs

Answer

Option 1: This is a correct option. The Executing process group is used to acquire program resources such as staff, contractors, and suppliers.

Option 2: This is a correct option. The Executing process group ensures that change requests are managed accurately and fast.

Option 3: This is a correct option. The Executing process group ensures that appropriate program information is distributed to stakeholders, and enables stakeholders to be actively involved in the program.

Option 4: This is a correct option. The Executing process group is supported by the program governance framework. It ensures that program management proceeds in accordance with the agreed governance plan.

Option 5: This is an incorrect option. The Executing process group deals with managing the execution of a program, rather than with project or component initiation. Processes for initiating projects or components form part of the Initiating process group.

Option 6: This is an incorrect option. The Executing process group deals with managing the execution of a program. Processes for managing risk and program costs form part of the Planning process group.

In this lesson, you will learn about the activities involved in the Direct and Manage Program Execution process in the Executing process group.

You will also learn about the activities involved in the Perform Quality Assurance process, and about aspects of the Information Distribution process.

Introduction to the DMPE process

The Direct and Manage Program Execution (DMPE) process ensures that the intended benefits of the program are delivered.

This process results in the accumulative deliverables of all the projects and it is used to resolve problems that appear in the program. The process manages risks, constraints, and inter-project issues.

After a change request is approved, the DMPE process is used to implement the changes. The DMPE process uses the program management plan and the program schedule as inputs.

The process results in change requests, work results, and program termination requests.

Recall the Quito Air program. The company is in the component testing phase of its development of a low-cost, mid-range aircraft.

The engine specification project team tests the engine and discovers that the commercial off-the-shelf (COTS) product that the program sponsor chose makes too much noise. If Quito Air's aircraft is too noisy, it may be denied access to airports such as London Heathrow because of failure to meet departure noise limits.

The program management office (PMO)

receives the request to change the engine component from the design integration team. In compliance with the program management plan, the list of engine vendors is re-evaluated.

After the PMO reviews the program schedule, it establishes that the engine project schedule cannot be pushed back to allow for in-house development of a new engine design.

So more resources are needed to purchase a more expensive engine type that is quieter. A change request is authorized to acquire the more expensive engines.

Question

What inputs are required for the DMPE process?

Options:

1. A program management plan
2. A program schedule
3. Work results
4. A project management plan

Answer

Option 1: This is a correct option. The DMPE process involves ensuring that program work is performed according to the program management plan, so this plan is an input for the process.

Option 2: This is a correct option. The DMPE

process involves ensuring that program results are delivered according to schedule, so it uses the program schedule as an input.

Option 3: This is an incorrect option. The DMPE process ensures that work results are delivered as an output.

Option 4: This is an incorrect option. The DMPE process uses a program management plan – rather than a project management plan – as an input. The process involves managing and integrating projects at the program level.

DMPE process activities

A program manager uses the DMPE process to integrate all of the activities and processes involved in program execution, to ensure the delivery of the intended program benefits to customers and other stakeholders.

The DMPE process involves daily work, to allocate resources and manage the trade-offs between objectives across all projects and program activities. It also involves the anticipation and resolution of potential issues.

The DMPE process involves managing and directing the four main activities that occur in the Executing process group.

Human resource management

A program manager needs to consider the human resource requirements of a program. Considerations include whether to use internal or external employees, and how to develop existing resources to the benefit of both the program and the employees.

To enable program-level human resource management, the DMPE process integrates the Acquire Program Team and the Develop Program Team processes.

Communication management

Communication management is crucial to the success of a program because stakeholders need to have access to important information. Stakeholder decisions also need to be delivered appropriately and fast.

Communication management ensures that information is distributed according to the planned program reporting channels. Information that needs to be distributed could address decision-making authority, responsibility for executing tasks, schedules for tasks and reporting requirements, and methods of information distribution. To manage communication, the DMPE process integrates with the Information Distribution process.

Procurement management

Procurement management is fundamental to program success because it involves ensuring that needed program resources are acquired – on time and within budget. Procurement management can be treated as a project and managed as such.

To enable effective procurement management, the DMPE process integrates the outputs of the Request Seller Responses process and the Select Sellers process. Together, these processes determine criteria for vendor selection and reduce procurement risks.

Quality management

Quality management at the program level involves ensuring that the quality management plans from the Planning process group are implemented. At the project level, it involves ensuring that project deliverables meet quality requirements.

Program-level quality management requires the integration of the component or project quality assurance outputs. It also involves ensuring the quality of business processes in the organization, to minimize rework, recall, and warranty costs. The DMPE process integrates quality management in program execution activities through the Perform Quality Assurance process.

Question

The DMPE process involves directing and managing all processes and activities involved in program execution. What activities are involved in the Executing process group?

Options:

1. Human resource management
2. Communication management
3. Procurement management
4. Quality management
5. Strategic management
6. Marketing management

Sorin Dumitrascu

Answer

Option 1: This option is correct. Executing process group activities include the management of human resources. Program managers need to consider the human resources that are required for a program, how to develop them, and how existing human resources will be affected.

Option 2: This option is correct. Executing process group activities include the management of communication. The program manager needs to ensure that stakeholders have access to important program information and that stakeholder decisions are communicated quickly and accurately.

Option 3: This option is correct. Executing process group activities include the management of procurement. Procurement management involves selecting the products or services that best suit a program from reliable suppliers or vendors at a suitable cost.

Option 4: This option is correct. Executing process group activities include the management of quality. The program manager needs to ensure the quality of each of the projects in a program and their collective output.

Option 5: This option is incorrect. Strategic management is addressed through processes in the Initiating process group, rather than through the

Executing process group. During Initiating processes, program managers use strategic management when initiating program components.

Option 6: This option is incorrect. Marketing management is a function that is usually performed as a project within a program.

Remember the aircraft development at Quito Air? The aircraft design is a consolidated effort of design teams around the world.

The teams use a collaborative 3-D modeling platform to reduce time-to-market and costs. However, many Quito Air employees do not have experience with collaborative computer-aided design (CAD). Through the DMPE process, program managers integrate human resource management with other program execution activities. They assign trainers to teach existing employees how to use the CAD system, and appoint staff to provide ongoing technical support during development.

During development, it becomes clear that the civil aviation market is in trouble. The company executives decide to launch a number of projects to develop a second model of the company's planned aircraft for military use.

Projects are launched to develop variations of

the aircraft design for cargo transport, troop transport, and medical evacuation. It is hoped that the new line will reduce the impact on the company of the downturn in the civil aviation market.

Through the DMPE process, the program management office (PMO) at Quito Air integrates appropriate communication management. It facilitates the communication of information about the new military projects between the program sponsors and the project managers, using weekly status reports and meetings. The PMO is also responsible for creating the information package that prospective clients will receive.

In order to meet military requirements, a turboprop engine must be used. Turboprop engines are more efficient at low speed, so they allow short takeoffs and landings. However, they are more expensive than the commercial turbofan engines.

The DMPE process also integrates procurement management in program execution. A series of requests for quotations (RFQs) for the turboprop engine are made, and the list of selected vendors is updated. The current vendor of the turbofan engines is able to offer the best combination of cost, schedule, and quality benefits for the turboprop engines, so that vendor is selected.

Through the DMPE process, the program

manager integrates quality management in program execution. Quality management plans for the new projects are created and the projects are launched. The program manager checks that quality activities are being implemented as planned, and assesses the quality of the collective project and component outputs.

The PMO initiates a project that streamlines the tool testing procedure before manufacture of the component prototypes begins. The 3-D modeling platform allows for the reduction of variation in goodness of fit of the aircraft components.

As a result, the team is able to begin testing and manufacturing tools sooner than expected in the program life cycle.

The Quito Air program manager used the DMPE process to integrate and manage the four main activities in the Executing process group.

Human resource management

Human resources were managed when the program manager decided to provide existing, internal employees with CAD training – rather than, for example, hiring experienced CAD technicians. This involved assessing individual employee career development in relation to the needs of the program. Here the DMPE process integrated the outputs of the Acquire Program Team process and the Develop Program Team process.

Communication management

Communication was managed to allow the smooth transfer of information about changes in the company's program to stakeholders and project managers.

Here the DMPE process integrated the Information Distribution process outputs within the program.

Procurement management

Procurement was managed after the need for a new military line was identified. RFQs were sent out to potential vendors and potential vendor criteria were used to create a list of selected vendors.

The DMPE process integrated the outputs of the Request Seller Responses process and the Select Sellers process.

Quality management

Quality was managed as the program manager actively assessed quality performance against the established quality management plans. A process quality improvement initiative was also initiated to reduce tooling time and costs.

The DMPE process integrated the outputs of the Perform Quality Assurance process with other program outputs.

Question

The Quito Air PMO learns that the aircraft cabling has repeatedly failed quality assurance testing. The PMO, sponsors, and design integration team meet and approve a change request to use lighter aluminum cables. The PMO negotiates a contract and chooses a vendor. In order to use aluminum cabling, the manufacturing process will require an ultrasonic welding step.

Match each program management activity in the Executing process group with its example in this scenario.

Options:

A. Human resource management

B. Communication management

C. Procurement management

D. Quality management

Targets:

1. A specialist is hired to work on one of the projects

2. The PMO schedules a meeting with the project manager and sponsor

3. The PMO negotiates a contract for an aluminum cable

4. The PMO staff consider increasing the average gauge of the cable to improve reliability

Answer

Human resources are managed when the program manager considers whether to hire externally or to develop skills internally.

Communication management is practiced when the PMO meets with the appropriate stakeholders and communicates its decision to change the cable.

Procurement is managed when a supplier is selected and the contract is negotiated using the procurement plan.

Quality is managed when the PMO manages quality considerations across projects and program components, for example by balancing weight and reliability requirements for cable.

The Perform Quality Assurance process

"Quality is not an act, it is a habit." Aristotle - ancient Greek philosopher

A program should involve a process of continuous improvement. Quality assurance is there to verify or determine whether program elements meet overarching customer expectations, and to ensure continuous improvement.

The Perform Quality Assurance process is part of the Executing process group. It identifies poorly performing systems and enforces planned quality standards. The process also develops process improvement initiatives.

The Perform Quality Assurance process uses the quality management plan, operational definitions, quality metrics, and work results as inputs. It produces findings and change requests as outputs.

The process can be used at any point in the program life cycle.

The Perform Quality Assurance process does not replace the quality assurance efforts for program components or projects.

Instead, it assures the quality of the outputs of the program as a collective of projects or components. It also assures the quality of the outputs of the individual projects, which may feed to other projects or to the program deliverables.

The program-level Perform Quality Assurance process focuses on fulfilling the quality requirements of the customer, whereas project output quality assurance seeks to meet the requirements of internal customers, such as other projects.

Four activities are commonly performed during the program-level Perform Quality Assurance process:

auditing

An audit is used to perform quality assurance. It can evaluate the effectiveness of a product or process, and it is usually performed by a person independent of the program or organization. The audit compares a system or product against planned standards such as customer requirements, statutes, or other regulations.

repeatability and reproducibility (R&R) techniques

The validity of the quality performance metrics is checked using a number of R&R techniques. The R&R analysis ensures the integrity of the metrics being analyzed by attempting to define a constant measurement error.

root cause analysis

Root cause analysis aims to identify the root cause of a problem. The tools used for root cause analysis attempt to define a problem and its related problems within a system. It then aims to identify corrective actions for all the related problems, rather than a quick fix of just the symptoms. Failure Mode and Effect Analysis (FMEA) can be used to perform root cause analysis.

interviewing

If a problem is found, the program employees and stakeholders close to the problem should be interviewed. This may reveal that alternative work methods are being used, and it allows more informed corrective action to be developed.

A company that manufactures consumer electronics launches a program to develop a line of products specifically for female consumers.

The product line includes personal digital assistants (PDAs), music players, and cell phones with associated branded accessories.

At the electronics company, the program manager oversees the four activities associated with the Perform Quality Assurance process:

auditing

An audit is performed on the quality systems of

the program. The auditors – internal program management office (PMO) staff – assess the effectiveness of the systems that manage manufacturing quality. They discover that the PDA products fail stress tests.

R&R techniques

The testing processes are checked using R&R techniques to verify the stress test results. The executives discover that 5% of the PDAs break if dropped from the height of an average desk onto a concrete floor. This performance metric fails to meet the quality standards that were planned for the product.

interviewing

The program management office (PMO) audit staff interview the casing designers, plastics engineers, and manufacturing staff in an attempt to discover variables that may have led to the quality failure. They discover that the plastic casing occasionally breaks in the mold in the same place as when it falls off a table.

root cause analysis

The program management office (PMO) calls a meeting of a cross-functional team of employees to perform an FMEA on the product to determine the root cause of the quality failure.

During the FMEA, the PMO quality assurance team discovers that altering the plastic and the housing design for a PDA reduces performance failure to within the planned acceptable limits.

The program team continues to use the Perform Quality Assurance process throughout the duration of the program.

Question

Ballentine Cosmetics launches a program to develop a line of hair-care products. The company aims to use natural and less controversial ingredients in the products, and to market them accordingly.

Match the activities involved in the Perform Quality Assurance process to the activities performed at Ballentine Cosmetics.

Options:

A. Auditing

B. R&R analysis

C. Root cause analysis

D. Interviewing

Targets:

1. The employees test that the products meet the planned shelf life requirements despite the reduction in the use of preservatives

2. A check is performed to ensure that the shelf

life estimations are, in general, indicative of the time it takes for the products to spoil

3. The team uses FMEA to discover that one product fails the shelf life tests because the preservative used is sensitive to light

4. The PMO staff learn from the production line employees that the preservative storage container in the factory is left open when not in use

Answer

This is an example of using auditing. An audit is performed to assess the quality of the products. Shelf life is one aspect of product quality.

This is an example of using R&R analysis. The validity of the quality performance metrics is assessed using R&R analysis tools.

This is an example of using root cause analysis. The root cause of quality failures is investigated, and corrective action is then recommended in the form of a change request.

This is an example of using interviewing. Interviews with the manufacturing staff members can reveal the root causes of problems by identifying alternative work methods.

The Information Distribution process

The Information Distribution process is a process in the Executing process group used to provide stakeholders, clients, and component managers with information.

The process uses communication messages, information requests, communications management plans, stakeholder analysis charts, and information for stakeholders as inputs.

The process outputs are the formal communication of program information, as well as the informal communication of information as it's needed.

The Information Distribution process distributes information to three groups, known as distribution channels:

1. clients
2. sponsors
3. project managers

Information that could be delivered using the Information Distribution process includes:

status information

Status information – such as schedule progress, risk analysis, or internal budgetary information– may be distributed through performance reports or updates.

notification of change requests

Change requests and responses to change requests are distributed by the process.

filings with regulatory bodies

The process is responsible for accurate and timely filings with government or other regulatory bodies.

public announcements

The process is used to communicate useful information to the public.

The Information Distribution process is successful if the information it distributes is relevant to the recipients, accurate, received on time, and presented in a format that is appropriate for the target audience.

Malltronic is a pension fund advisor company that was recently acquired by Callinsure. The executives initiate a program to deploy a customer relationship management (CRM) system that will improve service for individuals employed by the company's large commercial clients.

The program's Information Distribution process will include the following information:

status information

Program Management

The customer complaints project team submits status information in the form of a schedule report indicating that its deliverables will be one week early. Information flows from the project managers to the PMO and then to the sponsors.

notification of change requests

During the program planning phase, the PMO distributes a change request form for an alternative development platform to the program sponsor. Information flows from the PMO to the sponsors.

filings with regulatory bodies

The reporting standards for filings with regulatory bodies such as the Financial Accounting Standards Board (FASB) are distributed to the project managers. Information flows from the PMO to the project managers.

public announcements

Malltronic makes public announcements by sending brochures about new customer services to its corporate clients for distribution to customers. Information flows from the PMO to the clients.

Question

What criteria should all distributed information conform to?

Options:

1. Accurate

2. Punctual
3. Appropriate
4. Concise

Answer

Option 1: This is a correct option. The information must be accurate. Inaccurate information can lead to schedule delays, reduced quality, and increased costs, as well as stakeholder dissatisfaction.

Option 2: This is a correct option. The information must be received in time. Late information does not allow for immediate response or action.

Option 3: This is a correct option. The information must be presented in a format that is appropriate for the target audience.

Option 4: This is an incorrect option. The information can be as verbose as is required, as long as it is accurate, punctual, and presented in an appropriate manner.

Question

Chaplan Home Stores is a large home improvement retailer. The executives initiated a program to develop a new IT system for the company's chain of stores. The system will include a self-checkout system and will link the inventories of all the stores.

What are examples of appropriate distributed program information?

Options:

1. The support project manager reports projected cost savings to the PMO during the selection of support service vendors, using the PMO's standard reporting format

2. The PMO releases a draft for an advertisement to an advertising agency to promote the self-checkout system after the point-of-sale vendor delivery is assured

3. The database project manager reports to the sponsor during project closing that the servers purchased were more expensive than budgeted for

4. A risk analysis report that highlights the risk of the database being unavailable is distributed to the account holders

Answer

Option 1: This is a correct option. The information flows from the component manager to the PMO, and then to the sponsor. The information is received at the right time, and is in an appropriate format for the PMO staff to process.

Option 2: This is a correct option. Information flows from the PMO to the clients in an appropriate format. It is accurate and timely because the details of the delivery have been verified.

Option 3: This is an incorrect option. The information is late. It should have been distributed when vendor offers were being reviewed.

Option 4: This is an incorrect option. The risk analysis is not appropriate information for clients. It should have been distributed to sponsors and managers.

Developing a program team

"Effective program management begins and ends with people." – Edward Hoffman, director of NASA's Academy of Program, Project, and Engineering Leadership

A program's successful execution depends on the efficacy of its projects, and the projects underlying the program's execution are mostly performed by teams of people.

Once a program reaches the Executing phase, its successful execution becomes the responsibility of a program manager and program team.

The Develop Program Team process – part of the Executing process group of program management – supports the development of people by providing the necessary knowledge and skills people need to successfully perform duties for a particular program.

This process is an ongoing one for ensuring that program activities are performed competently and in accordance with a program's strategic objectives.

The Develop Program Team process develops the competencies of:

individuals in a team
A successful development plan needs to balance

the needs of the program with the needs of the individual. Through the Develop Program Team process, program managers prepare employees for current assignments and roles they need to take on.

Program managers can also prepare employees to assume different or larger roles within a program at a future date, or to be reassigned different roles when the program concludes.

the team as a whole

Typically, a program manager establishes the competencies a program team should have in order to perform activities in a specific program effectively.

Using the Develop Program Team process, the program manager supports the development of the team by providing it with the necessary knowledge and skills relevant to the program.

Building individual competencies and group competencies according to a team development plan ensures that:

- • required competencies for a program are present on the team,
- team members are properly trained for current and future roles.

By developing individual and group competencies, you can ensure that these competencies interact effectively to form a strong program team.

Among other things, you need to create an accessible and encouraging environment in which team members can contribute feedback on a program's progress, and interact with a program's stakeholders.

This will enable individuals to work well together, and help ensure that the program's execution goes smoothly.

Consider Callitel, a financial institution in which a program team is responsible for upgrading the company's database and web site.

The team developing the upgrade has to coordinate with other teams to ensure that the code and user interface used conforms to the needs and standards for the web-based databases in the industry.

Callitel's program manager neglected to pay attention to individual team members' needs, and individuals became unhappy, unfocused, and uncooperative as a result. People in the team were unable and unwilling to work together as a team, and this hampered the program's execution.

Program managers need to provide team members with the necessary skills and knowledge. Here Catherine, the program manager, assists Erika, a program team member.

Catherine: Hi Erika, you look worried. What's wrong?

Erika: I'm still updating the program management plan, and I'm not sure whether I'll be done in time for our next milestone briefing that's coming up.

Catherine: Well, I've done my fair share of updates in the past – what exactly are you struggling with? Maybe I can help.

Erika: There's been a radical change in one of the subsidiary plans, and I'm not sure who to ask for help.

Catherine: Well, besides me, there's Joe. He's experienced in risk management and change control. I'm sure he'll be more than willing to help.

Erika: Thanks, Catherine. I'll be sure to approach Joe on this issue.

Like Erika, members of a program team may have varying fields of expertise, and different skills necessary for a program's successful execution. When appropriate, a skilled program manager refers team members to other members who have needed skills, as Catherine did.

Without sufficient feedback and attention to their

needs, program team members can become disruptive and even leave a program team, which could negatively impact a program.

Developing a program team is important, especially considering the challenges all teams are faced with.

Problems on a program team that can affect program execution include:

- • a lack of motivation, or a "don't care" attitude,
- poor communication,
- a lack of trust or respect for a program manager,
- updates that become complaining sessions,
- program work that isn't fulfilling.

Question
What benefits can a program manager derive from developing a program team using the Develop Program Team process?

Options:
1. A work environment and team situation that is always conflict free

2. Team members who are properly prepared to take on current and future roles

3. A program team that has the competencies needed to execute a program

4. A well-developed program that has no chance of failing

Answer

Option 1: This is an incorrect option. Although effective teams may quarrel less and resolve conflicts fairly easily, the possibility that conflict can occur still remains, and conflict-free teams cannot be guaranteed.

Option 2: This is a correct option. A well-developed program team helps ensure that team members are prepared to fulfill the roles and responsibilities that their current and future assignments include.

Option 3: This is a correct option. In a well-developed program team, individuals within the team and the team as a whole have the competencies needed to execute a particular program effectively.

Option 4: This is an incorrect option. A well-developed team will not make up for poor program planning or ineffective program management techniques, which could still cause a program to fail.

Acquiring a program team

In order to see a program through successfully, you, as program manager, need to acquire the appropriate human resources to form a program team. To do this, you select suitable candidates from external or internal sources.

To assemble a program team in an orderly and suitable manner, you follow the Acquire Program Team process, which is part of a program's Executing process group.

When acquiring your program team, you need to decide whether to source your team from internal staff, or whether to source staff externally.

This is important, because you need to involve people with the required skills at the right time to execute program-oriented processes. If your own staff members do not have the required competencies, you'll have to look elsewhere.

The choice of whether to source staff internally or externally depends on various factors, including the:

- • length of time the skill is needed,
- availability of internal human resources with the appropriate skill,
- cost of external human resources,
- timing of the need for more staff.

There are a number of activities you need to perform, depending on whether you recruit your staff:

internally

Activities involved in recruiting staff internally include identifying the qualified staff, negotiating for their services with their current managerial staff members, and transitioning them into the program.

externally

To recruit staff externally, you need to identify and evaluate candidates. You then decide whether to hire them as full-time employees, on a contractual basis, or as consultants.

Before choosing how to hire externally, you should compare the costs involved in hiring external staff as subcontractors or consulting staff, and the potential cost of waiting until internal staff become available.

Callitel, a financial institution, wants to develop a new system to enable customers to submit user-entered data into a web-based database.

So the company's managers need to decide whether they have sufficient human resources with the adequate skills to perform the upgrade in-house, or whether they need to hire staff externally.

Program Management

As part of the Acquire Program Team process, Callitel's management needs to consider the length of time that they need skilled developers and expert software developers to help build a new database program.

Callitel managers need to determine whether they have sufficient internal resources with the appropriate skills available, or whether it would be less disruptive to the organization's daily functioning if they hired an external developing team to perform the database upgrade.

However, the cost of hiring external resources must be considered, to avoid exceeding the program budget.

The timing of the need for more staff is a contributing factor in the choice between hiring an internal or external development team.

Managerial staff at Callitel check with prospective off-site team members who are developing products whether the requested individuals would be available when the program schedule requires them. Internally, some of the Callitel staff members and developers are tied down with urgent projects, which complicates resource scheduling.

Some of the inputs for the Acquire Program Team process include:

Sorin Dumitrascu

staffing management plan

The staffing management plan is a subsidiary management plan that forms part of the program management plan.

Program managers need to consider this plan when assembling a program team to ensure that the people they recruit have skills relevant to the program's objectives.

program budget

When acquiring staff for a program, the program budget should be considered because it

defines how funds are laid out for the program and how funds can be applied to pay salaries.

The program budget also determines the funds for activities that program teams will perform.

program schedule

The program schedule includes a time line of various program components and activities in the program work breakdown structure (PWBS).

The schedule defines how program actions and human resources need to produce expected benefits within a limited time frame.

Callitel's managers decide that partnering with an offshore developer is their best option.

Management is confident that the company has

sufficient experience working with foreign developers and strong enough IT support to deal with the added administrative strain that monitoring an off-site program involves.

Question

Which factors should influence your decision to recruit staff internally as opposed to externally?

Options:

1. Duration of time for which particular skills are needed

2. Availability of internal resources with the appropriate skills

3. The proximity of external candidates to on-site facilities

4. The scope of the staffing management plan

5. The cost of external resources

6. Timing of the need for staff

Answer

Option 1: This is a correct option. When deciding whether to recruit staff members from an external or internal source, program managers have to consider if they will need the skills of these individuals for an extended period.

Option 2: This is a correct option. If adequate personnel with the appropriate skills are unavailable internally, program managers need to hire team members from an external source.

Option 3: This is an incorrect option. An externally recruited team member's proximity to the organization that hosts the program isn't necessarily relevant. Off-site team members are often hired to assist in a program's execution via a remote management team.

Option 4: This is an incorrect option. The scope of the staffing management plan outlines the skills and abilities needed for a project, but does not specify the source from which program team members should be hired.

Option 5: This is a correct option. When deciding whether to hire external or internally located team members, program managers need to assess if the cost of hiring staff can be covered by the program budget.

Option 6: This is a correct option. The time at which team members will be needed to assist in a program's execution is important, because it may coincide with times at which internal staff will be tied to working on other programs.

Developing a program team

The Develop Program Team process is ongoing throughout a program's life cycle. It involves developing program team members to prepare them for current assignments and roles, as well as for future, more advanced assignments.

The Develop Program Team process assists team members in becoming a more cohesive group while a program is underway, and in performing well individually once the program has ended.

Training is an important component of the Develop Program Team process. Relevant inputs for the process include:

a training plan

Program managers should compile a training plan that addresses teamwork concepts, such as skills and competency in dealing with products, services, and processes relevant to a program.

assigned training resources

Program team managers need to be assigned training resources to enable them to train program team members in a timely and structured manner, and to ensure that team members understand their responsibilities and perform according to expectations.

training records

Sorin Dumitrascu

A program manager needs to keep accurate training records to indicate what skills and competencies the team members have accumulated, and what training requirements still need to be met.

Remember Callitel's decision to hire an offshore developer to develop its new database system?

Upon receiving the offshore company's database design, Callitel's lead data architect declares it to be impractical, too time-consuming for web users, and unsafe from intrusion. As a result, the company's program fails to reach its first milestone.

If Callitel managers had provided the offshore development team with appropriate team development training, they could have ensured that the team had an understanding of the safety and usability requirements for the new system.

Team development needs to focus on developing each team member for their current role in a program

taking on a different role within the same program taking on new roles after the program's completion taking over a role from someone else

Team development is vital to ensure that all individuals within a program team are adequately prepared to fulfill their current roles and responsibilities. To this end, a program manager attempts to address many aspects of individuals' behavior and the dynamics of interacting professionally within the workplace.

In the case of Callitel, a successful team development effort will help prepare the offshore team for its role in the Callitel program's execution.

Management needs to highlight the preferred interpersonal and technical skills that work best within the program's particular environment. In particular, program members will benefit from a more complete understanding of team dynamics, leadership responsibilities, and the technicalities of ensuring that the enhanced database application is secure enough to be used in a financial environment.

Besides ensuring that program team members can fulfill their current roles and responsibilities, management needs to prepare team participants for the future.

Program team members need to have adequate training and skills to enable them to assume a different role within the same program, or a new role in a future program after the current program's completion.

The offshore experts developing software for the Callitel program will continue to work on other projects and programs once this program is finished.

So as well as ensuring that the program team is a

cohesive unit, the program manager needs to ensure that the team can regroup and take on more challenging roles as the program nears its end. Team members must be able to fulfill a variety of new duties as part of future programs.

In addition to training-related inputs, the Develop Program Team process uses inputs such as:

employee records

A program manager can use employee records to assess whether individuals are suited for a program. For example, an employee record will reveal information about a prospective team member's work background, including any disciplinary problems.

the program management plan

When developing a program team, a program manager can refer to the program management plan to ensure that the cost, time, and skill gains associated with hiring a particular individual as a program team member fit within the program budget, schedule, and skill requirements.

the staffing management plan

Program managers can refer to the staffing management plan when developing a program team to ensure that prospective team members meet the requirements for human resources laid out in the plan.

a roles and responsibilities matrix

The roles and responsibilities matrix identifies all the roles and responsibilities that program team members need to fulfill. A program manager can use the matrix to assess who to assign to a role.

A well-developed program team member is able to assume different roles within the same program, and to take over a role from someone else within the program team when necessary.

Although it is unreasonable to expect that all team members be able to take over from someone else at a moment's notice, team members do need to work closely together and share an understanding of their collective role within the program's execution. This enables teams to contribute significantly to a program and to work together as cohesive units.

Leonard was the leading technical expert of the offshore development team for Callitel's database application program. When Leonard assumed a new role to provide technical support for the marketing division, the developing team was at a loss to decide what to do.

To avoid this, managers at Callitel should have ensured that someone else on the development team had the technical skills to take over from Leonard.

Case Study: Question 1 of 4
Scenario

Mariner Computer Solutions wants to upgrade its web site so that the Customer Support Department can more effectively and efficiently resolve the issues that users of the company's applications experience.

The program manager for the new development takes into account that the program will span several weeks. In addition, people working on the program should ideally have a fixed contract with Mariner Computer Solutions to rule out the possibility of intellectual property issues. The program manager now needs to determine how to apply the Acquire Program Team and Develop Program Team processes.

Answer the questions that follow in order.

Question

The program gets off to a good start, but even before the first milestone review, a coding expert that is supposed to assist the development team is too caught up in another software program – from the Marketing Department – to be of assistance to the team.

What action should management have taken to prevent this?

Options:

1. Extended the duration for which the coding expert was assigned to the team

2. Focused more on internal and external hiring costs than on reaching milestones

3. Ensured that the timing of the program didn't coincide with other programs that team members may have been assigned to

Answer

Option 1: This is an incorrect option. Extending the duration of time the coding expert was assigned to the team would only have set the program's execution back further.

Option 2: This is an incorrect option. Milestones help to ensure that a program is executed on time and within the limited time frame, so they can't be ignored or treated as secondary to costs.

Option 3: This is the correct option. Ensuring that the program was timed well and didn't coincide with other programs that would require the skills of the coding expert at the same time would have prevented the problem.

Case Study: Question 2 of 4

Halfway through, the program falls behind schedule because Tom, the coding expert, has moved to another program. With only two weeks to spare, the program manager knows that the program won't be released on time.

What action should management have taken to prevent this?

Options:

1. Ensured that it knew the length of time that Tom's expert skill would be required

2. Ensured that another team member could take over Tom's role in his absence

3. Ensured that team members were hired only on a fixed-contract basis

4. Limited the possibility of concurrent programs when planning for the program

Answer

Option 1: This is a correct option. By considering the length of time that a skill is required for a program, management could have checked Tom's availability to ensure that it fit within the program schedule.

Option 2: This is a correct option. Ensuring that other staff members or external contractors are available to take over from an absent team member reduces the reliance on a particular individual during the execution of a program.

Option 3: This is an incorrect option. Binding team members to a fixed contract does not guarantee their availability. Unless management ensures that a skilled individual is available for the required length of time, their duties can still coincide with other program activities, thereby causing a delay.

Option 4: This is an incorrect option. Concurrent programs do not pose a problem unless a conflict occurs when a particular individual's skill is required on more than one program at the same time.

Case Study: Question 3 of 4

As a last resort, the program manager considers hiring an external code expert on a temporary basis to make up for Tom's absence from the team. However, management soon realizes that this will cause the program to exceed its budget and schedule.

What action should management have taken to prevent this?

Options:

1. Allowed for more time on the program schedule near the close of the program

2. Considered the costs and availability of hiring external staff to ensure the program does not exceed its budget or schedule

3. Advertised well in advance to source more staff as the program nears its end

Sorin Dumitrascu

4. Considered the availability of using internal human resources with the appropriate skills to replace

Tom on the program

Answer

Option 1: This is an incorrect option. Allocating more time as a program nears its close will only delay it further, unless a need for the delay has been taken into account during the initial planning of the program's schedule.

Option 2: This is a correct option. If adequate personnel with the appropriate skills are unavailable internally, program managers need to hire team members from an external source. By considering the costs of hiring external resources, a program manager can ensure that a program does not exceed its budget or schedule due to lack of funding or insufficient human resources.

Option 3: This is an incorrect option. Having more staff available as a program nears its close does not replace the need to consider the cost of hiring team members during the program's initial planning.

Option 4: This is a correct option. The time at which team members will be needed to assist in a program's execution is important, because it may coincide with times at which internal staff members

– such as Tom in this case – will be tied to working on other programs.

Case Study: Question 4 of 4

The program suffered due to the program manager's lack of skill when acquiring the team. To ensure that the program team's subsequent development is more successful, management has decided to promote Tom, the coding expert, to the position of team lead. Jane, a marketing executive, will also be moved to the marketing solutions program. What must management do to ensure good team development?

Options:

1. Prepare Tom for his new role as the team lead

2. Ensure that Janice, a team member, is ready to take on Jane's duties when she leaves

3. Delegate some of Tom's new duties to Jane

4. Ensure Tom is ready to assist Jane in her new duties

5. Ensure Jane is prepared for her new role in marketing once the program concludes

6. Prepare Simon, a marketing solutions program team member, for a customer service role in the program

Answer

Option 1: This is a correct option. Like Tom,

individuals within the program team need to be prepared to fulfill the role they will be assigned to and to meet the associated responsibilities.

Option 2: This is a correct option. Management should ensure that there is a team member available to take over the role of someone else, in order for the program team's development to be most effective.

Option 3: This is an incorrect option. Delegating some of Tom's responsibilities to another individual is not helpful in developing Tom's skills or in preparing him for future roles that require more responsibility.

Option 4: This is an incorrect option. Tom is not responsible for assisting Jane in her new role – she has to be prepared to fulfill the duties of the new role herself.

Option 5: This is a correct option. Management must ensure that individuals like Jane are prepared to assume different roles once the current program concludes, to assist them in their careers.

Option 6: This is a correct option. Like Simon, individuals in the program team need to be prepared to assume different roles within the same program to make the program team as versatile and effective as possible.

The Request Seller Responses process

An engineering company initiates a program to market its own corporate clothing range. The program's managers prize the rate of production above any other concerns when they select a seller, because they want the clothing to be produced in time to meet their busy program schedule. But because other criteria such as cost, quality, and the value of the clothing are overlooked, the program now runs the risk of failing due to complaints about the low quality of all the products.

When managing a program, it is important to select an appropriate seller, also called a vendor or supplier, from which to acquire a product, benefit, or service that meets the program's needs.

If a program's management uses inappropriate criteria to select a seller, the seller may not necessarily have the required level of experience, skill, or maturity to deliver the program's benefits. If a program's management chooses sellers solely on the basis of price, for instance, the sellers may fail to deliver adequate results in terms of quality.

When managing a program's execution, two formally structured processes in the Executing process group assist in selecting a suitable seller – the Request Seller Responses process and the Select

Sellers process.

During the Request Seller Responses process, management issues a number of requests to obtain formal documents from bidders for a sales contract.

These formal requests are used during the early stages of program execution to help management decide whether or not to buy a product or service from a particular seller. Seller responses also help a program's management to understand the qualifications of sellers bidding on the sales contract.

There are three kinds of requests issued during the Request Seller Responses process:

request for information (RFI)

An RFI is a formal document requesting a seller to supply written information regarding the products, services, or benefits it provides.

A request is submitted as a precursor to a sale, and it is a way to approach a seller without interacting in person or binding either party to a contract or price.

request for proposal (RFP)

An RFP invites a supplier to bid on a specific product or service via a structured bidding process.

A seller typically submits an RFP as a detailed report on how a job will be done and who will be performing the work activities, in an attempt to win the bid of buyers who already have a specific product, service, or benefit in mind.

request for quotation (RFQ)

An RFQ is a request for pricing details, typically issued when a buyer knows the seller and doesn't need to enter into a discussion to debate the deal.

With an RFQ, the price is generally the only determining factor in whether to accept a seller's bid for a product or service, because the buyer already knows all needed facts about the seller.

Management at LangPharma Industries, a pharmaceutical company involved in manufacturing generic drugs and healthcare products, has decided to publish a healthy living brochure in which to advertise the company's range of products.

Because LangPharma doesn't have experience in the publishing field, the company's management embarks on the formal Request Seller Responses and Select Sellers processes to help select the most suitable seller with whom to enter into a sales contract.

As part of the Request Seller Responses and Select Sellers processes, managers at LangPharma need to:

- • stipulate what they expect from the

seller and agree to what sellers expect in
return,

- compile a set of selection criteria and a
  process through which to select,
- the seller negotiate and agree on a suitable
  price for the brochure,
- compile formal legal contracts to satisfy legal
  requirements.

Once LangPharma's management knew what
form it wanted the brochure to take, it initiated the
Request Seller Responses process.

LangPharma's management set the selection
criteria against which prospective sellers' proposals
would be measured to include aspects such as
sellers' technical competency, financial history,
stock availability, and past performance records.

Because LangPharma's managers don't have
experience with key players in the publishing field,
they don't yet have a suitable seller in mind, and
need sellers to submit their proposals to bid for the
sales contract.

The managers decide to evoke seller interest
using an RFI, to obtain the widest range of seller
responses. This way, LangPharma's management
can determine the kinds of products and services
sellers provide in the marketplace without yet
binding the company to a contract, price, or bid.

Program Management

LangPharma's managers allocate sufficient time in which to execute the brochure's release, and this enables them to review all proposals – even those containing a high level of detail. To assist in decision- making, management asked that shortlisted candidates submit RFPs in which they stipulate how they
intend to fulfill the contract.

Once management has assessed all the candidates and has a few potential sellers in mind, they submit RFQs to the shortlisted candidates. Each seller then provides details regarding its range of prices and products to give LangPharma an idea of how suitable its quotation is in terms of the contract and program budget.

With the potential candidates earmarked, decision-makers at LangPharma are confident to continue with the next process in the program's execution – the Select Sellers process.

Question

A software company launches a program that aims to release an expanded range of software packages to the international market to expand the company's market share. Management is looking for a suitable seller to develop the software.

Match each example of a request that the

company makes to sellers with the type of request it represents. Not all examples will be used.

Options:

A. A request for a formal document from each prospective seller, outlining the software products it has developed in the past and its technical capabilities

B. An invitation to suppliers to outline how they plan to fulfill a contract to sell software packages to the company

C. A request for documentation in which prospective sellers provide pricing details about software products development

D. A request for documents in which prospective sellers outline their best and final technical and financial bids for the development contract

Targets:

1. Request for information (RFI)
2. Request for proposal (RFP)
3. Request for quotation (RFQ)

Answer

A request for information (RFI) is typically a formally written document requesting a prospective seller to describe the products, services, and benefits it can provide to meet program requirements.

A request for proposal (RFP) is a document inviting suppliers and sellers to submit proposals, outlining how they plan to fulfill a contract to a buying company.

A request for quotation (RFQ) is a document requesting a seller to submit proposed prices and costs for providing services and products to a buying company.

The Select Sellers process

Once a program's management requests that sellers respond to RFPs, management is ready to start the Select Sellers process.

Activities in the Select Sellers process include:

reviewing proposals from prospective sellers

When reviewing proposals from prospective sellers, a program's management assesses the suitability of each seller's proposal against the criteria a suitable seller is expected to match.

selecting a seller from prospective sellers

Once prospective sellers have been reviewed, a program's management can select a seller from prospective sellers by identifying the candidate most suited to the program's needs.

negotiating contract terms with the selected seller

When negotiating contract terms with a seller, a program's management needs to establish a mutual agreement with the seller in terms of factors such as proprietary rights, financing, technical solutions, schedule, payments, and price. The agreed terms are then stipulated in a contract.

After the selected sellers have been evaluated in

terms of their past performance, risk factors, and other preset criteria, a company's management can recommend a suitable seller to the company's CEO via the program governance body and other program stakeholders.

In the case of LangPharma, the company's management reviews proposals from prospective sellers to find an experienced seller who also has knowledge of the pharmaceutical industry. Because LangPharma wants the brochure's release to coincide with the release of a major drug onto the market, management wants a seller with the technical capability to produce the brochures on time.

At the program level, the Select Sellers process helps program managers to negotiate and finalize program-wide policies and agreements.

For instance, a program's management can establish an agreement with a seller that entitles the buying company to receive a discount for orders it places that exceed a particular volume.

Once the program's managers had reviewed all proposals from sellers, they selected the seller that best met the agreed criteria.

When negotiating the details of the contract, the managers and the seller established an agreement regarding technical terms and conditions, roles and responsibilities, deliverables, and the final cost of the deal.

To conclude the Select Sellers process, LangPharma's management signed a contract with the selected seller.

Question

Identify the activities in the Select Sellers process.

Options:

1. Requesting information from prospective sellers

2. Reviewing sellers' proposals

3. Asking sellers for proposals

4. Selecting the most suitable seller, given a program's objectives

5. Negotiating the terms of a contract

Answer

Option 1: This is an incorrect option. Requesting that prospective sellers submit information regarding the product, services, and benefits they can provide is an activity in the Request Seller Responses process, rather than in the Select Sellers process.

Option 2: This is a correct option. As part of the Select Sellers process, program managers review all proposals received from prospective sellers to determine which seller is most suitable, given specified requirements.

Option 3: This is an incorrect option. Requesting that sellers submit proposals outlining how they plan to fulfill a contract is an activity performed in the Request Seller Responses process, rather than in the Select Sellers process.

Option 4: This is a correct option. Once the submitted proposals have been reviewed, a program's management can assess the results and select the seller that most closely meets the established selection criteria. This activity is an important component of the Select Sellers process.

Option 5: This is a correct option. Once a suitable seller has been selected, a program's management needs to negotiate the contract and sign it with the seller as the final activity in the Select Sellers process.

CHAPTER 6 - Monitoring, Controlling, and Closing

The Monitoring and Controlling process group includes processes for obtaining and analyzing data from all the projects that make up a program, and for acting on this data where necessary to improve program success.

It's important to monitor and control a program to gain a clear picture of the program's benefit delivery status and to ensure that the program is modified when necessary, that program resources are allocated correctly across projects, and that the program stays within its budget.

The Resource Control process of the Monitoring and Controlling process group involves managing the human, non-consumable, and consumable resources for a program. Activities involved in this process include monitoring human resources to ensure commitment to the requirements of the program, monitoring both consumable and non-consumable resources to control expenditure, and allocating expenses between the program, components, and other contributing functions within an organization.

The Integrated Change Control process is for managing any changes to a program. It involves approving or rejecting requests for change based on whether the change is necessary, it's likely effects on a program in terms of cost, quality, schedule, and scope, and whether it will improve or reduce the chances of successful program completion.

The Monitoring and Controlling Program Work process involves collecting, measuring, and consolidating performance data about all the projects and activities that make up a program in order to assess how well the program as a whole is performing.

The Issue Management and Control process involves recording and reviewing program-level issues, escalating program issues to ensure they're resolved, and addressing unresolved issues escalated from constituent projects.

The Scope Control process involves controlling any requests for changes to the scope of a program. Activities it includes are recording and evaluating requested changes, determining the disposition of requested changes, communicating decisions to program stakeholders, archiving the change requests, and incorporating agreed changes in the program management plan.

The Schedule Control process involves tracking the commencement and completion of program activities, tracking important program events, and updating the schedule management plan to reflect progress.

The Cost Control process involves monitoring and controlling the cost of a program, to ensure it remains within budget and to identify opportunities for returning allocated funds to an enterprise.

The Performance Quality Control process involves monitoring and controlling the quality of program results and of program management, and removing sources of quality problems.

The Communications Control process involves ensuring that policies and procedures are recorded and conveyed to stakeholders. It also involves handling communications with stakeholders and resolving program issues that affect them.

The final three processes in the Monitoring and Controlling process group are the Program Performance Reporting process, the Risk Monitoring and Control process, and the Program Contract Administration process.

The Program Performance Reporting process is used to report on the program's performance to the stakeholders.

The Risk Monitoring and Control process defines how to track identified risks, identify new risks, and create and implement effective risk response plans.

The program management team uses the Program Contract Administration process to manage the relationship between sellers and buyers – as stipulated in legal contracts – at the program level.

The closing team implements three processes in the Closing process group – Component Closure, Contract Closure, and Close Program – to bring the program to an orderly end.

These processes enable the closing team to meet closure agreements, generate lessons learned, ensure that projects are closed properly and that all records are archived, and ensure that all contractual agreements are met.

The Closing process group consists of three processes – the Component Closure process, the Contract Closure process, and the Close Program process.

The Component Closure process and Contract Closure process occur at project and program levels. During the program-level Component Closure process, the closing team ensures that all projects and non-project activities in a program are properly closed and documented. During the program-level Contract Closure process, the team ensures that all contracts executed during the program are closed.

Once these two processes are complete, the closing team can close the program. During the Close Program process, the team gains acceptance for the program's outcome and achieves client or customer sign-off. This formally brings the program to an end.

Monitoring and controlling a program

In program management, the Monitoring and Controlling process group includes processes for obtaining data about the status of an existing program or a program package, and for acting on this data to optimize program success.

The Monitoring and Controlling process group enables managers to assess the current benefit delivery and projected future benefits of the combined projects that make up a program.

It ensures that programs – rather than only the individual projects of which they're composed – can be controlled and that preventive and corrective actions can be taken as required.

Five of the processes included in the Monitoring and Controlling process group relate to managing change, resources, work, issues, and scope at the program level.

Integrated Change Control

Integrated Change Control is the process of implementing changes to the program as a whole. These changes may relate to quality, schedule, scope, and cost.

Resource Control

Resource Control is the process of monitoring

and controlling the various resources – including human, non-consumable, and consumable resources – involved in the program.

Monitoring and Controlling Program Work

Monitoring and Controlling Program Work is the process of collecting and appraising performance data and – based on this data – of developing improvements to the program.

Issue Management and Control

Issue Management and Control entails identifying and resolving any problems that arise with the program. This may include issues that could not be resolved at the project level and so must be addressed at the program level.

Scope Control

Scope Control is the process of controlling requested changes to the scope of the program.

The Monitoring and Controlling process group includes an additional seven processes.

Schedule Control

Schedule Control is concerned with ensuring that the program's objectives are met within the scheduled time.

Cost Control

Cost Control is the process of controlling the

program budget, and of analyzing the consequences of any budget changes.

Performance Quality Control

Performance Quality Control involves monitoring the extent to which a program is meeting the objectives and quality requirements specified for it.

Communications Control

Communications Control is the process of ensuring that stakeholders are informed about the program's status and about any issues that pertain to their interests in the program.

Performance Reporting

Performance Reporting is the process of consolidating data related to program performance and conveying this information to stakeholders.

Risk Monitoring and Control

Risk Monitoring and Control involves monitoring risks that have been identified, recognizing other potential risks, and implementing risk response plans.

Program Contract Administration

Program Contract Administration involves handling the relationship with sellers and buyers at the program level. It includes the procurement of external resources needed for the entire program, rather than for specific projects only.

Importance of monitoring and controlling

It's important to properly monitor and control a program to ensure that:

- • you have a clear picture of the program's current benefit delivery status,
- you can modify the program as needed,
- you can properly allocate program resources,
- you follow the budget for the program.

The benefits of proper monitoring and controlling apply to individual projects, as well as to programs as a whole.

However, monitoring and controlling individual projects is an aspect of effective project management, rather than of total program management. It involves ensuring that projects are executed in line with their individual project management plans, rather than focusing on a full program – which may include multiple projects.

Poseidon Bank is a financial services provider. Through its mortgage program, it provides services for both residential and business clients.

Using processes in the Monitoring and Controlling process group, the company's managers develop a clear picture of the program's current benefit delivery status. They determine the returns on the residential and business mortgage projects, and identify areas in which the program is falling short of targets.

After collating data about the residential and business mortgage projects, Poseidon's managers are able to determine how the mortgage program should be modified. They identify a need to manage external data sources for the program better, to eliminate data entry errors in residential mortgage applications, and to increase the speed of the loan servicing procedure.

Using the Monitoring and Controlling process group, the managers are also able to determine how best to allocate program resources. For example, they decide to redistribute the budget to invest in an automated item processing system for the residential mortgage project, to improve speed and eliminate manual errors.

By monitoring and controlling the mortgage program, Poseidon's managers are able to keep to the budget for the program. They monitor program costs and, when necessary, take corrective action.

Through processes in the Monitoring and Controlling process group, managers at Poseidon determined how best to reduce costs, delivery times, and errors, while improving the value of the mortgage program to the company and its clients.

Question

You are a program manager at a large pharmaceutical company. You manage a research and development program that includes multiple projects for the development of new drugs.

Why is it important for you to monitor and control this program properly?

Options:

1. To ensure that project expenditure is in line with the allocated budget for research and development

2. To ensure that the program is modified when necessary

3. To ensure that all the projects are executed in line with their project management plans

4. To gain a clear picture of whether the program is delivering the expected benefits

5. To provide feedback between each phase of the individual development projects

6. To ensure resources are allocated optimally across the drug development projects

Answer

Option 1: This is a correct option. Proper monitoring and controlling enables the company to ensure that the program stays within the budget allocated for drug research and development. It enables you to allocate the available budget effectively and, when necessary, to take corrective action before program costs exceed the budget.

Option 2: This is a correct option. Properly monitoring and controlling the program enables you to identify any discrepancies between the program's targets and its actual benefit delivery, and to modify the program as necessary to address these discrepancies.

Option 3: This is an incorrect option. The execution of projects in line with their project management plans is a function of project management, rather than of program management, which focuses on performance across all projects in a program.

Option 4: This is a correct option. Monitoring the program ensures that you know the benefits it's having, and can compare these to the expected, required benefits. Where shortfalls exist, managers can then take corrective action.

Option 5: This is an incorrect option. Providing feedback between project phases is a function of project management, rather than of program management. Program management is concerned with how projects relate to each other and with their combined performance, instead of with how project phases relate to each other.

Option 6: This is a correct option. By monitoring

and controlling the program, you are able to determine whether resources are being allocated appropriately across the various projects, and to reallocate resources where necessary.

In this lesson, you will learn about the processes in the Monitoring and Controlling process group and their roles in successful program management.

Resource control

The Resource Control process of the Monitoring and Controlling process group is the process of managing all the resources for a program.

It also involves managing the costs associated with program resources, in line with the program management plan.

Three types of program resources need to be monitored and controlled.

Human resources

Human resources must be monitored and controlled to ensure that enough employees with sufficient skills are committed to meet the requirements of the program.

Human resources should be assigned and released from the program in accordance with the program's management plan.

Non-consumable resources

Non-consumable resources are fixed resources such as software programs, laboratories, office space, vehicles, and various types of equipment.

Non-consumable resources that are purchased must be monitored so that once they are no longer needed for a program, they are sold or made available for use elsewhere.

Resources that are leased also need to be monitored so that they are returned once they are no longer required or the lease has expired. This avoids unnecessary expenditure.

Consumable resources

Consumable resources are resources such as office supplies that are used up during the course of a program and, therefore, need to be replaced. These resources must be monitored as an expense.

Consider Gleeson Associates, an IT company that provides computer products, services, and solutions.

One of Gleeson Associates' key resources is its consulting personnel. Controlling this resource is essential to ensure that the right personnel – with appropriate skills and expertise – are assigned within the company's programs.

By monitoring where its personnel are located and their skills, the company can assign consultants to clients efficiently, thus reducing unnecessary expenditure.

Gleeson Associates has two offices – one in New York and one in Boston. The office premises in each location comprise part of the company's non-consumable resources. The costs associated with these resources – including the lease agreements for the office premises – must be monitored and controlled.

The company's consumable resources include the money it spends to run its operations, as well as resources such as office supplies. The company monitors the expenditure associated with these resources to ensure that it is in line with the budget.

The activities involved in monitoring and controlling resources include

- • monitoring human resources to ensure commitment to the requirements of the program,
- monitoring non-consumable resources to control expenditure,
- monitoring consumable resources as expenses,
- allocating expenses between program, component, and other contributing functions within an organization.

Blastara is an event-planning company that organizes functions.

Within its event-planning program, Blastara monitors and controls the following resource types:

human resources
The company allocates its human resources

according to where they are needed within the program. Certain staff members handle phone bookings for events, while others deal with catering, venue booking, and decor. Depending on the status of each project within the program, the company controls where it utilizes its staff members in the program.

non-consumable resources

The company's non-consumable resources include the venues that it hires for functions, its office premises, and equipment. It monitors the hiring of the venues, ensuring that once they are no longer needed, they are returned promptly to avoid added expenditure. Similarly, it monitors the leasing of its office premises and equipment.

consumable resources

The company's consumable resources include its promotional advertising through flyers and posters, the money it spends to run its operations – for example on phone calls – and the various supplies needed to run its office. The company monitors these resources as expenses and ensures that they are controlled according to the program's budget.

allocating expenses

Through monitoring its various resources, the company controls how it allocates expenses within the program and across the various operations that make up the organization.

Question

Consider Drive Easy, a car rental agency.

What activities will management at Drive Easy perform when controlling the company's program resources?

Options:

1. Allocating staff members within various departments according to program needs

2. Monitoring the costs of servicing the company's fleet of vehicles

3. Developing improvements to the program

4. Holding regular budget meetings to allocate expenses across the company

5. Accounting for costs associated with outlet premises

6. Holding regular meetings to ensure that program objectives are met in the scheduled time

Answer

Option 1: This is a correct option. The company monitors where its human resources are allocated within the program so that sufficient resources can be committed to meet program requirements.

Option 2: This is a correct option. The Resource Control process includes controlling consumable resources – such as the parts and materials used in servicing Drive Easy's fleet of vehicles – and the associated costs. These must be monitored and controlled as expenses.

Option 3: This is an incorrect option. Developing improvements to a program is an activity involved in the Monitoring and Controlling Program Work process, rather than the Resource Control process.

Option 4: This is a correct option. The company monitors how it allocates its resources across the program and the various components and functions of the organization to ensure that associated expenses are identified and distributed appropriately.

Option 5: This is a correct option. The company's outlets are one of its non-consumable resources. The costs associated with maintaining this resource – such as network administration and lease agreements – are expenses that must be monitored and controlled.

Option 6: This is an incorrect option. Monitoring whether program objectives are met is an activity in the Schedule Control process, rather than in the Resource Control process.

Integrated change control

The Integrated Change Control process of the Monitoring and Controlling process group is a continuous process that involves controlling any changes to a program across the program as a whole. These changes may include changes to cost, quality, schedule, and scope.

Consider Margaret's description of what happened in her company's program.

"I'm a manager at Award Sportswear, a clothing manufacturer that specializes in producing casual sportswear. Recently, we were asked to change our manufacturing process on one particular production line because the demand for a product had increased.

It seems that changes to this production line negatively impacted a few of our other production lines, and they haven't been meeting their deadlines."

Margaret's company lacks program-level change control. As a result, the changes it implemented in one area had negative effects on other parts of its program.

The functions of the Integrated Change Control process are to enable managers to

- • determine whether to approve or refuse requests for change,
- escalate requests for change that require more senior authorization in line with authority thresholds,
- determine when changes have occurred,
- influence factors that create changes,
- ensure that changes are beneficial and agreed,
- manage how and when approved changes are implemented.

The inputs for the Integrated Change Control process include requests or prompts for change from program-level activities, components, and non-project activities. The outputs result from the actions taken in response.

Inputs

Possible inputs for the Integrated Change Control process include change requests, performance reports, program management plans, the program scope statement, and the cost management plan. They also include recommended corrective or preventive actions.

Outputs

Possible outputs from the Integrated Change Control process include either approved or rejected change requests, updates to the program management plan or to the program scope statement, and a change register. They also include modified project priorities and updates to the benefits realization plan for the program.

When a request for change is put forward, it must be analyzed. The work that will result because of the change must be identified, estimated, and documented.

This includes determining which of the other program management processes will have to be carried out again as a result of the change. For example, a change may make it necessary to revise the program risk register or to update the program work breakdown structure (PWBS).

When determining whether or not to approve a request for change during the Integrated Change Control process, you should consider the following key questions:

- • Should the change be implemented?
- What cost will the change have in relation to project constraints?
- Will the benefits gained by making the change increase or decrease the chances of program completion?

Consider Award Sportswear's situation again. To

Sorin Dumitrascu

successfully implement the change to their program, managers at the company should have:

considered whether or not to implement the change

A significant part of the Integrated Change Control process is to determine whether or not to implement the change that has been requested. This decision should be based on the cost of the change to the program and on an analysis of the benefits of making the change.

Award Sportswear's management should have started by questioning whether a change to the production line was necessary for the functioning of the program, and whether the results of the change would be sufficiently beneficial to warrant the change.

determined the cost of the change to the project

If a change is approved, the cost of the change to the project in terms of its constraints – including cost, time, scope, and quality – must be considered.

In the case of Award Sportswear, management did not think about how the change to one production line would affect the quality of other product lines or the time constraints of meeting other deadlines.

538

analyzed the benefits of making the change

Managers need to analyze the benefits of making the change to ascertain whether they will increase or decrease the chances of successfully completing the program.

The change that Award Sportswear's management implemented affected the success of other projects. Although focusing resources and attention on the clothing line that was in high demand was beneficial to the success of that clothing line, it impacted negatively on other production lines.

Question

Earthfarm is a manufacturer of natural and organic food and beauty products. A proposal is made to change the labeling of the company's beauty products.

What are the questions that managers should consider as part of the Integrated Change Control process?

Options:

1. How costly will the change to the labeling be in terms of program costs, time, quality, and scope?

2. Will new labeling improve the success of the company's project for marketing beauty products?

3. Will the benefits gained from new labeling

improve the success of the company's program for delivering competitive beauty and food products?

4. Should the change to the labeling be implemented? 5. How can the request for modified labeling be denied?

Answer

Option 1: This is a correct option. Managers at Earthfarm need to consider how the proposed labeling change will impact on the company's program as a whole, given the program's constraints. These constraints include cost, time, scope, and quality. If the change will impact the program negatively – for example by preventing adequate investment in other program areas – the request for the change should be refused.

Option 2: This is an incorrect option. The Integrated Change Control process is designed to enable managers to monitor and control changes to a program. Each time a request for change is put forward, it should be considered in relation to the program as a whole, rather than only in relation to a particular project.

Option 3: This is a correct option. The Integrated Change Control process involves determining whether a proposed change will have beneficial or negative effects for a program as a whole. So Earthfarm's managers need to consider how a change to the labeling for the company's beauty products will impact all projects – including those related to food products – in the company's program.

Option 4: This is a correct option. The first question that managers at Earthfarm need to consider is whether the change to product labeling should be implemented, based on the likely benefits and on the impact of the change for the company's program.

Option 5: This is an incorrect option. The aim of the Integrated Change Control process is to enable managers to determine whether to approve or reject a request for change, based on how the change will affect a program as a whole. The process isn't designed to help managers reject requests for change they've already identified as unsuitable.

Monitoring and controlling program work

The Monitoring and Controlling Program Work process involves analyzing the performance of each project and non-project activity included in a program to obtain an assessment of how well the program as a whole is performing.

The process enables program managers to identify required changes and improvements to a program, and to report on program performance.

The focus of this process is similar to risk management – but instead of dealing with risks, it is concerned with performance.

Activities involved in the Monitoring and Controlling Program Work process include:

collecting performance information

The first step in the process is collecting performance information about each of the projects comprising a program, as well as about non-project components and deliverables that form part of the program.

measuring performance information

Once data has been gathered, the next step is measuring the performance information that has been collected. This information is analyzed to obtain an overall picture of the performance of the projects and other activities that make up the program.

This activity enables program managers to identify any conflicts between the various projects and non-project components that need to be rectified. It also enables managers to recognize opportunities for development and improvements.

consolidating performance information

The final step in the process is consolidating the performance information derived from the projects making up the program and from other program-level activities. This involves generating a report on each project's performance and then collating all the reports at the program level to provide an overall picture of the progress and performance of the program.

Once the performance information is consolidated, it can be made available to stakeholders through the Information Distribution process.

The inputs of the Monitoring and Controlling Program work process are performance reports, the program management plan, the program benefits statement, and the communications management plan.

The outputs include change requests, forecasts,

and communications with program stakeholders.

Consider Enterprises Now, a real estate development company. To monitor and control program work, program managers begin by collecting performance information about each of the company's development projects and about non-project activities related to the program.

The managers then measure the performance information. They analyze it to identify trends and possible improvements, and to determine how well each development project is meeting program targets.

Through this process, a need to reallocate human resources – from a housing development project coming to a close to another project in the initial phases of development – becomes clear. The process of addressing the need is then put into motion.

As the final step, the program managers consolidate the performance data from the different projects and activities, and use the consolidated data to create a report on the performance of the company's program. The relevant information can then be distributed to the program stakeholders.

Question

Which activities are involved in the Monitoring

and Controlling Program Work process?

Options:

1. Consolidating performance information
2. Evaluating each requested change to the program
3. Collecting performance information
4. Allocating expenditure across an organization
5. Measuring performance information

Answer

Option 1: This is a correct option. Once performance information about the projects and non-project deliverables included in a program has been collected and analyzed, the information must be consolidated to provide an overall picture of the performance of the program.

Option 2: This is an incorrect option. Evaluating requests for change is an activity in the Integrated Change Control process, rather than in the Monitoring and Controlling Program Work process.

Option 3: This is a correct option. As the first step in the Monitoring and Controlling Program Work process, performance information about each of the projects and about other activities in a program must be gathered. The information can then be analyzed and collated.

Option 4: This is an incorrect option. Allocating expenditure is an activity in the Resource Control process, rather than in the Monitoring and Controlling Program Work process.

Option 5: This is a correct option. Once performance data has been collected, it must be measured to determine how the performance of the projects and non-project activities in a program relate to program targets and overall performance. This activity enables program managers to identify any conflicts between program components and any opportunities for development.

Issue management and control

The Issue Management and Control process involves recognizing, tracing, and resolving issues not resolved at project level so that program activities and deliverables align with stakeholders' expectations. To achieve this alignment, program requirements, program scope, and organizational policies may be modified. Alternatively, stakeholders' expectations may be changed.

The Issue Management and Control process works alongside the process of controlling risk, particularly where risks are not dealt with at the project level and are escalated to the program level.

The activities involved in the Issue Management and Control process include:

recording issues in an issues register

An activity of the Issue Management and Control process is recording issues in an issues register. A reviewing body then analyzes these issues. conducting issue reviews

There should be a schedule that allows for regular issue reviews by the reviewing body. These reviews must be conducted regularly to monitor the progress of all pending issues.

escalating unresolved program issues

Sorin Dumitrascu

If an issue at the program level is not resolved, it must be escalated further up the scale of authority within the program until it is resolved. Each issue must be assigned to an individual with the appropriate level of authority who is responsible for resolving the issue. That individual must have the requisite authority to do so.

addressing unresolved issues escalated from constituent projects

The Issue Management and Control process deals with issues that could not be resolved at the project level. Procedures and a governance process must be put in place to selectively focus on unresolved issues escalated from constituent projects. This ensures that issues are given visibility and that their potential impact across projects can be monitored.

The inputs of the Issue Management and Control process are an issues register, performance reports, the program management plan, and work results.

The outputs are requests for change, escalated issues, an updated issues register, and proposed resolutions.

Consider Enterprises Now, the real estate development company. An issue arose when it was discovered that the site on which a commercial

548

building was being constructed contained more underground water than was initially reported in surveys.

This led to complications when laying the foundations, which resulted in more time and additional resources being used. The issue was escalated to the program level because it had far-reaching implications for the company's development program as a whole.

Program managers at Enterprises Now recorded and kept track of the issue using the Issue Management and Control process. The scope of the program had to be adjusted, and program stakeholders were informed of the issue and its projected impact on the deliverables of the project.

Because the issue was unforeseen, the company had to change stakeholders' expectations to align with a realistic time frame for meeting the project requirements.

Question

Which activities are involved in the Issue Management and Control process?

Options:

1. Resolving issues at the project level
2. Escalating unresolved program issues
3. Recording issues in an issues register

4. Addressing unresolved issues escalated from constituent projects

5. Evaluating requests for change

6. Conducting issue reviews

Answer

Option 1: This is an incorrect option. The Issue Management and Control process involves managing and resolving issues at the program level, rather than at project level. Issues that can't be resolved at project level may be escalated and then dealt with through this process.

Option 2: This is a correct option. If an issue at the program level cannot be resolved, it must be escalated up the scale of authority within the program until it can be resolved.

Option 3: This is a correct option. Any unresolved issues that may impact on the program must be recorded in an issues register so that they can be monitored and traced.

Option 4: This is a correct option. If an issue cannot be resolved at project level, it must be referred for resolution at the program level.

Option 5: This is an incorrect option. Evaluating requests for change is an activity in the Integrated Change Control process, rather than in the Issue Management and Control process.

Option 6: This is a correct option. A reviewing

body must regularly review the issues recorded in the issues register in order to track the progress of each issue and ensure that it is resolved.

Scope control

The scope of a program refers to the extent of the work that must be performed to deliver the program's intended results.

The Scope Control process involves controlling any changes made to the scope of a program. Activities involved in the Scope Control process include:

capturing requested changes to program scope

The first activity in the Scope Control process is capturing requested changes to program scope. Any requested changes must be recorded using a formalized change control system to ensure that change requests carry through the appropriate channels.

evaluating requested changes to program scope

The second step in the process is evaluating requested changes to program scope. An evaluating body must determine whether each requested change to project scope is necessary and should be implemented.

determining the disposition of each requested change

Program Management

After evaluating requested changes to program scope, the evaluating body must determine the disposition of each requested change. The disposition of a requested change refers to the potential of the change to require further, larger changes.

communicating decisions to change program scope to stakeholders

If the decision is made to accept a request for change to the scope of a program, it's necessary to communicate the decision to program stakeholders. Each decision should be recorded, backed up with documented analysis, and presented to stakeholders.

archiving accepted change requests

Once a requested change is accepted, it must be archived, together with supporting details. This information can then be referred to at a later stage, during program performance reviews.

incorporating changes to program scope in the program management plan

After a request for change to the scope of a program is accepted, it must be incorporated in the program management plan. All related documentation must be updated, and stakeholders must be informed of the change.

The inputs of the Scope Control process are

change requests, the scope management plan, the program scope statement, the program work breakdown structure (PWBS), the program budget, the program schedule, and performance reports.

The outputs are approved or rejected change requests, updates to the program budget, and change request status communications.

At Enterprises Now – the real estate development company – a manager suggests that all housing units currently in development be redesigned to comply with pending legislation. The legislation requires that each housing unit support reasonable structural modifications for accommodating people with disabilities. Examples of reasonable structural modifications include the installation of ramps, the lowering of entry thresholds, and the installation of grab bars in bathrooms.

If accepted, this change will alter the scope of the company's existing development program.

Program managers at Enterprises Now performed each of the following activities in the Scope Control process to manage the requested change:

capturing the requested change
First, the program managers captured the

requested change to the designs of housing units using the formalized change control process for the program.

evaluating the requested change

An evaluating body evaluated the request for change to determine whether the change should be implemented. The body decided that the change to the program's scope should be implemented to ensure compliance with pending minimum building requirements for housing units.

determining the disposition of the requested change

The evaluating body determined the disposition of the requested change. It identified more changes required when altering the designs of housing units, and evaluated the repercussions – including longer development times and higher costs for the company's development program.

communicating a decision to stakeholders

Once the evaluating body had accepted the change and determined its disposition, project managers communicated the decision and its expected repercussions to program stakeholders. This ensured that stakeholders' expectations changed in accordance with the intended change to the scope of the company's program.

archiving the change request and supporting

details

After communicating the decision to stakeholders, program managers archived the request for change and supporting documentation for inclusion in subsequent reviews.

initiating the activities required to incorporate the change to program scope

Finally, project managers incorporated the change to program scope in the program management plan to cover all required planning, and to ensure that the company's program satisfied the new minimum building requirements.

Question

Which activities are involved in the Scope Control process?

Options:

1. Updating the program management plan

2. Escalating unresolved program issues

3. Evaluating each requested change to the scope

4. Communicating scope changes to stakeholders

5. Identifying initial program scope

6. Determining the disposition of the requested change to program scope

7. Capturing requested changes to program scope

8. Archiving requested changes to program scope

Answer

Option 1: This is a correct option. Once a change to program scope has been accepted, the activities that must be carried out to implement the change must be reflected in the program management plan, and all documentation must be updated.

Option 2: This is an incorrect option. Escalating unresolved program issues is an activity in the Issue Management and Control process, rather than in the Scope Control process.

Option 3: This is a correct option. An evaluating body evaluates the proposed change and determines whether it is necessary and beneficial to implement it.

Option 4: This is a correct option. Once a change has been approved, the decision to proceed with it must be communicated to program stakeholders. The decision should be backed up with supporting documentation and analysis.

Option 5: This is an incorrect option. The Scope Control process involves controlling changes to the scope of a program, rather than identifying its initial scope – which will have been defined before work on the project started.

Option 6: This is a correct option. Part of the

task of an evaluating body is to determine the disposition of the requested change to program scope. This involves identifying what further changes will have to be made to accommodate it.

Option 7: This is a correct option. Once a request for change to the scope of a program is put forward, it should be recorded using a formalized change control system to ensure that the request carries through to the appropriate channels.

Option 8: This is a correct option. If a requested change to program scope is accepted, it must be archived together with supporting details. This information can then be referred to during program reviews.

Schedule control and cost control

The Schedule Control process works alongside the other program processes in the Monitoring and Controlling process group to ensure that program deliverables are produced on time.

The process identifies where deliverables are not being produced in the scheduled time and also recognizes opportunities to pursue within the program.

Activities involved in the Schedule Control process include

tracking the commencement and completion of program activities

tracking important program events according to the schedule management plan updating the schedule management plan

Inputs for the Schedule Control process include performance reports, the program and project schedules, the schedule management plan, and schedule information requests. They also include earned value performance, the earned value scorecard, and forecasts.

Outputs from the Schedule Control process include change requests, information for stakeholders, and updates to the schedule management plan.

Enterprises Now is a large real estate development company that develops commercial and residential property. Multiple development projects make up its program. Schedule Control is essential for the company so that it can monitor program deliverables and ensure they are produced on time.

Program managers at Enterprises Now follow the Schedule Control process by:

tracking the start and end of program activities

Enterprises Now's program managers track the start and end of program activities – such as conveyance and legal research – in the program work breakdown structure (PWBS) to ensure that program deliverables are produced on time.

tracking important program events

The program managers track important program events to ensure that they align with the schedule management plan. Important program events are those that relate to the deliverables and benefits of the program – for example the completion of development projects.

updating the schedule management plan

The program managers update the schedule management plan so that the progress of all the company's development projects can be tracked and compared to the original schedule. Managers can monitor if the program is on schedule, adjust the schedule where needed, and decide when stakeholders need to be informed of schedule changes.

The Cost Control process controls any changes to the program budget and enables budget reporting and monitoring.

The aims of the process are to ensure that a program remains within its budget and to identify opportunities to return funds allocated to the program to the enterprise.

Activities in the Cost Control process include:

monitoring and controlling actual costs in relation to budgeted costs

A proactive activity in the Cost Control process is monitoring and controlling actual costs in relation to budgeted costs. This enables program managers to identify and address any areas in which planned costs are being exceeded.

The process also involves trend analysis so that problem areas can be predicted and prevented from negatively impacting the program.

monitoring and controlling unplanned costs

Sorin Dumitrascu

A reactive activity in the Cost Control process is monitoring and controlling unplanned costs that affect the program budget.

This involves accounting for and minimizing the costs of unforeseen program activities to ensure that the program remains within its budget.

Inputs for the Cost Control process include the program budget, the actual costs of non-project activities, the cost management plan and cost performance reports, earned value performance, and expenditure forecasts.

Outputs from the process include change requests, cost estimates, updates to the program budget, and variance reports.

As a proactive activity in the Cost Control process, program managers at Enterprises Now monitor the company's real estate and marketing costs to identify where these costs have deviated from the planned costs in the program budget. They also control these costs, to prevent the total budget from being exceeded.

In addition, the program managers analyze real estate trends and interest rates to predict their likely future effects on the program costs and budget.

As a reactive activity in the Cost Control process, the program managers monitor and control unplanned costs. For example, they adjust the program budget to account for the costs involved in complying with new building legislation – costs that weren't foreseen when the program budget was first developed.

Question

Poseidon Bank is a financial services provider. It provides services for residential and business clients through its mortgage program.

Match the Schedule Control and Cost Control processes to the activities Poseidon's program managers monitor. You may use each process more than once.

Options:

A. Schedule Control

B. Cost Control

Targets:

1. Tracking important program events

2. Analyzing actual program costs in relation to budgeted costs

3. Updating a plan so that program progress can be assessed

4. Accounting for unplanned events in the program budget

5. Tracking the start and completion of program activities

Sorin Dumitrascu

Answer

In addition to tracking the start and completion of program activities, the Schedule Control process includes tracking important program events to ensure that they align with the schedule management plan. Important program events are those that relate directly to the deliverables and benefits of the program.

A proactive activity in the Cost Control process is monitoring and controlling actual program costs in relation to planned costs accounted for in the program budget. This activity also includes analyzing trends to predict and account for future costs.

Updating the schedule management plan is an activity in the Schedule Control process. The plan must be updated so that it reflects the progress of the projects that constitute a program and so that required changes to the schedule can be identified and implemented.

In addition to accounting for actual costs in relation to planned costs, the Cost Control process involves accounting for unforeseen costs that affect a program budget. These costs should be controlled, and – when necessary – the budget may have to be adjusted.

One activity in the Schedule Control process is

Program Management

tracking the commencement and completion of program activities in relation to the schedule management plan to ensure that the program stays on schedule.

Quality and communications control

The Performance Quality Control process is a continuous process for ensuring that the results of a program meet quality requirements.

Activities in the Performance Quality Control process include:

monitoring the quality of program results

The Performance Quality Control process involves continuously monitoring program results to ensure that they meet quality requirements in a quality management plan. It continues from when program requirements are identified through to assessment of whether these requirements have been satisfied.

Program results may include products and services, management results, and cost and schedule performance. The Performance Quality Control process ensures that any defective or inadequate outcomes are detected so that the causes for the problems can be addressed.

monitoring the health of project management

In addition to monitoring the quality of program deliverables, the Performance Quality Control process involves monitoring the health of project management to ensure it meets quality requirements.

Reviewing project management is important because of the central role it plays in the quality of project results and, therefore, in program success.

removing the sources of quality problems

Once quality problems or inadequacies are detected in program results at any stage of the quality loop, the Performance Quality Control process involves removing the sources of the quality problems.

This may, for example, involve adjusting an existing procedure or even eliminating a problematic project or program component.

Inputs for the Performance Quality Control process include a quality management plan, quality checklists, work results, and performance reports.

Outputs for the Performance Quality Control process include change requests, completed quality checklists, inspection reports, identified non-conforming work products, test result reports, and measuring results.

Program managers at Enterprises Now – the real estate development company – monitor the quality of program results and the quality of project management on a regular basis. This enables them to identify and address any quality problems.

Through quality monitoring, the program managers discovered that units in one of the company's residential development projects were not selling well due to a poorly planned marketing strategy. The marketing strategy was then reviewed and changed.

The Communications Control process is for managing communications with stakeholders. Activities included in this process are:

monitoring the receipt and recording of policies and procedures

All corporate policies and procedures relating to constituent projects are recorded and monitored by the Program Management Office (PMO) to ensure that they're accessible and that all program activities comply with them.

The policies and procedures are conveyed to the necessary recipients through the Information Distribution process.

conveying policies and procedures to stakeholders

Program policies and procedures must be conveyed to stakeholders to ensure they know the parameters in which project activities occur.

managing program issues and public relations with stakeholders

Program Management

The Communications Control process includes managing program issues and public relations with stakeholders through clear and effective communication. This ensures that stakeholders receive appropriate information, given their interests in a program.

The process may also involve resolving program issues that affect stakeholders' interests.

The inputs for the Communications Control process include approved requests for change, the communications management plan, management directives, performance reports, and the stakeholder analysis chart.

The output of the process is a communications management plan.

Program managers at Enterprises Now manage communications with stakeholders by following the Communications Control process.

Monitoring the receipt and recording of policies and procedures

The company's PMO maintains corporate policies and procedures, including particular real estate and legal compliance policies. The PMO also monitors the policies and procedures to ensure compliance with them.

Ensuring that policies and procedures are conveyed to stakeholders

The program managers ensure that the recorded corporate policies and procedures are conveyed to the appropriate stakeholders. They also communicate any changes to policies to stakeholders. This prevents any misunderstandings and ensures that stakeholders' expectations align with Enterprises Now's operations.

Handling issues and public relations relating to programs

Enterprises Now's managers need to consider neighboring communities and handle any issues or public relations concerns that arise.

Program managers communicate with residents near the proposed sites for certain industrial development projects to explain how the projects will proceed and how any negative impact on surrounding residential areas will be avoided. To deal with concerns expressed by nearby communities, the managers also initiate a project to build public parks and gardens as boundaries between the industrial and residential areas.

Question

Think back to Poseidon Bank, the financial services provider that provides mortgages to residential and business clients.

Match the Performance Quality Control and Communications Control processes to the activities that Poseidon's program managers monitor. You may use each process more than once.

Options:

A. Performance Quality Control

B. Communications Control

Targets:

1. Monitoring for defective program outcomes

2. Removing sources of quality problems

3. Monitoring the receipt and recording of policies and procedures

4. Handling program issues and public relations with stakeholders

5. Monitoring the health of project management

6. Conveying program policies and procedures to stakeholders

Answer

The Perform Quality Control process involves monitoring the quality of program results to ensure that defective outcomes are identified and addressed. Program results may include products and services, management results, and cost and schedule performance.

An important activity in the Performance Quality Control process is identifying and removing the causes of quality problems in program results. Together with quality monitoring, this activity should occur continuously to ensure that a program complies with quality requirements.

As an activity in the Communications Control process, the PMO must record, maintain, and monitor compliance with all corporate policies and procedures that affect the constituent projects in a program.

The Communications Control process includes handling program issues that affect stakeholders' interests and managing public relations with stakeholders to ensure they receive appropriate information about a program.

The Performance Quality Control process includes reviewing the quality of project management, as well as of program results. This ensures that management weaknesses can be identified and addressed so that they don't have a negative effect on program quality.

As an activity in the Communications Control process, corporate policies and procedures relevant to a program must be conveyed to program stakeholders. This ensures that stakeholders are aware of the parameters within which program activities occur.

Program performance reporting

The Program Performance Reporting process is used to cumulate performance data from the program's projects and non-project activities. The performance data includes how the program's resources are being used to execute the projects and other program activities.

The program's performance data is consolidated into a report that provides general and background information about the program's performance. This report can then be presented to stakeholders via the Information Distribution process.

A number of inputs are required to create the performance reports:

- the program management plan,
- the program's budget,
- the program schedule,
- program performance data and status reports,
- actual work results,
- variance reports.

Outputs from the Program Performance Reporting process include:

- updates to the program's budget,
- forecasts,
- performance reports for stakeholders,
- communication messages.

Sorin Dumitrascu

Fresh Earth is an environmental agency dealing with all aspects of conservation and environmental protection and improvement. Managers at Fresh Earth want to embark on a new program to promote the general public's environmental awareness.

This program involves several projects, including the production of video advertising and the development of consumer literature and a web site.

As part of the Program Performance Reporting process, Catherine, a program manager at Fresh Earth, is reviewing the performance of the projects in the company's program. She first compares the actual expenditure to budgeted expenditure, and realizes that the project managers for the literature and web site projects underspent allocated funds.

While reviewing the project management plans, she notes that there were difficulties with retaining staff members to work on the web site.

While reviewing the schedule for the web site project, she picks up that deadlines were frequently missed, mainly due to the developers redesigning the web site after testing it and after receiving user feedback.

Catherine uses the information she has gathered and the budget and schedule management plans to create variance reports.

Program Management

Catherine uses the variance reports and the other inputs for the Program Performance Reporting process to create a program performance report for Fresh Earth's program stakeholders.

She also updates the budget and – because the goals of the literature and web site projects were achieved – reallocates the available funds to the project for producing video advertising. She uses the schedules and program management plan data to create new forecasts.

Last, she sends out various communication messages – for example to set up meetings with the project managers to determine why there was such a high turnover of staff and to address the design, development, and testing process for the web site.

Question

LangPharma Industries is a company that grows herbs and medicinal plants for bulk sale to other companies. Rosa is the manager of LangPharma Industries' program for identifying and researching new, commercially viable medicinal plants, and for growing and marketing these plants.

Which activity is an example of how Rosa completes the Program Performance Reporting process?

Options:

1. Consolidating performance data about the company's research, horticultural, and marketing projects – and about its non-project activities – in a single report

2. Reporting on how each project team's activities were tracked during the past three months

3. Reporting on how the scope of the program changed when a nationwide franchise ordered stock of a particular plant

4. Collating information about the horticultural project into a report for the program team

Answer

Option 1: This is a correct option. Rosa completes the Program Performance Reporting process by reviewing the performance of all projects and non-project activities included in the program against the management plans, program schedule, and budget. She uses this review to create a consolidated performance report for the program's stakeholders.

Option 2: This is an incorrect option. This is an activity that Rosa would complete during the Schedule Control process. It involves tracking important program events to ensure that they correlate with the schedule management plan.

Option 3: This is an incorrect option. This is an activity that Rosa would complete during the Scope

Control process to establish what work must be performed to achieve the program's goals.

    Option 4: This is an incorrect option. Rosa would complete this activity in the Resource Control process because this activity describes the resources used in the program.

Risk monitoring and control

The Risk Monitoring and Control process involves identifying risks to the success of a program and implementing and assessing solutions to mitigate these risks.

This process is an ongoing one. Ideally, it should be followed throughout the duration of a program to ensure that risk response plans remain appropriate and account for new risks that emerge.

The activities included in the Risk Monitoring and Control process are as follows:

tracking identified program risks

The Risk Monitoring and Control process involves tracking the program risks identified in the risk response plan to monitor any changes to these risks, to ensure that response plans are in effect, and to monitor the effectiveness of actual responses to the risks.

identifying new risks to the program

The Risk Monitoring and Control process includes identifying any new risks to the program and adding these risks to the risk register. New risks are identified by pinpointing any misalignment between identified risks and the actual risks encountered during the program's different phases.

executing risk response plans

The Risk Monitoring and Control process involves managing any developing or existing risks by executing the appropriate risk response plans – including planned response actions and contingency plans.

evaluating the effectiveness of risk response plans

The Risk Monitoring and Control process includes evaluating the effectiveness of risk response plans by completing reviews that detail the program's risk situation, status, and plans, and the effectiveness of ongoing or completed risk responses.

These reviews are used to address any unresolved risks or ineffective response plans, and to update the risk register.

Inputs for the Risk Monitoring and Control process include risk response plans, a list of identified and prioritized risks, a program work breakdown structure (PWBS), performance reports, and the risk register.

Outputs from the process are any change requests and updates to the risk register.

At Fresh Earth, Catherine starts the Risk Monitoring and Control process by tracking risks identified in the risk response plan for her company's program. In consultation with other program and project managers, she confirms that planned responses for each prioritized risk are in effect. She also evaluates how well these responses are working in mitigating the risks.

Next, Catherine identifies any new risks – risks not already identified in the risk response plan – for the program. To do this, she reviews the PWBS and compiled performance reports, and consults with project managers.

Once new risks to the program have been identified, Catherine ensures that appropriate risk response actions are implemented.

She then uses feedback from project managers and performance reports to evaluate whether the responses were effective.

Finally, Catherine uses the information and feedback she has gathered to issue appropriate change requests and to update the risk register for the program.

Question

Rosa, the program manager at LangPharma Industries, is assessing two incidents her field team experienced while conducting clinical trials of an herbal drug in Africa – a flood that caused extensive damage to the team's camp, and a serious allergic reaction one of the participants in the trials had to the test drug.

The project managers focused on the clinical trial risks and not on the field conditions when they created risk response plans.

Match the activities involved in the Risk Monitoring and Control process to examples of her activities during this process.

Options:

A. Tracking identified program risks

B. Identifying new risks to the program

C. Executing risk response plans

D. Evaluating the effectiveness of risk response plans

Targets:

1. The results from the clinical trials, including any emergencies

2. The team's physical work conditions in remote countries and the associated risks

3. The team's response to the allergic reaction and transferring the participant to hospital

4. The team's speed when responding to the medical emergency, and the result of their actions

Answer

To begin, Rosa tracks the program risks already identified. In this case, the results from the clinical trials.

To identify unforeseen program risks, Rosa evaluates the program's performance data. She updates the risk response plan to include new risks – in this case natural disasters.

Part of the Risk Control process is how Rosa's team responds to any risk, given the response actions and contingency plans detailed in the risk response plans.

Rosa evaluates the effectiveness of the risk response plans if any identified risks actually occur. In this case, it's the team's speed in responding to the medical emergency.

Program contract administration

The program management team uses the Program Contract Administration process to manage the relationship between sellers and buyers – as stipulated in legal contracts – at the program level.

This includes managing the procurement of external resources that span the program.

Because this process occurs at the program level, it relies on effective interaction between program and project processes.

Activities in the Program Contract Administration process include:

managing the buyer and seller relationship

Program managers use the Program Contract Administration process to manage the buyer and seller relationship involved in a program.

This involves ensuring that both parties abide by contract terms and that these terms remain beneficial to the program.

considering any legal, political, and managerial implications

The program management team must consider the legal, political, and managerial implications when managing buyer and seller relationships.

Sorin Dumitrascu

This helps prevent any contractual issues impacting on the program's execution – for example through increased overheads, missed deadlines, or negative publicity.

communicating with stakeholders

The program management team must communicate with stakeholders to receive the inputs required to manage buyer and seller relationships.

The program stakeholders include sponsors, sellers, governing bodies, and the project and other program management teams.

Inputs for the Program Contract Administration process include:
- • contracts with buyers and sellers,
- the contracts management plan,
- the program management plan,
- seller invoices,
- actual work results,
- performance reports.

Outputs from the Program Contract Administration process are:
- • adjustments to resources accounting,
- approved payment requests,
- contract changes,
- program reports,

- change requests,
- communication messages.

Consider Catherine's activities as the program manager for Fresh Earth. Her responsibilities include overseeing the buyer and seller relationships in the development of consumer literature, a web site, and a video project.

For this project, the principal buyer is Fresh Earth's Marketing Department, which has contracted an external agency to create the required content. The agency is the principal seller.

Catherine meets with the project managers to review the buyer and seller contract. The review focuses on ensuring that the responsibilities and contractual obligations stipulated in the contract align to the project's goals. Then she reviews whether these responsibilities and obligations were met and how they were met.

Based on this review, she determines whether any contractual amendments are necessary to account for any changes in the project's goals or work requirements.

Catherine uses this review to help her address any of the legal and managerial implications arising from the contracts. For example, she determines the impact of the Marketing Department's delay in sending a draft of the consumer brochure to an agency for the final write-up. She then issues any necessary change requests.

She also checks the agency's invoices to determine that the work completed was what was required and at the correct standard, that the work was charged for as per contract stipulations, and that charges fell within the project's budget. Finally, she approves payment of any accepted invoices.

Question

Contracted horticulturists are the main sellers of medicinal plants to LangPharma Industries laboratories, which are the buyers of the plants.

Match the activities involved in the Program Contract Administration process to examples of how Rosa – the program manager at LangPharma Industries – performs them. One activity will not be used.

Options:

A. Managing the buyer and seller relationship

B. Considering any legal, political, and managerial implications

C. Communicating with stakeholders

D. Allocating resources between the program's team members

Targets:

1. Reviewing the terms of the contract between

buyer and seller

2. Evaluating the impact arising from the late supply of plants to the laboratories when the seller fails to meet contract terms

3. Sending reports to the program's stakeholders detailing the buyer and seller relationship

Answer

To manage the relationship between the buyer and seller at the program level, Rosa reviews the terms of the contract to ensure that all parties abide by them and that the terms are beneficial for the program.

Rosa must consider any legal, political, and managerial implications that arise from the contractual relationship between the buyer and seller. In this case, she assesses the impact of the seller's failure to meet contract terms.

Rosa communicates with the program's stakeholders by sending them reports about the buyer and seller relationship.

Benefits of managing program closure

The Closing process group is a set of processes for managing the closure of a program effectively. Consider the following scenario. Kudu Films has decided to bring its program for a series of documentaries on African wildlife to a close.

To close the program, a closing team of program managers creates reports that provide quantitative and qualitative data showing which benefits met or exceeded the initial program targets. For example, the benefit of increased product sales exceeded the target level by 10%.

They hand over the financial records to verify that all costs for the program have been covered, and provide records of what data has been archived.

The closing team at Kudu Films releases all program team members and sets availability indicators on resources – such as editing suites – in the company resource database.

The customer service team is briefed on specifics of the documentary series and the closing team ensures that all copyrights on the research and finished documentaries are in place.

During the closing process, the closing team at Kudu Films ensures that all:

- • program benefits have been delivered,
- payments have been made,
- project records are archived,
- resources are released,
- support functions are in place,
- intellectual property is protected for future use.

To manage program closure effectively, the closing team at Kudu Films used the three processes in the Closing process group.

Component Closure process

During the Component Closure process, the closing team ensures that all projects and non-project activities within a program are closed at project level.

Contract Closure process

During the Contract Closure process, all contractual agreements with outsourced vendors for a program are closed.

Close Program process

During the Close Program process, acceptance of the program's outcome from the customer or program sponsor is formalized.

The benefits of using the Closing process group are that it enables the closing team for a program to:

Sorin Dumitrascu

meet closure agreements

The closure agreement lists all the deliverables of the program. During the closing processes, the closing team demonstrates that all the program benefits have been delivered and that the work has been completed. The team also documents the current state of the program if it was terminated due to unforeseen circumstances.

To meet closure agreements for the Kudu Films documentary program, the closing team provides the program sponsor – the company's CEO – with reports containing quantitative and qualitative data about which program benefits met or exceeded their target levels. The CEO then agrees that the required benefits have been delivered, and the program is officially closed.

generate lessons learned

The closing team generates lessons learned during the program. Documented details of what went well for the program and what did not can then serve as inputs for the next program.

During the filming project in the Kudu Films documentary program, members of the outsourced filming crew requested that they be paid half their fees up front. This was unexpected and required adjustments to the program budget. The lesson learned was documented and can be used as input during budgeting for the next project.

ensure project closure

The closing team ensures that project closure has taken place at project level. This involves ensuring that all project information and records are captured and archived, that each project and non-project activity is signed off, and that project resources are released. In this way, valuable program information is retained and the program meets all the deliverables listed in the closure agreement. Project closure also occurs when a project is terminated due to a program benefits review or unforeseen circumstances.

The closing team at Kudu Films verifies that all the information and records for the research, filming, narration, production, and editing projects in the documentary program have been captured and archived.

meet contractual agreements

The closing team ensures that all contractual agreements have been met with outsourced vendors and that all payments are made. The team also verifies that all financial records are documented. This ensures that the information is readily available if a procurement audit or legal action is initiated. If early termination of a contract occurs, the closing team documents the work done, the work outstanding, and the reason for contract termination.

The closing team at Kudu Films ensures that the outsourced filming crew is paid in full and that all invoices and payment records are updated in the contract records.

Question

Philipa is a program manager for an IT marketing company. Identify the reasons why using the Closing process group is important to her management of programs.

Options:

1. To show that the agreed list of program benefits have been delivered

2. To ensure that information about program successes and failures is documented

3. To ensure that project closure has occurred

4. To ensure that all contractual obligations have been met

5. To ensure that team members who have achieved their targets are rewarded

6. To reassign program team members to new programs

Answer

Option 1: This is a correct option. During the closing processes, the closing team shows that program benefits have been delivered and that all required program work is complete. This brings formal closure to the program and ensures that the closure agreement is met.

Option 2: This is a correct option. During the closing processes, the closing team documents lessons learned during the program. This information about the program's successes and failures serves as input for the next program.

Option 3: This is a correct option. The closing processes ensure that all projects in the program are officially closed, that valuable program information from the projects is retained, and that the program meets all the deliverables listed in the closure agreement.

Option 4: This is a correct option. Using the closing processes, the closing team verifies that all contractual agreements are met, that all payments have been made, and that financial records are documented. This ensures that information about the proper closure of contracts is up to date and readily available.

Option 5: This is an incorrect option. Although it is important that team members are rewarded for program success, this isn't an activity in the Closing process group. Recognition and reward is a function of human resource management.

Option 6: This is an incorrect option. One purpose of using the Closing process group is ensuring that all human resources are released from a program. However, the task of reassigning team members after program closure is part of transition management.

In this lesson, you will learn more about the three processes of the Closing process group – Close Program, Component Closure, and Contract Closure.

You will also learn how program management processes interact and how each process group correlates to defined program management knowledge areas.

The Closing process group

Program closure is an important part of the overall program life cycle. It brings a program to an end in a formal, approved way.

The closing team is responsible for carrying out the closing processes. The Project Management Institute (PMI®) Combined Standards Glossary defines closing processes as "those processes performed to formally terminate all activities of a program or phase, and transfer the completed product to others, or close a canceled program."

Easy Nomad Travel is bringing its program to promote travel to Eastern Europe to a close.

The closing team for the program implements the three closing processes in the Closing process group:

Component Closure process

The Component Closure process involves ensuring that all projects and non-project activities within the program have been closed at project level. It is conducted at the end of each project life cycle or when a project is terminated prematurely.

The closing team at Easy Nomad Travel ensures that the budget, mid-range, and luxury travel package projects are closed at the end of their life cycles.

Contract Closure process

The Contract Closure process involves ensuring that all contractual obligations with outsourced vendors have been met, and then closing the contracts. The process should also be completed if a contract is terminated prematurely.

The closing team at Easy Nomad Travel closes all contractual agreements. The team ensures that all brochures are printed and delivered and that the printers have been paid in full.

Close Program process

The Close Program process involves achieving formal acceptance of the program's outcome. The end result is the signing off by the customer or sponsor.

The closing team meets with the program sponsor, the CEO of Easy Nomad Travel, to review the deliverables of the program. The CEO agrees that the program benefits – such as increased revenue, increased market share, and improved strategic relations with Eastern European tourism agencies – were achieved, and signs off the program as complete.

The Component Closure process ensures that all projects and non-project activities within a program

are closed, and the Contract Closure process ensures
that all contracts with outsourced vendors are
closed.

You need to close a program component or
contract before you can gain acceptance of the
program's outcome for that component or contract.
So each component or contract is closed at two
levels – first at component or contract level, and
then at program level.

Question

Disposall Corp, a waste management company,
is closing its safety program. The deliverables of the
program are to improve employees' skills and
capabilities in meeting safety requirements. Projects
in the program include the development of a safety
manual and the provision of workplace safety
training to all employees.

Match the activities of the closing team for the
program to each of the processes in the Closing
process group.

Options:

A. Review the improved safety practices and
obtain sign-off from the company's CEO

B. Document and close the safety manual and
training projects

C. Close the contract with outsourced trainers

Sorin Dumitrascu

Targets:

1. Close Program process
2. Component Closure process
3. Contract Closure process

Answer

During the Close Program process, the closing team gains formal acceptance of the program's outcome from the program sponsor – in this case, the company's CEO. To do this, the team reviews the program deliverables – such as improved safety practices – and obtains a sign-off on the program deliverables from the sponsor.

During the Component Closure process, the closing team ensures that all projects – such as the safety manual and training projects – and any other non-project activities are properly closed at the ends of their life cycles.

During the Contract Closure process, the closing team closes all contracts with outsourced vendors, such as outsourced trainers who facilitated the training sessions.

Component closure

A major component of program closure is the process of formally closing all the projects and non-program activities within the program at program level.

Program-level Component Closure is performed after project closure has taken place at project level, or in the case of early termination. To close a component at program level, the closing team should validate and ensure that project closure has taken place at the end of the project life cycle.

During the program-level Component Closure process, the closing team should:

close projects and archive project records

During project closure, project managers submit their final report reflecting the projects' success and lessons learned. The closing team reviews and validates the final report and ensures that it includes the required variance reports, status reports, cost and schedule accountability reports, and team member performance reviews.

Once the closing team is satisfied that all project records are complete, it closes the projects and archives project records for future reference. These records are archived in paper form, electronically, or

– preferably – both.

ensure that resource availability has been updated

As tasks within projects are completed, project managers should reassign team members to new activities or projects and indicate the resources that have become available for reallocation.

The closing team ensures that all resource availability has been updated and that freed resources are ready for reallocation to other components or programs.

communicate closure status to a larger set of stakeholders

During project closure, project managers are responsible for communicating project closure status to project team members, customers, and program team members.

However, during the program-level Component Closure process, the closing team needs to communicate the closure status of the program to a larger set of stakeholders. These include all internal and external stakeholders – such as the program director, program board, suppliers, or interest groups.

Cedar Lake Canyon National Park wishes to close its environmental program, which aimed at increasing awareness of conservation issues, meeting the Environmental Protection Agency (EPA) conservation standards, increasing revenue by 30%, and increasing customer satisfaction.

The program comprises a park conservation project, an education project, and a recreation project.

The park conservation project is to achieve compliance with the EPA standards for conservation. The education project is to create a six-part television series that explores the ecosystems in the park, and the recreation project is to create a recreation park alongside the lake, including picnic areas and a children's play park. Ongoing work for this program includes maintaining a web presence.

During the Component Closure process, the closing team reviews and validates the final reports of the park conservation project, education project, and recreation project as they come to the end of their project life cycles. The team ensures that each final report includes a variance report, a status report, a cost and schedule accountability report, and team member performance reviews, and then closes each project.

The closing team archives the project records by filing all paper-based documentation and copies of all electronic correspondence.

The closing team ensures that all team members have been released from the program. The team then updates resource availability by setting availability indicators on freed resources in the company's resource database.

Finally, the closing team communicates the closure status of the park conservation project, the education project, and the recreation project to a large set of stakeholders, including the program director, program board, the conservation board, and the EPA.

Question

Poseidon Bank is closing its Young Savers program, aimed at attracting customers between the ages of 7 and 13.

The closing team is implementing the program-level Component Closure process. Identify the activities that should be executed during this process.

Options:

1. Review the final reports of the in-house training projects and file the records

2. Ensure that availability indicators are set on freed resources in the bank's resource database

3. Communicate project closure status to the

program director and program board

4. Complete the procurement documents detailing how much money was spent during each project

5. Reassign project team members to new projects in the bank

Answer

Option 1: This is a correct option. During the program-level Component Closure process, the closing team reviews and verifies the final reports for each project in the program to ensure that they include all the required data and that project closure has indeed taken place at project level. The team then officially closes the projects at program level and archives the project records.

Option 2: This is a correct option. During the program-level Component Closure process, the closing team ensures that resources used for the program are made available for reallocation to other components or programs.

Option 3: This is a correct option. During the program-level Component Closure process, the closing team communicates the closure status of each project to all internal and external stakeholders, such as the program director and program board.

Option 4: This is an incorrect option. The project

manager is accountable for the money that has been invested in a project and is responsible for completing all procurement documents, including cost and schedule accountability reports.

Option 5: This is an incorrect option. The task of reassigning project team members after project closure is part of transition management, which is usually conducted by the project manager or the Human Resource Department.

Contract closure

A component of program closure is the process of formally closing all the contracts entered into for the program at program level.

During the Contract Closure process, the closing team ensures that all contracts with outsourced vendors were executed according to their terms and conditions, and officially closes these contracts.

During the program-level Contract Closure process, the closing team should:

verify that contracted work was done

During the Contract Closure process, the closing team reviews and verifies the work that was done by outsourced vendors to ensure that it meets contract terms and conditions.

update all contract records

During Contract Closure, the closing team updates all contract records and ensures that the contracts and all progress reports, financial records, invoices, and payment records are updated and filed in the contract files. The contract files should form part of the complete program file.

In the case of early contract termination, the closing team is required to document the work done, the work outstanding, and the reason for contract termination, and to update relevant contract records.

Once the closing team is satisfied that contracted work is completed and that all contract records for a particular contract are updated, the team issues a certificate of contract completion to indicate contract closure.

During the Contract Closure process, the closing team at Cedar Lake National Park reviews the contracts with the builders who were outsourced to build the picnic areas and children's play park. The team verifies that the work was done and that it meets the contract terms and conditions, which specify that the benches in picnic areas and the play park must be safe and durable.

The closing team updates all contract records and ensures that the contract with the building company and all the progress reports, financial records, invoices, and payment records are updated and placed in a contract file.

Finally, the closing team issues a certificate of contract completion to indicate contract closure, and hands the recreation project over to a maintenance committee.

Question
Poseidon Bank has already performed

component closure of its Young Savers program. The closing team is implementing the Contract Closure process. Identify the activities that the team should execute during this process.

Access the learning aid Young Savers Program to answer the question. Options:

1. Review the new web site and verify that it was built according to agreed specifications

2. Ensure that all the invoices and payment records with Mariner Computer Solutions are updated

3. Make payments to Mariner Computer Solutions for their services

4. File the records for the in-house training project

Answer

Option 1: This is a correct option. During the Contract Closure process, the closing team reviews all the contracts with outsourced vendors, such as Mariner Computer Solutions, to ensure that all the work was done according to contract terms and conditions.

Option 2: This is a correct option. During the Contract Closure process, the closing team ensures that all contract records have been updated and that the contract and all associated documentation – such as progress reports, financial records, invoices, and payment records – are updated and filed in the contract file.

Option 3: This is an incorrect option. Project managers are responsible for ensuring that all payments to outsourced vendors have been made at project level. During the Contract Closure process, the closing team is responsible for ensuring that all progress reports, financial records, invoices, and payment records are updated and saved in the contract file.

Option 4: This is an incorrect option. Filing records is an aspect of the Component Closure process, during which the closing team closes and archives all projects as they end their life cycles. Furthermore, the in-house project didn't require any contracts with outsourced vendors.

Close program

Once all the projects, non-project activities, and contracts within a program are closed, the Close Program process can begin.

During the Close Program process, the closing team achieves formal acceptance of the program's outcome by:

reviewing the program scope with the program sponsor or customer

During the Close Program process, the closing team and the program sponsor or customer review the program scope against what each project and non-project activity has delivered. They do this to ensure that all program work is complete.

reviewing the closure documents with the program sponsor or customer

Once the program scope has been reviewed, the closing team and the program sponsor or customer compare the program scope with the work that was actually performed, as documented in the closure documents. They verify that the program deliverables were met.

After the review, the program sponsor or customer is asked to sign the closure document. Once this is complete, a certificate of program completion is awarded. This indicates final acceptance of the program's outcome.

reviewing the lessons learned

During the Close Program process, the closing team reviews the lessons learned during the program, and generates a lessons learned report. This report is incorporated into the closure report and archived so that it can be used as input for future programs.

generating human resource reports

The closing team verifies the final performance reviews and updates the personnel records of the program team members. The team then compiles this information to generate a human resource report, which is sent to the Human Resource Department. The Department then assigns team members to new projects or programs.

Once all projects in the environmental program and all contracts with outsourced vendors have been closed, the closing team at Cedar Lake Canyon Park is ready to conduct the Close Program process.

The closing team meets with John, the program sponsor and head of the program board. They review the program scope by assessing the outcomes of the park conservation, education, and recreation projects, and of the ongoing web site project, to ensure that all program work is complete.

The closing team presents John with closure documents that provide quantitative and qualitative data about the extent to which the targeted program benefits have been achieved.

John and the team go on to compare the program scope with the actual work that was carried out. They find that the program has increased the awareness of conservation issues, met the EPA standards, increased customer satisfaction, and exceeded its target of increasing revenue by 30%.

John signs the closure document and the program team receives a certificate of program completion.

The closing team reviews the lessons learned during the program. These lessons include the need to provide a higher budget for contingencies and to allow more flexibility in scheduling. Due to bad weather, the construction team for the recreation project had to be on stand-by for four days, and this added to program costs and time.

The closing team then documents these lessons and generates a lessons learned report. The team ensures that this report is filed in the closure report and archived in the program folder.

Finally, the closing team generates a human resource report, which includes final performance reviews for all program team members and their updated personnel records. This report is sent to the Human Resource Department.

Question

Poseidon Bank is closing its Young Savers program. The closing team has already ensured that all program components and contracts are closed. The team is now implementing the Close Program process. Identify the activities that the team should execute during this process.

Options:

1. Review the program scope against the work done in the awareness, marketing, and training projects

2. Ask the CEO to sign off on the reports detailing increased customer awareness

3. Create a report detailing lessons learned through the success of the advertising campaign

4. Submit a human resource report, containing final performance reviews and personnel records

5. Ensure that all records of payments to Mariner Computer Solutions are filed in the program contract file

6. Inform the Human Resource Department that the marketing project manager can be reassigned

Answer

Option 1: This is a correct option. During the Close Program process, the closing team and the program sponsor or customer ensure that all agreed program work is complete. They do this by reviewing the program scope and comparing it with the outcome of each project and non-project activity.

Option 2: This is a correct option. During the Close Program process, the closing team and the program sponsor – the CEO, in this case – review the benefits that were achieved. The CEO is then asked to sign the closure document and to award a certificate of program completion.

Option 3: This is a correct option. During the Close Program process, the closing team reviews the successes and failures of the program and generates a report that includes all the significant lessons learned. These documented lessons are used as input for future programs.

Option 4: This is a correct option. During the Close Program process, the closing team generates a human resource report that includes the final performance reviews of the program team members and their updated personnel records. This report is handed over to the Human Resource Department for transition management.

Option 5: This is an incorrect option. The

closing and archiving of contracts occurs during the Contract Closure process. This process should be completed before the Close Program process occurs.

Option 6: This is an incorrect option. During the Component Closure process, the closing team ensures that program resources are made available for reallocation to other projects. This process should be completed before the Close Program process occurs.

Julio and Rosa have discussed what processes you need to follow to close the African program. This involves closing the contracts, closing the components, and finally, closing the program.

Process interactions

A process is a set of interrelated actions and activities performed to achieve a specified set of products, services, or other results.

The various processes in program management do not work independently of each other. They continuously interact and overlap so that the outputs of one process become the inputs of another process.

It is also possible for an output of a process to become an input of the same process. For example, this occurs when a plan is updated continuously throughout a program.

An output of a program process may logically progress from one process through to another until it reaches an end point.

For example, an output such as lessons learned from a program continues to be generated across processes, until it forms completed output from the Close Program process. During the Close Program process, this information is collated and analyzed in a program closure report, and then archived.

Conversely, an output may progress through multiple processes and return to the original process that produced that output, but this time as an input to the first process.

The interrelationship between program processes is complex. Not only is there a relationship between the inputs and outputs of program processes, but project inputs and outputs may progress to the program domain, and even to the portfolio domain.

Consider four examples of process outputs that become inputs in other domains.

Project schedule

A project schedule becomes an input to the Schedule Control process at the program level. As an input of this process, it is used to update the program's master schedule plan. So a shift in the schedule of one project may affect the overall schedule of the program.

Project risks

Project risks are an output in the project domain but flow to the Risk Management Planning and Analysis process of program management as an input. When a risk analysis is done at program level, the results of this analysis will then flow back to the project level as new inputs.

Corrective action

A corrective action is an output of the processes in the Monitoring and Controlling process group and is filtered down as an input at the project level.

For example, the name of a contractor that did

not perform well in a program task will be passed along to the program managers of other projects so that the contractor will not be used again in the future. Another example would be if one project manager recognizes the need for an IT subject matter expert and passes this information on as an input for other ongoing projects.

Funding availability

Funding availability flows as an output from the portfolio domain to the program's Cost Control process as an input. For example, a major funder may pull out of a company and so affect the viability of certain programs.

LangPharma Industries is a company that grows medicinal plants, which it sells to other companies that use them to make products.

A request for change is put forward to invest in more land for growing echinacea – a plant thought to boost the immune system – given increased demand for echinacea products.

The request is considered and then accepted through the Scope Control process, which provides an approved change request as an output. The approved change request is passed as an input to the Communications Control process, which involves handling communications about the program with stakeholders. The approved change then becomes part of the communications management plan.

Question

Identify examples of ways in which program processes interact.

Options:

1. The program management plan is an output of Integrated Change Control and becomes an input of Resource Control

2. Organizational process assets are used throughout a project to influence its success

3. Performance reports are an output of Performance Reporting and become an input of Communications Control

4. Historical data about previous programs is used to analyze the success of a program

5. The program budget is an input of Cost Control and an output of Cost Control when it is updated, and is also an input of the Performance Reporting process

Answer

Option 1: This is a correct option. The Integrated Change Control process involves approving or refusing requests for change to a program. When changes are approved, they are reflected in updates made to the program management plan. The updated program management plan is simultaneously an input to the Resource Control process, which involves monitoring and controlling program resources in line with the program management plan.

Option 2: This is an incorrect option. Organizational process assets are an input and output of the project domain, rather than at the program level. They do not interact with program activities and processes. These assets include historical information, plans, procedures, policies, and guidelines.

Option 3: This is a correct option. The purpose of the Performance Reporting process is to amalgamate performance data relating to the program into reports to be presented to stakeholders. These performance reports then become an input of the Communications Control process, which involves handling communications with stakeholders.

Option 4: This is an incorrect option. Using lessons learned from previous projects to evaluate the success of another project doesn't involve an interaction between program-level processes. However, lessons learned are an output of more than one process within a program.

Option 5: This is a correct option. The Cost

Control process controls changes to the program budget and produces data from it by analyzing actual expenditure in relation to planned expenditure. The program budget is an input to the Cost Control process as well as an output of the process when changes are made and it is updated. The program budget also becomes an input of the Performance Reporting process, which consolidates performance data for stakeholders.

The Project Management Body of Knowledge (PMBOK®) Guide – Third Edition identifies nine project management areas. These include Integration Management, Scope Management, Time Management, Cost Management, Quality Management, Human Resource Management, Communications Management, Risk Management, and Procurement Management.

In turn, processes in each of the five groups of program management processes identified by the Project Management Institute (PMI®) Standard for Program Management relate to the project management knowledge areas.

The processes in the program management process groups do not work in isolation. They interrelate and overlap, with the outputs of one process logically becoming the inputs of another.

Program Management

There is also an interrelationship between processes in the project, program, and portfolio domains, with outputs progressing up and down the domain levels to become inputs.

There is a further correlation between the program management processes and the nine knowledge areas of project management.

Made in the USA
Coppell, TX
12 November 2020